Applied Research
in Child
and
Adolescent
Development

Applied Research
in Child
and
Adolescent
Development
A Practical Guide

Edited by

Valerie Malhomes, Ph.D., CAS
Eunice Kennedy Shriver National Institute of
Child Health and Human Development

Carmela Gina Lomonaco, Ph.D.
Inspire USA Foundation

The opinions and assertions presented in this paper are those of the authors and do not purport to represent those of the Eunice Kennedy Shriver National Institute of Child Health and Human Development, the National Institutes of Health, the US Department of Health and Human Services or the Inspire USA Foundation.

Psychology Press
Taylor & Francis Group

New York   London

Psychology Press
Taylor & Francis Group
270 Madison Avenue
New York, NY 10016

Psychology Press
Taylor & Francis Group
27 Church Road
Hove, East Sussex BN3 2FA

© 2010 by Taylor and Francis Group, LLC
Psychology Press is an imprint of Taylor & Francis Group, an Informa business

Printed in the United States of America on acid-free paper
10 9 8 7 6 5 4 3 2 1

International Standard Book Number: 978-1-84872-814-1 (Hardback) 978-1-84872-815-8 (Paperback)

Library of Congress Cataloging-in-Publication Data

Applied research in child and adolescent development : a practical guide /
    editors, Valerie Maholmes and Carmela Gina Lomonaco.
        p. cm.
    Includes bibliographical references and index.
    ISBN 978-1-84872-814-1 (hard back : alk. paper) -- ISBN 978-1-84872-815-8
    (pbk. : alk. paper)
    1. Child psychology--Research. 2. Adolescent psychology--Research. I.
Maholmes, Valerie. II. Lomonaco, Carmela Gina.

BF721.A693 2010
155.4072--dc22
                                                              2009054335

Visit the Taylor & Francis Web site at
http://www.taylorandfrancis.com

and the Psychology Press Web site at
http://www.psypress.com

Contents

SECTION II Challenges and Issues Conducting Applied Research on Child and Adolescent Development

Chapter 6 Challenges and Issues in Designing Applied Research 101

Robert B. McCall, PhD
Christina J. Groark, PhD

Chapter 7 Ethical Issues and Challenges in Applied Research in
Child and Adolescent Development 131

Celia Fisher, PhD
Adam L. Fried, PhD

SECTION III Conducting Research in Applied Settings

SECTION IV How to Make the Most of Your Applied Research

Preface

Basic research holds the promise of yielding scientific advances and discoveries regarding conditions that affect children and adolescents. To reduce the burden of these conditions, research findings must be translated into practical application. In biomedical research this translation leads to tools and strategies to improve clinical practice. In research designed to understand and elucidate child and adolescent development, these translations lead to applications that promote health and well-being in the specific contexts within which children grow, learn, and develop.

Despite the growing body of work on the importance of contextual influences on development, questions remain, particularly among early career researchers, as to how best study these influences on children and adolescents. What are the most appropriate designs and what happens when there are challenges to ideal research designs? The authors in this volume address these and other questions by discussing the challenges they have encountered conducting their own applied research. They each put forward approaches, definitions, theories and concepts about applied research based on their unique and varied experiences. They refer to translational research (Guerra & Leidy, Knox), applied research (Spicer, Schonfeld), practice research (McCall & Groark), and developmental science (Lerner, McCabe, Liben) as a way to underscore the importance of bringing scientific evidence to bear on the compelling public health issues affecting children and adolescents and in so doing, create effective strategies designed to improve their developmental outcomes.

By assembling this volume, we aim to encourage thoughtful and provocative discussions about the most efficient and effective ways to use theory and appropriate methodology to develop practices, interventions, or materials to affect positively the lives of children and adolescents. We recognize that the social, educational, economic, and public health issues confronting children and adolescents can not be addressed by a single disciplinary perspective or methodological approach. Strategies and insights from multiple disciplines are needed to capture the essence of phenomena observed in naturalistic settings and translate these observations into culturally sensitive and developmentally appropriate interventions and strategies. The authors draw upon diverse perspectives ranging from anthropology, pediatrics, sociology, and psychology to ask and attempt to answer key developmental questions from different scientific vantage points.

This book is organized in four sections. The first section, Getting Started with Applied Research on Development, elucidates the reciprocal process between basic and applied research by using questions most salient to the applied researcher as the focal point for inquiry and analysis. As early career investigators, Blachman and Esposito lead Section I of the book by responding directly to questions most frequently asked among their contemporaries and provide advice for guiding their peers through the obstacles and opportunities for launching careers in applied research. Topics discussed include questions like these:

- How do I gain a firmer grounding in the developmental perspective, including how psycho-social and bio-social developmental processes interact with proximate environments, such as family, school, and peers?
- How can researchers, even if in a position of "authority" take measures to ensure that the "voice" of the participants is heard, even at the level of planning the data collection methods?
- How do I frame my applied questions within a developmental paradigm and integrate multiple methods and data sets to investigate young adult development?
- Because I am early in my career, I am framing questions using academic processes more than community inputs. I feel that I shouldn't stray too far from my academically defined questions, or I risk slowing progress towards tenure. However, I want my community relationships to be productive for the community, not just for my academic career. How do I negotiate this?

Chapter 3 provides an overview of applied developmental science and a theoretical framework upon which investigators can build ideas for their research. Lerner refers to applied research in child and adolescent development as the utilization of behavioral and social science theories to optimize the course of development. He emphasizes that the application of developmental science is predicated on developmental systems models of human development. These models stress that the basic process of human development involves mutually influential relations between children and contexts, and emphasize the potential plasticity of these relations. This, in turn, enables an optimistic view to be taken to promote positive development. Pamela Cole's chapter (Chapter 4) chronicles her pre- and post-doctoral experiences and discusses how questions that arose in the conduct of her studies put her on an inquisitive path toward understanding emotions and emotion regulation. She puts forward the notion that the process of inquiry is ongoing, regardless of career stage and that this process leads to new discoveries and even more questions. Now a distinguished professor, she offers advice as to how one extrapolates applied questions from basic clinical research.

Section II, Challenges and Issues in Conducting Applied Research on Child and Adolescent Development, focuses on methodological approaches utilized in applied research and most importantly the particular challenges encountered in the conduct of applied research in child and adolescent development. Paul Spicer leads this section and discusses in Chapter 5 the important cultural issues involved in planning and carrying out applied research within vulnerable populations. Here, he presents examples from work with Native American Indian populations to highlight effective strategies for working with particular populations including sampling techniques, recruitment, and retention issues. McCall and Groark (Chapter 6) provide references to specific methodological techniques and theoretical frameworks most suitable for guiding the applied and "practice" research processes. In Chapter 7, Fisher and Fried give examples of how these techniques and methods may be modified to carry out the study in applied settings while maintaining the integrity of the data. They further illustrate the ethical challenges of conducting research in applied settings and with vulnerable populations. Fisher and Fried urge that researchers take these techniques and strategies into consideration at the design stage of applied research and not once data collection has started.

In Section III, we pay particular attention to Conducting Research in Applied Settings. Research in child and adolescent development is often learned in controlled settings giving researchers in training the opportunity to learn applied research theories and methods under optimal conditions. However, the real world of conducting applied research brings unique challenges, most of which are not learned in classrooms or controlled settings. Inherent in this research are compromises to ideal research designs, which most beginning investigators may not be adequately prepared to manage.

In addition, research conducted in applied settings calls for a unique set of *attitudes*, *skills*, and *knowledge* that will enable the researcher to forge partnerships, develop innovative approaches, and take on new perspectives to address compelling public health problems of local and national significance. Guerra & Leidy (Chapter 8) emphasize cultural competence as both a necessary frame of mind and an important attitudinal perspective essential for establishing the relationships needed to engage in applied research. In Chapter 9, David Schonfeld talks about humility and mutual respect as among the most important attitudes for early career investigators to exhibit in their work in schools. With respect to the skills needed for applied research, Lyndee Knox shares some of her mistakes as a young investigator in Chapter 10 and how these lessons strengthened her skills as a researcher. Each of the contributors to this section in his or her own way emphasizes persistence, focus, and maintaining an appropriate balance between the needs of members of the community and the needs of the researcher as essential skills needed to successfully plan and carry out applied research in various contexts. Finally, with respect to knowledge, the authors emphasize the importance of knowing the community with which the research will be conducted and being knowledgeable of the theoretical frames that guide community practices and perceptions. Aside from scientific knowledge, early career investigators must also be knowledgeable of ethical codes of conduct to protect vulnerable populations while at the same time engaging these individuals in studies designed to inform practices and policies that could have a bearing on their life circumstances.

Thus each of the chapters in this section provides applied researchers with the tools to respond to and manage the unpredictable nature of real world research. The authors also provide an overview of the importance of multidisciplinary collaborations needed to forge successful and mutually beneficial research collaborations essential for working successfully in applied settings.

How to Make the Most of Your Applied Research is the focus of Section IV, the final section in this volume. Here, the authors talk about the researcher's responsibilities as a member of the advocacy, policy, and academic communities. The applied researcher is in a unique position to bring these constituencies together, inform the public, develop prevention and intervention strategies, and, most importantly, give voice to issues affecting children and their well-being. The applied research enterprise is both labor and time intensive. In Chapter 11, Berch gives a thorough discussion of strategies for seeking funding for applied research and the ways in which investigators obtain support from their institutions for release time and resources to conduct applied research. The authors discuss how applied research can be effectively disseminated and how it ultimately informs basic research. McCabe & Browning (Chapter 12) and Liben (Chapter 13) discuss methods for disseminating research-based knowledge on child, and adolescent development. These methods include journals and other publications, as well as strategies for communicating research findings so that policy, practice and education decisions will benefit from leading edge scientific information.

The perspectives advanced in this volume reflect each author's experience and scholarship regarding the issues and challenges they encounter while conducting applied research on children and adolescents. Although writing from diverse disciplinary perspectives, research interests, and experiences, the authors share insights that reflect common themes and lessons that we hope are instructive to the reader.

As we discuss in the concluding chapter, this is not intended to be an exhaustive text, but rather a practical resource for answering specific questions from early career investigators about the conduct of applied research. Readers should already have a working knowledge of child and adolescent development and should have had some practical experience conducting research so that they have a basis for understanding the questions and the examples provided. Masters level and pre-doctoral students preparing their theses and dissertations will find this book accessible and beneficial, as will postdoctoral fellows and early career investigators moving toward applied research careers. In addition, faculty who prepare students to do research will find the resources and case studies useful for helping students manage the complexities of real world research.

This book is intended to complement technical and theoretical texts. The book can be used as a guide and quick reference for answering questions about the conduct of applied research as it relates to child and adolescent development. Advanced undergraduate and graduate level courses on Research Methods, Theories of Child and Adolescent Development, the Ethical Conduct of Research, Child and Family Processes, Neighborhoods, Schools and Social Contexts, as well as proseminars on Vulnerable Populations, Multiculturalism, and Cultural Competence may use this book as a supplement to assigned texts.

Unique features of this book include the various learning tools to make the topics more accessible to the reader. First, each chapter begins with an autobiographical discussion describing how and why the author began her career in applied research. Issues such as navigating the tensions between seeking promotion and tenure and pursuing an applied line of inquiry are recounted in very compelling detail. Next, the chapters are organized around actual questions from investigators making their first foray into applied research. The authors draw upon case examples of authentic applied research experiences to directly answer some of the questions, while others are highlighted in sidebar callouts. Finally, the chapters conclude with lessons learned and references and resources for specific techniques, and theoretical frameworks most suitable for guiding the research process. Where appropriate, the contributors give examples of how these techniques and methods may be modified to carry out the study in applied settings, while maintaining the integrity of the data and taking into account ethical considerations.

There were many directions we could have taken in conceptualizing this book, but we learned from participants at our Summer Institutes on Applied Research in Child and Adolescent Development (see Chapter 1) that information on the more practical elements of conducting applied research was sorely needed. We asked each author to write about the specific content and context related to their research, and to shed light on some of the decision-making processes they use in conducting research in less than optimal, largely uncontrolled environments. We think this was most important because as these contexts become more complex, having a realistic picture of what may be involved in examining how the direct and the nuanced influences of families, schools, communities and other settings shape the lives of children and adolescents is vital. As you read these personalized explanations of complex processes, we encourage you reflect on the challenges and opportunities for charting your career and conducting your own applied research on child and adolescent development.

Acknowledgments

This volume is based on the Inaugural NICHD Summer Institute on Applied Research in Child and Adolescent Development held in Bethesda, MD. This week long Institute was co-sponsored by the NIH Office of Behavioral and Social Sciences Research (OBSSR) with support from the Association for Psychological Science (APS) and the Society for Research in Child Development (SRCD). The editors wish to acknowledge these partners for their support of our efforts and ultimately for making this volume possible.

We would also like to acknowledge the individuals who advised us on the first Institute and served as faculty-in-residence—Dr. Jeanne Brookes-Gunn, Dr. Richard Lerner, Dr. Robin Morris, and Dr. David Schonfeld. Their substantial contributions helped make the Institute a reality, and in large measure led to the conceptualization of this volume. We are also grateful for the guidance and support of Dr. Peggy McCardle, the Chief of the Child Development and Behavior Branch at NICHD.

We offer a special note of gratitude to our concept reviewers Linda Baker, University of Maryland Baltimore County, Natasha Cabrera, University of Maryland, and Scott Hofer, University of Victoria. Most especially we acknowledge the support and cheer-leading we received from Debra Riegert, our acquisitions editor, whose enthusiasm for the subject of this book was instrumental in having Taylor & Francis publish this volume!

CHAPTER 1

Introduction

Valerie Maholmes, PhD
*Eunice Kennedy Shriver National Institute of Child
Health and Human Development*

Carmela G. Lomonaco, PhD
Inspire USA Foundation

Many of the public health and social challenges confronting our society have their basis in child and adolescent development. Having an understanding of the developmental underpinnings of such issues as obesity, bullying, academic achievement, violence, and the like could lead toward designing of programs, practices, and policies to ameliorate the affects of these problems.

More and more, universities are establishing departments of applied developmental science or are creating opportunities for students to have cross-disciplinary training to frame the research questions and design applied studies. While these opportunities are becoming more available, many young scholars interested in pursuing careers in applied research have lingering questions about the processes by which such studies are actually carried out.

In an attempt to address these questions, program scientists in the Child Development and Behavior, and Demographics and Behavioral Science Branches at the *Eunice Kennedy Shriver* National Institute of Child Health and Human Development (NICHD) along with program scientists in the National Institutes of Health (NIH) Office of Behavioral and Social Sciences Research collaborated to develop the Summer Institute on Applied Research in Child and Adolescent Development. We chose this title to call attention to the importance of studying development—the factors and contexts that promote optimal development and those that might place a child onto a less optimal course of development. We also wanted the title to reflect the fact that interest in and the study of development does not only reside in the traditional departments of human development or psychology, but that researchers in other disciplines also have interest in many of the same issues, but ask these questions from different points of reference. It is this convergence of perspectives and coalescing of ideas around child and adolescent development issues that we wanted to foster in order to accelerate the pace of developing preventive interventions and to increase the number of researchers in the pipeline who are well trained to conduct applied research.

The idea for this book grew out of our experiences during the first Summer Institute on Applied Research in Child and Adolescent Development. We invited prospective participants to ask questions they would like the Institute to address and to indicate the aspects of conducting applied research with which they needed the most help. The responses led us to tailor the Institute to the specific questions raised and the particular interests and concerns of the participants. The majority of the authors contributing to this book participated in the Institute and the topics addressed at the Institute correspond to the chapters in this book.

An important goal of the Institute was to call attention to the theoretical and conceptual frameworks that support applied research. We deemed it important to help early career investigators become acquainted with developmental and systems theories that guide applied methodological approaches. Rich Lerner's, and Bob McCall and Christina Groark's presentations underscored this goal. Their chapters (Chapters 3 and 6, respectively) in this volume continue this theme and outline essential skills needed to propose and carry out studies leading to the development of interventions and the implementation of programs and practices that may improve the lives of children. Each of the authors discusses the need to build bridges between research and practice and provide guidance as to the most effective strategies to make these connections. They discuss the challenges they have encountered conducting applied research and the lessons they have learned throughout their respective careers.

Another important goal of the Institute was to provide an opportunity for investigators making their first foray into applied research to have a forum where they could ask the critical questions that would help them to negotiate and advance along their respective career paths. The Institute used a series of interactive presentations, plenary sessions, and small-group interaction to support the acquisition of advanced skills needed to plan and conduct applied research with children and adolescents. Accordingly this book is written in nontechnical, practical terms so that early career researchers can access information most relevant to their research goals and career stage.

A unique feature of the book is that it uses actual questions from early career investigators as an organizing framework. The authors attempt to provide answers to specific and pragmatic questions rarely addressed in research methods texts. The book starts with a chapter by Blachman and Esposito (Chapter 2), both early career investigators, who put forward some of the most frequently asked questions by their peers. Both fellows at the NIH at the time of this writing, Blachman and Esposito draw upon the breadth of their exposure to cutting-edge research and demystify the mechanisms by which new investigators can move toward this standard. Cole (Chapter 4) elaborates on the circuitous paths careers may take to find answers to compelling challenges affecting children and adolescents.

Applied research is often complicated by challenges to ideal designs outlined in traditional texts or utilized in controlled settings. We sought to help Institute participants gain knowledge of real-life challenges encountered in the conduct of applied research and how these challenges may be managed while maintaining the integrity of the science. McCall and Groark (Chapter 6) give a provocative analysis of various methodologies used to address these challenges and discuss their utility for answering particular applied questions. In keeping with this theme, authors in this volume enumerate the attitudes, skills, and knowledge needed to employ these methods in schools, underresourced communities, clinics, and with special populations.

Support for applied research often comes from a variety of sources. Federal funding is one of the avenues through which early career investigators can get their work supported. There are alternative sources available to support applied research focusing on children and families. The Institute brought together federal officials from a variety of agencies as well as representatives from foundations and organizations that have a mutual interest in advancing important research agendas that address their respective priorities and mission. Also discussed were outlets for disseminating and publishing funded research. These topics are addressed in this volume as well. Chapter 11 written by Berch lays out strategies for seeking funding to conduct and extend the research, while McCabe and Browning (Chapter 12) highlight techniques for disseminating research-based knowledge on infant, child, and adolescent development. These methods include strategies for communicating research findings so that policy, practice, and education decisions will benefit from state-of-the-art scientific information. Liben (Chapter 13) focuses on strategies for publishing research findings in relevant journals for child and adolescent development.

In summary, this book is not intended to be a substitute for research design and methods texts, but rather serve as a practical companion to these texts.

We hope that this volume will provide critical insights to help guide your career. As we continue to learn from our training institutes and conferences, we will continue to provide commentary and guidance on the theories, effective strategies, methods, and approaches to improve the lives of children and adolescents.

GETTING STARTED WITH APPLIED RESEARCH ON CHILD AND ADOLESCENT DEVELOPMENT

CHAPTER **2**

Getting Started
Answering Your Frequently Asked Questions About Applied Research on Child and Adolescent Development

Dara R. Blachman, PhD*
National Center for Health Statistics, Centers for Disease Control and Prevention

Layla Esposito, PhD
Eunice Kennedy Shriver National Institute of Child Health and Human Development

Introduction

Let us begin this chapter by introducing ourselves. Dara Blachman is currently employed at the National Center for Health Statistics, Centers for Disease Control and Prevention. At the time of this writing, Blachman was a Society for Research in Child Development Executive Branch Fellow at the Office for Behavioral and Social Sciences Research (OBSSR) in the Office of the Director at the National Institutes of Health for 2 years. During her time at OBSSR, she was involved in a range of cross-cutting initiatives, including in the areas of dissemination and

* Written while a Society for Research in Child Development fellow at the Office of Behavioral and Social Research, National Institutes of Health.

implementation science, adherence, and health disparities. She also participated in the planning of the first Summer Institute on Applied Research in Child and Adolescent Development (which OBSSR cosponsored). Blachman's research interests center on understanding the interactive role of peer, family, and community/cultural influences on children's socio-emotional adjustment and mental health, with an emphasis on the promotion of healthy development among minority children living in poverty. Reflective of her desire to conduct research that attempts to bridge the gap between science, policy, and practice, Blachman has been involved in several community-based, collaborative efforts in the areas of school-based mental health services, family-based HIV prevention programs, and foster parent retention. Blachman received her PhD in clinical/community psychology from the University of California, Berkeley. She completed her predoctoral internship at the Institute for Juvenile Research (IJR) at the University of Illinois at Chicago and a postdoctoral fellowship at the Family Institute and School of Education and Social Policy at Northwestern University.

While writing this chapter, Layla Esposito was in her second year of the Society for Research in Child Development (SRCD) Policy Fellowship at the *Eunice Kennedy Shriver* National Institute of Child Health and Human Development (NICHD). In this role, she focused on numerous issues related to child development and behavior and the interface of science and social policy. She is currently the coordinator for the Obesity Research Strategic Core and is involved with NICHD's second Summer Institute on Applied Research in Child and Adolescent Development. Prior to the fellowship, Esposito was involved in research evaluating middle school programs developed for violence prevention and drug and sex education; and her clinical work focused on children with emotional and behavioral disorders. Other research interests have included peer victimization, gender differences in aggression, violence prevention, psychosocial adjustment, and mental health in children. Esposito received her master's degree in child clinical psychology and her PhD in social psychology from Virginia Commonwealth University.

In authoring this chapter, we hope to bring our unique perspective to many of your questions. We are both early career professionals ourselves, yet have also had the opportunity to work in government with issues of applied child and adolescent development for

2 years each. Additionally, we both come from psychology backgrounds. We have done our best to include examples from other fields and provide resources from nonpsychology disciplines when possible. Yet, we clearly could not cover all possible resources and examples. We encourage you to use the resources as a starting point and a guide and to ultimately seek out other sources of information that may be more relevant to your field or area of interest.

We hope that our perspective will be useful to you as you begin your career in applied child and adolescent development research. We recognize that ours are only some among many possible answers, and we certainly do not claim to have the years of experience and fully developed expertise of the more senior authors featured in this volume. Yet, as early career researchers we believe that we are closer to the experiences and questions that you bring. In addition, we have struggled with many of them ourselves and have had the fortune to be able to blend our academic expertise with policy relevant experiences through our fellowship. We offer our insights as guidance and thoughts to ponder, in the hopes that it may be useful to you. In answering these questions we will often reflect on our own experiences, struggles, and wrestling with many of the same issues presented herein. We only hope that your journey can perhaps be informed by ours. We have by no means completed ours. We have only just begun and believe that the process of writing this chapter has assisted in our own professional growth and development.

This chapter is organized in sections that correspond to the sections in this book. The questions were chosen from those submitted by participants in the first Summer Institute in Applied Child and Adolescent Development sponsored by the *Eunice Kennedy Shriver* National Institute of Child Health and Human Development. Participants submitted questions prior to the Summer Institute, and these questions were utilized as discussion guides during the course of the week. We have chosen questions that we thought best covered the broad range of relevant topics and those that we believed we were best able to address from our individual vantage points and experiences.

Getting Started in Applied Developmental Research

In an environment that has typically operated from a medical model, and that is familiar with physical health outcomes, research that focuses on psychological constructs is often perceived as "less scientific."

How would you suggest bridging the "cultural divide" between the medical (pediatric) perspective and the psychological/developmental perspective of research?

This question is one that is on the minds of many behavioral and social scientists at the National Institutes of Health (NIH) and across the country. Unfortunately, many in the biomedical community still harbor perceptions of behavioral and social science (BSSR) that are in may ways outdated, that is, the science is somehow "soft" or that it is simply common sense that does not need to be studied. This is understandable given that the primary mode of training and research in the biomedical community is that of the individual, with a linear, deterministic way of explaining phenomenon as well as a focus on specific diseases. In contrast, the behavioral and social sciences involve multiple, interacting levels that cannot be controlled and often focus on overall growth, development, and well-being as opposed to specific disease states.

Yet, the reality is that BSSR is key to solving the nations top public health problems. Nearly half of all deaths in the United States can be attributed to preventable behaviors (e.g., smoking, poor diet, physical inactivity; NIH, 2008). Huge contributions have been made by BSSR over the last few decades, including the dramatic decrease in tobacco use, the reduction in sudden infant death syndrome (SIDS), and the slowing of the HIV/AIDS epidemic (Mabry, Olster, Morgan, & Abrams, 2008; NIH, 2008). Although perceptions are not changed overnight, we think there is evidence that the tide may be turning. The value of BSSR seems to be rising in public awareness and is obtaining increasing support in major NIH initiatives such as the National Children's Study; the Science of Behavior Change; and Genes, Behavior, and the Social Environment.

In addition, there are increasing calls for interdisciplinary work, given the recognition that to truly solve the complex issues facing our nation such as health disparities and obesity, then we need the input of multiple perspectives and disciplines. Related to the call for interdisciplinary work is the realization that to truly move the science of health and well-being forward, we need integration across multiple levels, from the cellular and molecular through the psychological and behavioral up to the economic, cultural, and social (Mabry et al., 2008). Until now, much "interdisciplinary" work involves what some have called "horizontal" integration, such that fields working within the same "level" are collaborating. For example, biologists will collaborate with chemists or sociologists will work with economists. "Vertical" or multilevel integration in which molecular geneticists are working with psychologists and sociologists on a common problem is much more difficult to achieve, yet is what is ultimately necessary. The increasing recognition of the need for this integration provides an opportunity for behavioral and social scientists.

Given this backdrop, we believe that it is an exciting time to be a scientist interested in bridging this gap, and there are likely to be increasing opportunities. The key to more fully integrating the biomedical with the behavioral and social sciences does not lie in complaining about a lack of respect. Instead, we need to be able to demonstrate what we have to contribute to our quest to understand health, disease, prevention, and well-being. This involves being open to reframing our questions into language that more biomedically focused colleagues can understand and to make it clear how our techniques, methods, and subject matter expertise can significantly complement their inquiries. Perhaps one of the best examples of how this can work is in the study of genes and environment. Few would argue today that it is a question of nature or nurture. Clearly both matter. But, we are learning more about how critical the environment (particularly the social environment) is in "turning on or off" certain genes. In a series of studies, Caspi and Moffitt (2006) have demonstrated that the presence of certain genes moderates the impact of significant life stressors, including child abuse, in the development of depression and antisocial behavior. In other words, it is not the gene in isolation; it is the gene in combination with adverse (childhood) experiences that produce later psychopathology. Many are coming to realize that the genetic "revolution" cannot fully be realized without a better ability to define and measure the role of the environment in such processes.

How do I get started conducting applied research?

Probably the best place to start is to find one receptive colleague who is open to collaboration and have conversations about how you see your work as relevant to a particular genetic or biological question. Start small and take it one step at a time. If you have demonstrated you can contribute, even in a small way, then other opportunities are likely to present themselves. Do not be afraid to find people outside of your university who seem to be doing the type of work you are interested in and have been successful in bridging these worlds. Talk to them and obtain their advice and insights. Try not to be defensive; instead, work on reframing questions in a mutually understandable language.

We are not trying to be naïve. There are likely those within the medical and behavioral and social science research communities who may not see the benefit of multilevel integration. Yet, it is our experience that when the science is discussed in a language that is understandable to both communities and when you are able to identify problems that both perspectives are needed to understand, then progress can be made.

Challenges and Issues in Applied Research Designs

What are some strategies for maximizing recruitment and retention?

Why are recruitment and retention so important? Well, for starters, you need to have an adequate sample size to have enough power in your study to detect differences if they exist. Validity of the study or the results can come into question if statistical power is insufficient. In addition, the time needed to recruit additional participants (maybe extend the study) can be costly. The characteristics of the final sample you end up recruiting can influence the interpretation and generalizability of the study results. We want to emphasize that spending sufficient time on recruitment strategies when designing the study is critical.

There are some general barriers to successful recruitment and retention. Awareness of these potential barriers can help you take some proactive steps to avoid problems that can arise from a small sample size. Barriers can be related to the participant, investigator, or the project itself.

One barrier to any type of research, but especially to research with children, is that the participant (or parent of the participant) has concerns with the study. Participation in research is a novel experience for many, and there may be unrealistic expectations of what is involved. The best solution to this barrier is related to informed consent. Detailed informed consent for the parent and informed assent for the child is necessary. Although the child's assent is not necessary for participation, it helps build rapport with the child, and lets her feel part of the process. There should also be a thorough verbal explanation of the study, its purpose, the amount of effort required from the participant, and possible risks and benefits. Participants should be aware (and reminded) that withdrawal from the study is an option at any point in time and without penalty. Additionally, make yourself available to answer any questions that may arise at a later point in time.

Next, consider the convenience of the study for your participants. The easier it is for people to participate, the greater chance that they will. Be flexible with time and consider the schedules of participants. Make the study location easily accessible if participants need to come to a lab, preferably near public transportation. If possible, offer reimbursement for travel for those who need it. Provide childcare for parents who have other children who may need to accompany them to the visit. Make snacks available if study participation is around a meal time. Consider home visits to collect data if participants cannot travel to the site.

It is very important to consider cultural factors when recruiting for a study. Consider possible language barriers and whether information or measures need to be available in another language. Certain communities may view research skeptically, depending on their history, so developing trust and building relationships within the community are key (see section in this chapter on Conducting Research in Applied Settings and Section III in this volume).

The investigator can also (unintentionally) hinder recruitment. First, do not underestimate the time it will take to recruit your sample. Build in enough time on the front end of this process. Consider designing a recruitment strategy that addresses the locations for recruiting, partners or staff who can assist in the daily effort, advertising (e.g., fliers), procedure of informed consent/assent, and incentives, if used. Another pitfall for investigators is lack of motivation. Some aspects of a study are naturally more exciting and engaging than others. Do not put the cart before the horse. In order for the study to have the best chance of succeeding, you have to put significant effort into this initial phase of the study.

Retention

Subjects drop out of research for many different reasons. Recognizing the challenges of participation in your specific study is the first step. Ask yourself, if you were participating in this study, what would make it challenging or difficult? Consider how the family is affected, not simply the individual participant.

When conducting longitudinal research, you may have a difficult time reconnecting with participants for follow-up assessments due to a move, phone disconnection, or school change. Therefore, when you recruit your participants, ask them for the names, addresses, and phone numbers of two people who could help you locate them if they move or cannot be reached. Another strategy is to send annual birthday cards to the children, which is a nice way of keeping in touch and reminding them that their participation is valued.

What are the venues for subject recruitment? How do you get others (i.e., parents, schools, communities) to collaborate?

Tips for Maximizing Recruitment and Retention

We have provided several suggestions for recruiting and retaining study participants.

1. Form partnerships with individuals or groups who have relationships with the pool of potential participants of interest. Participants are more likely to listen to a trusted source than an anonymous researcher. Therefore, since the subjects in applied developmental research are almost always children, it is important to make connections with those who serve as gatekeepers to this population. Aside from parents, partnerships can be formed with pediatricians, family physicians, community clinics or outreach services, daycares, schools, after school/community programs (e.g., Boys and Girls Clubs), and religious establishments. For this strategy to be successful, the partner organizations (or gatekeepers) must buy in to the program; researchers need to spend adequate time explaining the study, including benefits to participants and greater society. Sometimes researchers give small incentives for these gatekeepers for helping recruit, such as a small gift card or an entry into a raffle.

2. Use different mediums of communication and recruitment strategies. Recruiting through the mail is one way to spread information to a large group of people. For children, consider recruiting through a school if a partnership with the school can be formed. The school can provide information

to parents about the study or provide researchers with opportunities to recruit directly. Schools may also be willing to give addresses or phone numbers of students so that mail and phone recruiting is possible. Of course, the various ethical issues of this type of recruitment must be managed in conjunction with the institutional review board (IRB) overseeing the research. Be aware, however, that forming a new partnership with a school can be challenging, time intensive, and frustrating. Given that schools are often trying to balance multiple competing demands with limited amounts of time, administrators are sometimes hesitant to allow researchers to use class time for recruitment or data collection. Connecting with professionals within the school, such as a school psychologist, may also facilitate gaining access to this population. In addition to traditional recruitment strategies, consider signs, posters, or other public displays.

3. Provide incentives. Consider giving incentives for enrolling or participating in the study. For example, give a small incentive to the students for bringing back their consent form signed, regardless of whether the parent says yes or no to their child's participation. If the child was able to participate in the study, he or she can also receive a small incentive after completing the pretest and posttest survey. As previously mentioned, small incentives can also be given to those who assist in the recruiting effort, like teachers.

Conducting Policy-Relevant Research

What are some ways in which applied research on child and adolescent development can inform policy?

Policy research is a good example of an extension of applied child and adolescent development research. Whereas applied research usually addresses the causes, correlates, or consequences of a specific problem, policy research attempts to determine which concrete actions will address the problem. In other words, policy researchers are trying to create and evaluate public policies that will positively influence child development and the daily lives of children and families.

One of the main disconnects between researchers and policy makers is in the types of research questions that are studied.

Researchers are influenced by a variety of internal and external factors that shape the nature of their work, such as intrinsic interest, funding availability, and the pressures of pursuing research that will lead to tenure. Relevance to policy is one of the areas that is not on the radar screen of most academics.

So how could your research inform policy? Policy makers are looking for a few fundamental types of answers. First, what are the social conditions that influence behavior and development *and* are amenable to change via public policy? Second, what steps need to be taken to change these conditions? In other words, how do we improve the quality of current programs while demonstrating cost efficiency? What innovative policy actions can be identified and studied? Policy makers are much more interested in how a change in some program can positively influence development rather than the underlying processes behind development. Thus, in order for research on child and adolescent development to be applicable to policy needs, your research questions and hypotheses need to be structured around issues that public policy can reach. In addition, one of the most valuable pieces of evidence to a policy maker has to do with the economic efficiency and sustainability of a program using public expenditures. Currie (1997) discusses four criteria for evaluating child policies. First is how efficient is one policy compared to an alternative. Which policy will provide the largest benefit per dollar? The second is investment. Can you demonstrate that by investing in a specific intervention now, we will reduce the incidents of very costly problems in the future? The third criterion is equity, which evaluates if the policy distributes resources fairly. For example, is there enough funding available so that every child who qualifies for a specific benefit can receive it? Last, it is important to evaluate whether a policy has unintended consequences. We suggest that policy-relevant research is best suited by a multidisciplinary approach, and partnering with an economist to address these types of questions would definitely be advisable.

What is the value and significance of conducting policy research? How does that relate to child and adolescent development?

Consider the primary goals of policies aimed at youth. These goals include the enhancement of physical and mental health, intellect and language development, healthy relationships with others, and general well-being. In addition, some child policies attempt to ensure that children are raised by stable, responsible, and caring adults. In light of these goals, public funding is used to support a variety of programs for children, many of which address poverty, malnutrition, schools, and early education. Understanding these goals can help you design a study that both satisfies your research question but also provides useful information for policy makers.

The following are some other issues to consider in designing policy-relevant research:

- Focus on studying populations most directly impacted by policy and social programs (e.g., lower SES, minority children).
- Correlational analyses alone are not very useful to policy makers.
- *p*-Values should be reported with effects size, direction, and analysis of practical significance of the finding (McCartney & Rosenthal, 2000).
- Conduct cost–benefit analyses of specific policies or programs.

Conducting Research in Applied Settings

What is the best way to create a feeling of investment in research among people in the community and to integrate communities' interests? When I begin work with community organizations, I am concerned that I don't promise something I can't do without funding. How do you develop relationships when funding is so uncertain?

This set of questions gets at the heart of the challenges involved in conducting research in partnership with communities. Questions about building collaborations, balancing community and academic needs, and funding are all critical. For a detailed discussion and consideration of these issues, we refer you to the chapters on conducting research with special populations (Chapter 5) and translational research in community settings (Chapter 8). Here, we provide a few key issues to consider and point you to a few specific resources.

There are many definitions and approaches to community involvement in research. NIH has adopted the common *community-based participatory research* (CBPR) term, which appears to be most utilized in health circles. There are other approaches and terminology utilized in fields such as education, community psychology, and prevention research, but most share the fundamental principle that true collaboration involves the community as an active and equal participant in the entire research process, from concept development through implementation and evaluation. According to NIH, CBPR is defined as

> scientific inquiry conducted in communities and in partnership with researchers. The process of scientific inquiry is such that community members, persons affected by the health condition, disability or issue under study, or other key stakeholders in the community's health have the opportunity to be full participants in each phase of the work (from conception–design–conduct–analysis–interpretation–conclusions–communication of results). CBPR is characterized by substantial community input in the development of the grant application. (PAR 08-074, *Community Participation in Research*, http://grants.nih.gov/grants/guide/pa-files/PA-08-074.html)

Engaging in active and full collaboration with communities in the development, design, implementation, evaluation, and implications of research is not easy. We firmly believe in its value and its ability to improve the quality and impact of research, and thus, ultimately public health and well-being. It is also our experience that involvement in this type of collaboration can be a personal and professional growth and development experience and can be incredibly rewarding. That being said, it is not a straight and narrow path and this type of community-based research can be quite "messy." So, it is not something that is meant for everyone and should not be entered into lightly, as it involves a huge commitment on many levels. Of course, there are many alternatives between the extremes of the continuum from strict CBPR to ignoring community concerns and being the "typical" academic who conducts research without regard for community needs. This book provides many thoughtful explorations of ways to engage communities and conduct meaningful, policy-relevant research that can both advance knowledge and have an impact on the communities you are aiming to serve. We note that CBPR is one valuable, but challenging approach to achieving this goal.

In our experience, humility lies at the core of true CBPR. The key to successful and true partnership and collaboration with community organizations or populations means that the researcher must be able to leave his or her comfort zone as holding the position of power and authority. You must be able to appreciate and actually behave in ways that demonstrate recognition that both sides have something to contribute to the endeavor. You will bring content and scientific expertise and the ability (sometimes) to obtain funding, while the community will bring its sense of the true needs of the population as well as a sense of what has or has not worked in the past and what is feasible. Although many will espouse this in theory, it is difficult to actually practice, since in many ways it goes counter to how scientists are trained to think.

Because I am early in my career and concerned about tenure, I am framing research questions using academic processes more than community inputs. How do I foster relationships so that they are productive for the community, not just for my academic goals?

It is critical to always be mindful of the history that the community you are working with has with research, particularly when you are working with minority or traditionally underserved populations. This applies whether you are talking about their actual experience or simply historical knowledge of how their population has been treated by the research community. It does not matter whether you or your university were involved in any of these past interactions, it will have an impact on how you are viewed when you approach them to participate in your research. Most of the time, being very open and up front in addressing any past wrongdoings or bad experiences (in the form of asking what their concerns about research are) can be quite helpful in clearing the air. Ultimately, this process comes down to relationships and trust. You need to spend time "hanging around" and getting to know individuals in the community so that they can begin to see you are genuinely interested in working with them and understanding their perspective.

Inevitably the aforementioned questions emerge, particularly for young investigators. Honestly, conducting CBPR can be quite challenging, especially at the early stage of one's career. Partnerships take time to develop, and this is not the type of work that is going to lead to lots of publications in a short period of time. It does seem that the tide is changing slowly, and some departments are increasingly recognizing and valuing this type of research and even offering tenure "points" for policy and community relevant service. Yet, this is still the exception and not the rule. We are not trying to discourage you from entering this work, but it is important to be mindful of the realities. Sometimes it can be helpful to have another line of research going that may be able to give you needed, more "traditional" publications while you can slowly start building partnerships with communities for more long-term work. Collaborating with senior investigators who already have working relationships with communities can also be helpful.

Funding Resources

Funding for any research is always a primary issue, but for CBPR it is even more critical. First, as mentioned earlier, you often have to begin the collaboration process before you have a sense of the status of funding. Additionally, it is often the case that an intervention project is funded and then once the funding is gone, the community is no longer able to sustain the project. Conversations and plans for sustaining funding once the formal project is over must be addressed from the beginning.

CBPR as a focused approach and methodology is relatively new on the scene to NIH. But, NIH is making clear efforts to support this approach to research. Currently there are several program announcements specifically targeting this type of work:

> PAR 08-074, *Community Participation in Research* (R01), http://grants.nih.gov/grants/guide/pa-files/PA-08-074.html
>
> PAR 08-076, *Community Participation Research Targeting the Medically Underserved* (R01 and R21), http://grants.nih.gov/grants/guide/pa-files/PAR-08-076.html

The background information and research objectives are useful to reference, even after these notices expire. A recent OBBSR-led technical assistance workshop provided an excellent overview to the approach and very helpful step-by-step instructions for navigating the grant application process for CBPR investigations. All of the presentations are available on the Web (http://grants.nih.gov/grants/training/esaig/cbpr_workshop_20080229.htm) and we strongly encourage you to make use of this resource. Also, talking to a program officer in a particular NIH institute can help point you to other, institute-specific opportunities for CBPR work. Given the nature of the work, an exploratory grant mechanism (R21) is often well suited for beginning community collaborations.

The issue of needing to have the partnership before you get funding and then being unsure of what you will actually be able to do is one that often emerges. As more CBPR-specific funding opportunity announcements emerge and the realities of conducting this research become more apparent, it may get easier. But, if you speak to those who are most successful at CBPR, you will find that their funding has often been pieced together from a wide range of public and private sources. You may need to get some funding initially to focus on building the relationship before you design an intervention and apply for NIH funding. It is also important to be up front with communities about the realities of this process, so that you are not overpromising. Communities may be able to help brainstorm ideas for local- or state-level seed money that can offer smaller grants to keep things moving or can support pilot or coalition building work. Refer to the "Funding for Early Career Investigators" section in this chapter and the question on funding for ideas of private foundation and other government agencies that may be interested in supporting such work. Another resource may be found at Community-Campus Partnerships for Health (http://www.ccph.info/).

Interdisciplinary Collaborations

I believe that applied projects in one field can inform developmental processes in another (e.g., sexuality program evaluations can inform other sorts of prevention programs). I am uncertain how to maximize this cross-pollination of research findings and translation into practice.

This concern touches on a critical issue in most areas of scientific inquiry. We are all trained in a content area, and the way science moves forward is to continue to operate in these "silos." Just as biology, psychology, and sociology operate within their silos (hence the need for interdisciplinary work), just as NIH is divided up by diseases or body parts (or in two cases, life stages), so too are those who study violence separate from those who study mental illness or sexuality. We realize that there are necessary reasons for this segregation and some clear advantages to in-depth knowledge of a content area, particularly in training. Yet, we also know from decades of successful early intervention research that oftentimes programs that specifically target one outcome (e.g., drug abuse) may also have impacts in other areas. This makes sense if one believes in theoretical models that focus on, for example, social emotional learning or parenting, as key constructs or mechanisms of action. However, the catch is that sometimes specificity is needed. We need to better understand what types of interventions can have impact on multiple outcomes and which ones need to be more specific. This comes from the development and testing of strong theories guiding our interventions.

The good news is that there is increasing recognition of the importance of such overlap and there are currently a number of collaborations both at the NIH and at the individual researcher level, examining, for example, links between violence, substance use, and risky sexual behavior or between bullying and relationship violence. Given this state of affairs, if you are looking to conduct research, which addresses multiple content areas, one strategy is to look for "calls for research" that seek to integrate across the areas you are interested in. Another approach is to find colleagues who are working in the areas you would like to branch into and see if they are interested in collaborating.

A good place to start when looking for those who are currently conducting research in your area of interest is the NIH RePORTER (Research Portfolio Online Reporting Tool; http://report.nih.gov). RePORTER is a listing of biomedical and behavioral research currently being funded by NIH as well as other Health and Human Services (HHS) agencies such as the Agency for Healthcare Research and Quality (AHRQ), the Centers for Disease Control and Prevention (CDC), Substance Abuse and Mental Heath Services Administration (SAMHSA), Health Resources and Services Administration (HRSA), and the Food and Drug Administration (FDA). This database has a wealth of information and will be much more current than simply conducting a literature search, as projects often take years to reach the publication stage. For those of you interested in interventions with a preventive focus, you may consider exploring the Society for Prevention Research (http://www.preventionscience.org/). It has a very active network for early career professionals, which includes an electronic mailing list.

If, however, you are primarily seeking to use research evidence obtained in one content area to develop a program in another, then we think you must be more careful. Although some theories may suggest this type of overlap, if there is not at least some preliminary evidence for this crossover effect then you may be walking into risky territory. There are a lot of programs out there based on good will and common sense that do not work or may even have counterintuitive effects (e.g., DARE). As scientists, we must be careful not to contribute to this list. On the other hand, if you are already evaluating a program designed to target one outcome, then by all means measure other outcomes (within reason). If it is not measured, we will have no way of knowing if it does in fact have these cross-domain impacts. The R21 mechanism is often used for these kinds of high risk-high payoff studies. But be sure to pick outcomes with logical or theoretical basis for impact. Oftentimes what you decide to measure will depend on what the key issues and concerns are of the particular community you are working in (see question on CBPR in the section in this chapter titled "Conducting Research in Applied Settings").

Disseminating Applied Research Findings

Academic institutions place a high value on peer-reviewed publications. What is the best way for a researcher to publish in respectable journals while still reaching stakeholders involved in applied research with children?

One of the main goals of publishing is to communicate your findings with the outside world. What you publish and where you publish should reflect careful consideration of the audiences you would like to target. Given the importance of publishing in scientific journals for career advancement, it is important to try to get your articles into a reputable journal. This facilitates your responsibilities as a researcher to share your findings with your colleagues and allows for others to replicate your work or build off your ideas. However, as an applied developmental researcher, it is also important to share your findings with the general public and consider less traditional places to publish.

Deciding which journal or medium to submit to requires some background preparation, even before you begin your manuscript. First, find the class of journal where your work fits (academic specialty) and review several of the journals in that class. Look at the subject content that the journal caters to, the types of articles that are published in each, and what tier the journal is considered. Ask advice from more experienced colleagues who have served not only as authors, but also reviewers or journal editors. After this review, narrow your focus to two or three potential journals. Tailor your manuscript to the style of your first choice (review multiple issues of the journal for examples and see journal guidelines). Some examples of journals that publish applied developmental research include *Child Development, Journal of*

Applied Developmental Psychology, Journal of School Psychology, Pediatrics, Journal of Developmental Psychology, Journal of Applied Sociology, Journal of Social Work, Developmental Review, and *Developmental Science.*

Disseminating your work to the scientific community through academic journals is certainly the mainstream way of building your research credibility and career. However, the audience of scientific journals tends to be quite homogeneous: academics and researchers. Whereas communicating findings with your colleagues is important, there are many other audiences that can greatly benefit from a tailored description of your work. Indeed this is one of the main problems with dissemination; research findings are not easily available or interpretable by other stakeholders including policy makers and the general public. Therefore, we need to think creatively about other avenues for sharing information about child and adolescent development with those who can best utilize the information.

Aside from publishing in peer-reviewed scientific journals, consider other audiences who would benefit from learning about your research. If your findings have practical implications, find a way to get the information to those who work directly with children and youth, such as pediatricians, teachers, daycare providers, and other practitioners. Try to publish an article into a trade journal or magazine that targets the audience you are trying to reach. Communicating significant findings with the public can be challenging but it is very important. Think creatively about ways to reach parents, using plain language and explaining the significance of your findings in ways that are meaningful to them. Consider local papers and newsletters. See if local community organizations have publications to which you can submit a small article. In addition, there are often press offices at academic institutions, which may be helpful as well. These media offices may be able to help publicize your work, inform the community about participating in research, or provide advice about dealing with the media.

Last, we want to emphasize the need to disseminate your work to policy makers (see section in this chapter called "Bridging the gap between research policy and practice"). A few organizations, like the SRCD, American Psychological Association (APA), and the American Academy of Pediatrics (AAP), play an intermediary role between science and policy. Often, these organizations publish material specifically for policy makers (e.g., SRCD's Social Policy Report). Do not assume that findings you publish in an academic journal will reach practitioners, parents, or policy makers. Be proactive, creative, and persistent.

Funding for Early Career Investigators

How do young researchers survive in an environment where research funding is limited? Are there special funding opportunities for early career researchers?

Given the increasing difficulty of obtaining research grants from government funding agencies, early career researchers often face the grim reality of trying to get their project funded. Luckily, in recent years, there has been an attempt to assist early career professionals in successfully obtaining grants. We have outlined this question by discussing several of the main funding sources for research, and specific funding mechanisms, which are geared toward early career professionals. Take note, however, that this is not an exhaustive list of resources.

National Institutes of Health (NIH)

The NIH puts forth funding opportunity announcements (FOAs) of two primary kinds, requests for applications (RFAs) and program announcements (PAs). The RFA is typically a one-time solicitation for grant applications addressing a defined research topic. The PA, on the other hand, usually solicits applications over an extended time period and is used when an institute wants to increase its research program in a specific area. Another difference is that with an RFA, there is already a sum of money set aside for the best applications on the topic of interest. With a PA, there is usually no specific set aside of funds qualified grants get funded from a general fund. Many researchers also apply for "investigator initiated" grants, which are those *not* in response to a specific FOA. These grants, formally called "unsolicited" applications, are submitted under a "parent" announcement, a general application for a specific funding mechanism. The majority of grants are submitted under a parent announcement.

Understanding the types of grant mechanisms that NIH offers is important in helping you decide what to apply for. Take note, however, not all of the institutes and centers at NIH use the same mechanisms nor do they use them in the same way, so check with the institute first. That said, the most relevant NIH grants mechanisms for early career researchers are as follows:

F31—F mechanisms are for individual fellowships. The F31 mechanism is an individual fellowship award for predoctoral students. Applying for this type of grant can help you fund your dissertation research and give you experience in grant writing. Currently at NIH, there are a few different types of F31 grants, and you must find out if the institute to which you are applying supports the F31. In general, these grants are given to support promising doctoral candidates conducting research in the scientific-health fields.

F32—The F32 is a postdoctoral fellowship supported by many of NIH institutes. This mechanism is to support promising postdoctoral applicants who want to become independent researchers in science-health related fields.

R03—This is a small research grant. The *R* in the R mechanisms stands for research. These grants offer $50,000 each year for two years, and are not renewable. This is a small amount of funding for a short amount of time for things like pilot studies, collection of preliminary data, secondary data analysis of already collected data, and so forth. An R03 is often used as a pilot study that will lead to an R01 grant application. (The R01 is the most common research program grant and provides funding for up to five years and up to $500K in direct costs per year. R01 grants are not "starter" grants so we recommend considering the other mechanisms first.)

R15 (Academic Research Enhancement Award [AREA])— The R15 grant mechanism is good for small research projects conducted at schools or research institutions that have not been major recipients of NIH grant funds. The goals of this research grant are to support meritorious research, to strengthen the research environment of the institution, and to expose students to research opportunities.

R21—This is called the Exploratory/Developmental Research Grant Award and is used to "encourage new, exploratory and developmental research projects by providing support for the early stages of the project." This mechanism provides funding over two years up to $275,000. The various institutes and centers use grant mechanisms in different ways, and depending on which you apply to, the R21 might not be the best choice for a new investigator. As always, seek guidance from a program officer in the institute or center you are interested in applying to.

K99/R00 ("Kangaroo Award")—Pathways to Independence Award. All K grants focus on career development. This grant mechanism provides two types of funding support for those who are transitioning from being mentored to independent research. During the first year or two years of support, grantees are to complete their mentored research, with a focus on publishing their work and searching for an independent research position. After obtaining an assistant professorship (or equivalent), the "independence" phase of the grant begins. Funding is offered for up to three years to continue working on research that will lead to the independent R01 application.

There are a variety of other mechanisms at NIH, but NICHD funds the majority of the child development research. A full list of the mechanisms that NICHD supports can be found online at http://www.nichd.nih.gov/funding/mechanism/index. cfm. Also look for funding announcements at the National Institute on Drug Abuse (NIDA), the National Institute of Mental Health (NIMH), National Institute on Nursing Research (NINR), the National Cancer Institute (NCI), and the National Institute on Alcohol Abuse and Alcoholism (NIAAA).

National Science Foundation (NSF)

There are special funding announcements for undergraduates, graduates, and postdoctoral fellows in the area of social, behavioral, and economic sciences. http://www.nsf.gov/funding/

Substance Abuse and Mental Health Services Administration (SAMHSA)

SAMHSA provides grants for research to facilitate their mission of "building resilience and facilitating recovery for people with or at risk for mental or substance use disorders." http://www.samhsa .gov/grants/2009/

Department of Education (DOE) and Institute of Education Sciences (IES)

IES (http://ies.ed.gov/funding/) and DOE (http://www.ed.gov/ fund/grant/apply/grantsapps/index.html) fund research on academic achievement and other educational issues.

Administration for Children and Families (ACF)

ACF is in charge of federal programs that encourage the economic and social well-being of children and families and fund research that promotes this research (e.g., Head Start research). http://www.acf.hhs.gov/grants/index.html

National Institute of Justice (NIJ)

NIJ funds research related to crime control and justice issues, which includes violence against women and family violence. http://www.ojp.usdoj.gov/nij/funding/current.htm

Foundations

The Web site http://foundationcenter.org/findfunders/ will let you search a variety of foundations that award grant funding. Examples of foundations that cater to applied developmental research include the William T. Grant Foundation, the Foundation for Child Development, and the Robert Wood Johnson Foundation.

To search for all federally funded grants and additional information, go to http://www.grants.gov/.

To search for behavioral and social science funding, go to http://www.decadeofbehavior.org/finding-funding.cfn/.

Now that you have some information about where you might apply for a grant, you will have to spend time familiarizing yourself with the grant writing process. Even the best research ideas cannot get funded if the application is not well written. Here are some basic principles to help you develop this specific and important skill:

1. If possible, take a grant writing class or workshop. Often the hardest part of getting a grant is navigating the application and learning the skills of how to convey the right information in a specific way. If there is a graduate school grant writing class, this is a great opportunity. Take the class! You may even be able to write a grant for your dissertation. This will also help you in your job search if you choose to stay in academia. Having sat on a search committee for new faculty members, we can say that individuals with a track record of writing and receiving grants in the past (even as a graduate student) were considered much more competitive than those

who do not. There are also several books that guide you through writing grant applications. One example of such a book is the *Guide to Effective Grant Writing: How to Write a Successful NIH Grant Application* (Yang, 2005).

2. Many large-scale conferences have informational sessions on federal funding and the grant application process. Make a point to attend these types of sessions and speak to the program officers in attendance about your work and ideas.

3. Before applying for any funding, speak to a designated program officer in the area to which you are applying. Program officers will be able to help you understand the details of funding opportunity announcements and the application process. The program officer can also help you understand the current research priorities of the institute and suggest ways of improving your application. It is also good to have a relationship with your program officer because once your application is reviewed, she or he will be the contact person and should help you understand the critiques of the grants and how to make appropriate changes if necessary.

4. Have your application reviewed by colleagues who have a proven track record of receiving grant funding and those who have sat on review committees.

5. If at first you don't succeed ... A large number of grant applications are not accepted the first time around. Carefully review the critiques of your application and discuss them with the program officer. Addressing these critiques concretely in your revised application is necessary. If you cannot make the suggested change, you should state why the change is not possible or appropriate. Do not simply ignore reviewers' comments. New rules at the NIH will allow only one resubmission of a grant. Again, your program officer will be a good person talk with about the weaknesses of your application and how to approach resubmission.

Bridging the Gap Between Research, Policy and Practice

How do the agendas of researchers and policy makers differ? How does one serve as a bridge in the gap between research, policy, and people? How does one package and disseminate research findings to practitioners and policy makers?

This series of questions gets at the heart of what applied research on child and adolescent development is all about. After all, most of us who are involved in this enterprise ultimately want our research to be useful in improving the lives of children and families. Our perspective on these questions reflects our fellowship experiences, which include specific training about the interface of science and policy. We would also direct you to Chapter 12 for the reflections of those with more "real world" experience in this exciting, but challenging, endeavor. And, remember, thinking about the policy implications of your work should be considered in the conceptualization of the research (see the section in this chapter titled Conducting Policy-Relevant Research).

Perhaps the most important thing to understand when embarking on this journey is that science, policy, and practice are three unique cultures in the truest sense of the word *culture*. Each has its own set of norms and rules governing behavior, language and communication patterns, and general approach to the world. Specifically, they each possess different rules about evidence, time frame in which they operate, basic purpose and orientation, standards for accountability and reward, and language and communication styles. Fundamentally, science is designed to understand and explain and uncover what we do not know. In contrast, the ultimate goal of policy (and practice) is to act and make decisions, and it is focused on what we must do (Nelson, 2005; Shonkoff, 2000). This fundamental difference, combined with a much shorter time frame and a focus on relationships and personal stories in communication, makes the policy world seem quite foreign to many scientists. Indeed, one must really think of entering the policy world as a cross-cultural experience and be willing to learn and respect other's way of being while working to find common ground and shared purpose (Shonkoff, 2000).

It is also important to understand that in the policy arena, science is only one of many sources of input and knowledge that goes into decision making. Social, economic, political, and personal motivations clearly play a role in policy decision making. It is our observation that many scientists have a difficult time appreciating this and often believe that science should be the only, or at least the primary, source of information used to guide policy decisions. It is believed by many that if they (policy makers) only had the information, they would make decisions based on sound science. Certainly, many politicians and policy makers respect science, want to understand the evidence, and attempt to use it when they are able to in making the best decisions they can. But, as an individual scientist attempting to make it in this "foreign" world, you must be able to come to terms with the realities of how decisions are made. There are efforts to base policy decision making more on the scientific process, such as the evidence-based policy movement. Yet, the policy-making process is likely always going to involve some level of personal, political, and social/economic inputs. Thus, your goal is to become a valuable and respected participant in the process.

In trying to make a way in the policy world, the general advice given to us was to be humble and learn the rules and culture of the policy world. Go out of your way to learn how to communicate effectively in this environment, by using the right language, and being honest, respectful, and diplomatic. Share what you know, but also the limits of your knowledge. Communication is key and it is important to recognize that it is a two-way street. You are not only there to give information but to listen and hear what policy makers really need to know. In the end, it really comes down to relationship building and using your interpersonal skills. People in the practice and policy world like to have individuals they know, trust, and respect to call when they need information. If you can become one of those people, then you are likely to be able to ensure that relevant scientific information about children and families is brought to the table when critical policy decisions are being made. Also, as mentioned several times already, seek out mentors who are doing this kind of work. It is our experience that most are more than willing to share their experiences and talk with junior people who want to get involved. Start with the authors of the chapters in this book.

In observing the science–policy interface at the federal level, our conclusion is that there are two kinds of nonfederal scientists who become involved (since as a federal employee, you are prevented from advocating to influence specific policies). Understanding the differences and potential risks involved is critical. There are those researchers who have come to be viewed as experts in a particular area. They are trusted and respected and called to give testimony. They are able to share knowledge about the state of the field and the status of the evidence as well as the limits of it. These scientists most often will stop short of endorsing a particular policy decision, noting that such decisions are out of their realm of expertise. They see their job as providing the evidence, answering questions, and perhaps, if possible based on knowledge, predicting what might happen with certain policies in place. On the other hand, there are some scientists who also are seen as experts and are often called to give testimony on the state of the science and the status of evidence. However, these researchers see their role more as advocates and in addition to presenting evidence will also recommend a specific policy based on their experience.

Clearly, this is a fine line and it is often difficult to tell when the line into "advocacy" has been crossed. Most of us probably do have specific ideas about what policies may work given our knowledge of the area as well as our own political leanings. In addition, it is important to remember that, despite what many would like to believe, the idea of "value free" science (especially social science) is really an illusion (Shonkoff, 2000). Each individual's values and experiences shape one's research questions and approach. We do not wish to tell you how to conduct your professional life or which "camp" you should place yourself in. However, it is our belief that really understanding the implications of both paths is critical for anyone venturing into the policy world. We suggest that you take the time to stop and think and make a conscious decision about which role you would like to play, if you are interested in becoming an "expert" witness of one form or another. Once you have established yourself in one camp (particularly the advocacy camp), it is likely to be difficult to "switch" approaches.

Finally, although we have less direct experience at this level, consider that most policy actually happens on the local level. Policies may be made at the federal level, but they are implemented at the state and local levels. It is often much easier to access the local level, particularly as a beginning point.

Resources

Many professional organizations can serve as a way station between the research and policy communities by activities such as publishing policy briefs, organizing briefings for congressional staff, and keeping their members informed of policy-relevant issues. Although they vary in intensity, most also offer some sort of "advocacy training" for those in their scientific community who are interested in becoming more involved but are not sure where to start. Many also offer media training for researchers whose work has attracted media or press attention or are interested in reaching out to broader audiences. Professional groups we know of that are involved in such activities include, but are not limited to, the APA, SRCD, AAP, American Public Health Association (APHA), Society of Behavioral Medicine (SBM), and American Sociological Association (ASA). The best place to start is with the professional organization that you consider your "home" base.

In addition, there are a broad range of nonprofit research, policy, and advocacy groups that conduct (or fund) policy-relevant research and work to disseminate relevant research to policy makers through research reports and policy briefs. Familiarizing yourself with the organizations that touch on your area of interest can provide you with a great deal of background information about the policy arena. They can also provide you with a large sample of policy briefs in order to learn the style, format, and language used in such documents. Writing a policy brief is quite different than writing for scientific audiences and takes practice. Policy makers require short, concise, and nontechnical language.

The following is only a partial list of such organizations:

Child Trends (www.childtrends.org)
Center for Law and Social Policy (www.clasp.org)
National Association for the Education of Young Children (www.naeyc.org)
National Women's Law Center (www.nwlc.org)
Robert Wood Johnson Foundation (www.rwjf.org)
Annie E. Casey Foundation (www.aecf.org)
William T. Grant Foundation (www.wtgrantfoundation.org)

As mentioned, oftentimes it can be more simple and less overwhelming to begin your policy quest at the state or local level. Consider organizations such as the National Governors Association (www.nga.org), the National Conference of State Legislatures (www.ncsl.org), or the National League of Cities (www.nlc.org) to help you get started. Find out what issues are currently on the table in your local community and determine if there is something that you can contribute based on your expertise.

Finally, there are a number of centers at major universities, which bring together interdisciplinary scholars interested in conducting policy-relevant research and bridging this gap. Three such examples include the Center on the Developing Child at Harvard University (www.developingchild.harvard.edu/), Cells to Society at Northwestern University (www.northwestern.edu/ipr/c2s/), and the National Center for Children in Poverty at Columbia University (www.nccp.org). However, there are many others as well, and we encourage you to seek them out, as they can provide a wealth of resources.

Conclusion

What we have provided is merely a starting point for answering your questions and providing the resources you will need for conducting applied research on children and adolescents. The chapters that follow provide case examples from the writers' experiences conducting applied research, and they address questions that early career investigators have posed in greater detail.

Acknowledgments

The opinions and assertions presented in this chapter are those of the authors and do not purport to represent those of the *Eunice Kennedy Shriver* National Institute of Child Health and Human Development, the National Institutes of Health, the US Department of Health and Human Services or the Inspire USA Foundation.

References

Caspi, A., & Moffitt, T. E. (2006). Gene–environment interactions in psychiatry: Joining forces with neuroscience. *Nature Reviews: Neuroscience, 7*, 583–590.

Currie, J. (1997). Choosing among alternative programs for poor children. *Future of Children, 7*, 113–132.

Mabry, P. L., Olster, D. H., Morgan, G. D., & Abrams, D. B. (2008). Interdisciplinarity and systems science to improve population health: A view from the NIH Office of Behavioral and Social Sciences Research. *American Journal of Preventive Medicine, 35*, S211–S224.

McCartney, K., & Rosenthal, R. (2000). Effect size, practical importance, and social policy for children. *Child Development, 71*, 173–180.

National Institutes of Health. (2008). *OBSSR fact sheet: Public health achievements of the behavioral and social sciences: Improving health at home and abroad.* Bethesda, MD: Author.

Nelson, S. (2005). *The contrasting cultures of science and policy-making and what they mean for your fellowship year.* Paper presented at the Orientation Program for the AAAS Science and Technology Policy Fellows, Washington, DC.

Shonkoff, J. (2000). Science, policy, and practice: Three cultures in search of a shared mission. *Child Development, 71,* 181–187.

Yang, O. (2005). *Guide to effective grant writing: How to write a successful NIH grant application.* New York: Springer-Verlag.

CHAPTER 3

Applied Developmental Science
Definitions and Dimensions

Richard M. Lerner, PhD
Tufts University

Introduction

Human development involves organized, systematic, and successive changes within a person across the life span, and the study of development involves therefore the description, explanation, and optimization of such intraindividual changes and, as well, the identification of interindividual differences in intraindividual changes across the life span (Baltes, Reese, & Nesselroade, 1977). While the goals of description and explanation are shared by all instances of science (for instance, from physics to genetics through astronomy), the optimization goal of applied developmental science stands in contrast to many other instances of science, where explanations are tested in the context of the researcher's ability to control or predict the full range of phenomena pertinent to a given scientific domain (e.g., physical particle movement, molecular change, neuromuscular connections, economic expansion in developing nations, or the orbits of comets).

Although developmental scientists are interested in prediction and control, through laboratory-based experiments or community-based interventions, the full range of variation of a phenomenon is not ethically available in the study of humans. For instance, learning ability or moral functioning may be normally distributed from low to high; however, the applied developmental scientist cannot ethically try to test the validity of his or her theory-based explanations by acting to decrease people's capacity to learn or to lower moral functioning or diminish character. The scientist is obligated to act to improve behavior, to make it more optimal, and not to act to deteriorate it. In short, in developmental science the only ethical option available to the researcher seeking to test his or her explanations of why the changes he or she has described appear as they do is to attempt to move human functioning in a more positive or healthier direction, to attempt to move human behavior toward more optimal functioning. This chapter will outline the theoretical framework of the core of applied developmental science, including a brief history of the origins of the field. In addition, I will discuss the instantiation of applied developmental science in studying children and adolescents.

These theoretical frameworks have guided my work. My theory of relations between life span human development and social change, and my research about the relations between adolescents and their peers, families, schools, and communities have contributed to knowledge about positive youth development. My work integrates the study of public policies and community-based programs with the promotion of positive youth development and youth contributions to civil society.

Applied Developmental Science: An Overview

At its core, the nature of applied developmental science involves the integration of basic issues of description and explanation with issues about how developmental science may be applied (e.g., through enacting community-based intervention programs or evaluating or testing the effects of social policies) to improve the human condition (and, as well, in the context of these applications, to test basic ideas about the individual and contextual bases of human development; Lerner, 2006). In short, contemporary developmental science involves a fundamental integration between basic and applied scientific work.

The conceptual foundation for this integration is predicated within modern developmental science by *developmental systems theories*. Today, these models of the mutually influential relations between individuals and their contexts (represented within the literature as individual ←→ context relations; Lerner, 2006) are at the cutting-edge of theory and research in contemporary developmental science (Damon & Lerner, 2006). As described in Table 3.1, these theories focus on *relations* among variables within and across the integrated levels of organization that comprise the ecology of human development (Bronfenbrenner & Morris, 2006; Overton, 2006).

TABLE 3.1 Defining Features of Developmental Systems Theories

A relational metamodel

Predicated on a postmodern philosophical perspective that transcends Cartesian dualism, developmental systems theories are framed by a relational metamodel for human development. There is, then, a rejection of all splits between components of the ecology of human development, e.g., between nature- and nurture-based variables, between continuity and discontinuity, or between stability and instability. Systemic syntheses or integrations replace dichotomizations or other reductionist partitions of the developmental system.

The integration of levels of organization

Relational thinking and the rejection of Cartesian splits are associated with the idea that all levels of organization within the ecology of human development are integrated or fused. These levels range from the biological and physiological through the cultural and historical.

Developmental regulation across ontogeny involves mutually influential individual ←→ context relations

As a consequence of the integration of levels, the regulation of development occurs through mutually influential connections among all levels of the developmental system, ranging from genes and cell physiology through individual mental and behavioral functioning to society, culture, the designed and natural ecology, and, ultimately, history. These mutually influential relations may be represented generically as Level 1 ←→ Level 2 (e.g., Family ←→ Community), and, in the case of ontogeny, may be represented as individual ←→ context.

Integrated actions, individual ←→ context relations, are the basic unit of analysis within human development

The character of developmental regulation means that the integration of actions—of the individual on the context and of the multiple levels of the context on the individual (individual ←→ context)—constitute the fundamental unit of analysis in the study of the basic process of human development.

Temporality and plasticity in human development

As a consequence of the fusion of the historical level of analysis—and therefore temporality—within of the levels of organization comprising the ecology of human development, the developmental system is characterized by the potential for systematic change, by plasticity. Observed trajectories of intraindividual change may vary across time and place as a consequence of such plasticity.

Plasticity is relative

Developmental regulation may both facilitate and constrain opportunities for change. Thus, change in individual ←→ context relations is not limitless, and the magnitude of plasticity (the probability of change in a developmental trajectory occurring in

TABLE 3.1 Defining Features of Developmental Systems Theories *(Continued)*

relation to variation in contextual conditions) may vary across the life span and history. Nevertheless, the potential for plasticity at both individual and contextual levels constitutes a fundamental strength of all humans' development.

Intraindividual change, interindividual differences in intraindividual change, and the fundamental substantive significance of diversity

The combinations of variables across the integrated levels of organization within the developmental system that provide the basis of the developmental process will vary at least in part across individuals and groups. This diversity is systematic and lawfully produced by idiographic, group differential, and generic (nomothetic) phenomena. The range of interindividual differences in intraindividual change observed at any point in time is evidence of the plasticity of the developmental system, and makes the study of diversity of fundamental substantive significance for the description, explanation, and optimization of human development.

Optimism, the application of developmental science, and the promotion of positive human development

The potential for and instantiations of plasticity legitimate an optimistic and proactive search for characteristics of individuals and of their ecologies that, together, can be arrayed to promote positive human development across life. Through the application of developmental science in planned attempts (i.e., interventions) to enhance (e.g., through social policies or community-based programs) the character of humans' developmental trajectories, the promotion of positive human development may be achieved by aligning the strengths (operationalized as the potential for positive change) of individuals and contexts.

Multidisciplinarity and the need for change-sensitive methodologies

The integrated levels of organization comprising the developmental system require collaborative analyses by scholars from multiple disciplines. Multidisciplinary knowledge and, ideally, interdisciplinary knowledge is sought. The temporal embeddedness and resulting plasticity of the developmental system requires that research designs, methods of observation and measurement, and procedures for data analysis be change sensitive and able to integrate trajectories of change at multiple levels of analysis.[a]

---

[a] Representative instances of change-sensitive methodologies may involve (a) innovations in sampling (e.g., theoretically predicated selection of participants and of x-axis divisions, or inverting the x-axis and the y-axis, that is, making time the dependent variable; (b) using measures designed to be sensitive to change; to possess equivalence across temporal levels (age, generation, history), different groups (sex, race, religion), and different contexts (family, community, urban–rural, culture); to provide relational indices (e.g., of person–environment fit); and to provide triangulation across different observational systems (convergent and divergent validation); (c) employing designs that are change-sensitive designs, such as longitudinal and sequential strategies, person-centered, as compared to variable-centered, analyses ("P" versus "R" approaches); and (d) data analyses that afford multivariate analyses of change, for instance, procedures as structural equation modeling (SEM), hierarchical linear modeling (HLM), trajectory analysis, or time series analysis.

For instance, genes contribute to the development of mind and behavior but, at the same time, behavior and the broader ecology of human development influence the function and role of genes in development (Garcia Coll, Bearer, & Lerner, 2004; Gottlieb, Wahlsten, & Lickliter, 2006; Lewontin, 2000). Suomi (2004), for example, has found that variations in infant–mother and in peer group relations in rhesus monkeys accounts for whether specific genes are associated with either aggression and poor social skills or with socially skilled and peaceful behaviors. Shiner and Caspi (2008) reported that analogous interactions between genes and the social context have comparable outcomes in human development.

How do I gain a firmer grounding in the developmental perspective, including how psychosocial and biosocial developmental processes interact with proximate environments, such as family, school, and peers?

Accordingly, whether studying infancy, childhood, adolescence, or the adult and aging portions of the life span, the cutting edge of contemporary scholarship in human development involves attempting to integrate information from the several levels of organization comprising the ecology of human development (Bronfenbrenner & Morris, 2006). Such work aims to explain how mutually influential (i.e., bidirectional, reciprocal, or fused; e.g., Thelen & Smith, 2006; Tobach & Greenberg, 1984) relations between individuals and their contexts provide the basis for behavior and development. As such, to describe, explain, and optimize developmental changes, the applied developmental scientist focuses on systematic and successive alterations in the course of the relations an individual has with the multiple levels of the ecology of human development, ranging from the inner-biological level through the sociocultural and historical levels (Bronfenbrenner & Morris, 2006; Lerner, 2002, 2006). In short, through conducting research that is focused on or, at the least, informed by individual ←→ context relations, developmental scientists can describe, explain, and optimize trajectories of developmental changes across the life span (Baltes et al., 1977).

Not all developmental scientists pursue all three goals (describe, explain, and optimize) at one time (or even within one career).

Nevertheless, all goals are needed to have a complete and vibrant developmental science. Indeed, the view that the application of developmental science is regarded as a foundational component of the contemporary study of human development is evidenced both by the broad interest in the conceptual facets of developmental systems models (e.g., see Volume 1, "Theoretical Models of Human Development," in the 6th edition of the *Handbook of Child Psychology*; Damon & Lerner, 2006) and by the active research associated with issues of application of developmental science (e.g., see the four volumes of the *Handbook of Applied Developmental Science: Promoting Positive Child, Adolescent, and Family Development through Research, Policies, and Programs*; Lerner, Jacobs, & Wertlieb, 2003; the two-volume *Applied Developmental Science: An Encyclopedia of Research, Policies, and Programs*; Fisher & Lerner, 2005; or the articles published in the quarterly journal, *Applied Developmental Science*, which at this writing is now in its 12th volume year). Given the centrality of the application of developmental science within the field of human development, it is useful to review briefly the history and defining features of this domain of scholarship.

Applied Developmental Science: A Brief History

Applied developmental science seeks to advance the integration of developmental research with actions that promote positive development and enhance the life chances of vulnerable children, adolescents, young and old adults, and their families (e.g., see discussions by Eccles, 1996; Fisher & Lerner, 1994; Lerner, 2006; Lerner, Fisher, & Weinberg, 2000; Sherrod, 1999; Takanishi, 1993). Given its roots in developmental systems theory, applied developmental science challenges the usefulness of decontextualized knowledge and, as a consequence, the legitimacy of isolating scholarship from the pressing human problems of our world.

Accordingly, when focused on the first two decades of the life span, scientists applying developmental science use biological, behavioral, and social science theory and data to describe, explain, and optimize the course of child and adolescent development, and to enhance the key settings where young people develop. These settings are families, schools, after-school programs, community social service settings, or health settings. Section III of this book is devoted to a discussion of these settings.

The Scope of Applied Developmental Science Activities

In the late 1980s, scholars from several disciplines (ones associated with the American Psychological Association, the Society for Research in Child Development, the Society for Research on Adolescence, the International Society for Infant Studies, the Gerontological Society of America, the National Black Child Development Institute, and the National Council on Family Relations) came to the realization that issues of child, youth, and adult development; of family structure and function; of economic competitiveness; of environmental quality; and of health and health care were interdependent. To understand these phenomena requires creative and integrative research. To improve the status of these issues involves the design, deployment, and evaluation of innovative public policies and intervention programs. Moreover, as a consequence of the presence of the interrelated problems confronting global society, there has been over the last decade increasing societal pressure for universities, and for the scholars within them, to design and deliver knowledge applications addressing the problems of individuals and communities across the life span (Boyer, 1990; Chibucos & Lerner, 1999; Ralston, Lerner, Mullis, Simerly, & Murray, 1999).

These applications involve the ability to understand and assist the development of individuals who vary with respect to cultural and ethnic background, economic and social opportunity, physical and cognitive abilities, and conditions of living (e.g., in regard to their family, neighborhood, community, and physical settings). Moreover, infants at biological or social risk (e.g., due to being born into conditions of poverty), gifted children or those with developmental disabilities, adolescents considering health-compromising behaviors, single- and dual-worker parents, the frail elderly, and ethnic minority and impoverished families are just some of the populations requiring applications of knowledge based on the work of scholars—in fields such as psychology, sociology, nursing, human ecology/human development, social work, criminology, political science, medicine, biology, anthropology, and economics—who adopt a developmental perspective to their science.

The multiplicity of disciplines called on to apply their scientific expertise in the service of enhancing the development of individuals, families, and communities resulted in collaboration among the aforementioned learned societies. These groups organized a

National Task Force on Applied Developmental Science to synthesize research and applications aimed at describing, explaining, and promoting optimal developmental outcomes across the life cycle of individuals, families, and communities.

To accomplish these objectives, the National Task Force defined the nature and scope of applied developmental science. The Task Force forwarded these definitions in the context of convening a national conference (at Fordham University in October 1991), on "Graduate Education in the Applications of Developmental Science Across the Life Span." The conference inaugurated applied developmental science as a formal program of graduate study and specified the key components involved in graduate education in this area (Fisher et al., 1993). The National Task Force indicated that the activities of applied developmental science span a continuum of knowledge generation to knowledge application, which includes, but is not limited to

1. research on the applicability of scientific theory to growth and development in "natural," that is, ecologically valid contexts;
2. the study of developmental correlates of phenomena of social import;
3. the construction and utilization of developmentally and contextually sensitive assessment instruments;
4. the design and evaluation of developmental interventions and enhancement programs; and
5. the dissemination of developmental knowledge to individuals, families, communities, practitioners, and policy makers through developmental education, written materials, the mass media, expert testimony, and community collaborations.

In addition, applied developmental science has involved an embracing of an approach to scholarship that merges basic and applied research within an integrated developmental system (Lerner, 2002, 2006).

Accordingly, consistent with a developmental systems perspective, applied developmental scientists seek to synthesize research and outreach in order to describe, explain, and enhance development in individuals and families across the life span (Fisher & Lerner, 1994). Fisher et al. (1993) characterized the principles or core substantive features of applied developmental science into five conceptual components.

What are the best ways to analyze the interactions between social and individual factors over time and situation?

The first component is the temporality of change. There is a temporal dimension—a chronosystem (Bronfenbrenner & Morris, 2006)—that pertains to individuals, families, institutions, and community experiences. Simply put, things change.

Some temporal features of individual and contextual development or historical variation reflect continuity; other features may reflect discontinuity. Continuous or discontinuous changes may occur at different rates across different levels of organization of the human development system. For example, this requires that x-axis divisions of time be different for gauging the pattern of change for infant neuromuscular development, adolescent identity development, the family life cycle, or the course of school reforms subsequent to the introduction of new educational policies (Lerner, Schwartz, & Phelps, 2009).

Accordingly, the temporality of change has important implications for research design, service provision, and program evaluation. Because of temporality, generalizations across historical periods or birth cohorts may not be warranted (e.g., Elder, 1974; Elder & Shanahan, 2006).

The second component is sensitivity to individual differences and within-person change. Interventions must take into account individual differences. The diversity of racial, ethnic, social class, and gender groups and other important variations may moderate how an intervention may influence development (e.g., such variation may involve family socialization practices, youth motivation, or youth intellectual functioning). Applied developmental science must be attentive to both intraindividual change (i.e., within-person changes) and to interindividual differences in intraindividual change (i.e., between-person differences in within-person changes; Baltes et al., 1977). Given this focus on change, variation within and among people, that is, diversity, is a core, substantive component of developmental science theory and research. Indeed, diversity *is* the essence of human development.

The centrality of context in individual and family development is the third component. Predicated on the relational focus of developmental systems models, the basic unit of analysis in developmental science is the relation between features of the individual and features of the context (Bronfenbrenner & Morris, 2006). Context pertains to all levels within the developmental system, that is, the biological/physiological, individual (psychological/behavioral), social relational (e.g., dyadic or peer group), family, community, cultural (e.g., educational, religious, political, economic, etc.), and physical/ecological levels of organization. The focus on the individual ←→ context relation requires scholarship that involves systemic, multilevel approaches to research and program design and implementation.

The fourth conceptual component of applied developmental science has two areas of emphasis related to the description of normative developmental processes and primary prevention and optimization. The first area of emphasis focuses on diversity within applied developmental science, while the second area focuses on the promotion of positive development rather than a focus on remediation (Damon & Lerner, 2006; Lerner, 2006). Historically, the study of human development has all too often been equated with the study of White, middle-class American samples (e.g., Graham, 1992; Lerner, 2006). Consequently, considerably less is known about the normative development of other racial, ethnic, and national/cultural groups. For instance, normative information about the life-span development of Native Americans, Kenyans, Venezuelans, or Singaporeans does not exist, and normative descriptions of the family life cycle of African Americans, Cubans, Norwegians, Indians, or Chinese do not exist. Despite the absence of such normative information about the diversity of humanity, the normative study of White, middle-class American samples was often mistakenly construed as research identifying the characteristics of what was normative for all of humanity and what was reflective of optimal or ideal development. Such egregious overgeneralization is inconsistent with the core principles of applied developmental science. The need to identify what is normal and optimal among diverse individuals, families, communities, and cultural groups is regarded as a fundamental goal of the field.

The optimism about promoting positive human development, the second area of emphasis, derives from the concepts of plasticity and temporality and means that individual ←→ context relations can be found or created to enhance the likelihood of positive, healthy development (see Table 3.1). As a consequence, applied developmental science emphasizes that programs and policies may be aimed at promoting positive development and not only on reducing or remediating problems. Accordingly, deficit perspectives are eschewed within applied developmental science (e.g., Lerner, 2005; Lerner & Steinberg, 2007). Although problems of, and challenges to the healthy development of, human development do exist, such issues are not regarded as inevitable or as necessarily characteristic of particular age, racial, ethnic, or cultural groups. While work continues to need to be done to prevent or to reduce problems of development that do arise, especially because features of both positive and problematic development can develop at the same time (e.g. Phelps et al., 2007), researchers and practitioners using an applied developmental science perspective to frame their work emphasize the possibility of promoting positive human development across the life span (e.g., Baltes, Lindenberger, & Staudinger, 2006). Indeed, a goal for the field is to describe, explain, and optimize the life course of the diversity of humanity.

What is the best way to frame applied questions within a literature review of theory and practical application?

Finally, the fifth component of applied developmental science is respect for the bidirectional relationship between knowledge generation and knowledge application. Fisher and Lerner (1994, p. 7) have discussed this component by noting that

> there is an interactive relationship between science and application. Accordingly, the work of those who generate empirically based knowledge about development and those who provide professional services or construct policies affecting individuals and families is seen as reciprocal in that research and theory guide intervention strategies and the evaluation of interventions and policies provides the bases for reformulating theory and future research ... As a result, applied developmental [scientists] not only disseminate information about development to parents, professionals, and policy makers working to enhance the development of others, they also integrate the perspectives and experiences of these members of the community into the reformulation of theory and the design of research and interventions.

In sum, together, the components of applied developmental science foster a dynamic agenda of collaborations between researchers and practitioners that involves developmental, contextually sensitive research, and applications directed to enhancing the individual ←→ context relations characterizing the course of development of diverse individuals and groups. Applied developmental science scholarship inherently takes a life-span approach to human development in that individuals always interact in a social context composed of people of diverse age levels. In other words, part of any person's development involves relations with individuals who may be at any one of many other stages of life. These social relations are a basis of the course of intraindividual changes a person will experience in life.

Moreover, the life-span perspective of applied developmental science means also that research and application may be focused on understanding and promoting the positive development of individuals at any portion of the life course. To illustrate the character of applied developmental science research focused on a specific age level or stage of development, the following sample case is provided.

Instantiating Applied Developmental Science With Children and Adolescents

How may the components of applied developmental science describe, explain, and optimize the lives of diverse children and adolescents? Researchers need to conduct theory-predicated studies that explore the processes reciprocally linking youth and their contexts. Such research would be aimed at identifying and enhancing policies and programs intended to promote healthy child and adolescent development. Depending on the specific theory-predicated questions that are asked about developmental processes, a systematic research program should involve a range of research settings (from the laboratory to components of the actual ecology of youth development, e.g., families, schools, faith institutions, out-of-school-time activities, places of employment, community organizations, or the homes of friends or neighbors). Similarly, a range of research designs, measurement methods, and quantitative and qualitative data analytic procedures would be expected to be involved in studying the individual ←→ context relations involving youth. Any methodology selected for use *must* be change sensitive. Development cannot be studied, and tests of its enhancement cannot be made, unless designs, measures, and data analytic techniques are capable of observing and measuring change (for reviews, see Collins, 2006; Lerner, Dowling, & Chaudhuri, 2005; Little, Card, Preacher, & McConnell, 2009; Teti, 2005).

Several specific and substantive foci reflect the instantiation of applied developmental science to understand and enhance youth development. These include

- the assessment of the individual ←→ context processes involved in the course of healthy, positive youth development;
- the development, implementation, and evaluation of interventions to promote healthy child and adolescent development;
- the empirical evaluation of the impact of existing and emerging policies on youth and family development; and
- the dissemination of best practice information about youth development to policy makers, practitioners, and community members.

Furthermore, in that research in applied developmental science is directed to not only understanding but also improving the course of human development, any research program may eventually be expected to involve building collaborations between academic researchers and community organizations. Implicit within applied developmental science is an interest in developing, enhancing, and sustaining community-based activities that promote positive child, adolescent, and family development. To optimize youth development, this interest derives from developmental systems thinking on enhancing relationships among all organizational levels within the ecology of human development. Researchers in universities are parts of the system typically involved in building these community collaborations. However, other organizations such as research-oriented think tanks (for instance, the Brooking Institution, the Heritage Foundation, the American Enterprise Institute for Public Policy Research [AEI], or the Progressive Policy Institute), state-level research organizations (e.g., the Public Policy Institute of California), or community-based research organizations (e.g., Public/Private Ventures, Search Institute, Child Trends, or the Education Development Center [EDC]) also play a role optimizing youth development.

How does one begin to facilitate an interdisciplinary dialogue to translate research findings into practice?

These collaborations are necessary to bring about long-term, sustained benefits to youth and the communities involved. Applied developmental science is an approach to understanding how appropriate programs for diverse demographic characteristics of populations of youth, in diverse communities, optimize positive youth development.

An Applied Developmental Science Model for Studying and Enhancing Youth Development Programs

In the late 1990s, scientists at the National Institute of Mental Health (NIMH) suggested that the predominant research model used to conduct applied research and program evaluations was flawed, and suggesting that its use may be the reason effective youth development programs have not been sustained (Jensen, Hoagwood, & Trickett, 1999).

Jensen et al. (1999) described two distinct models for positive youth development that have been funded by National Institutes of Health (NIH). The first model, predominant in American social and behavioral science, was termed by Jensen et al. (1999) the efficacy research model. A key question addressed is: What programs works under optimal, university-based research conditions?

Studies using this model are aimed at demonstrating what is maximally effective under "optimal" (i.e., university-designed, as opposed to real-world) conditions, in regard to:

1. preventing the onset of behavioral or emotional problems;
2. ameliorating the course of problems after their onset; and
3. treating of problems that have reached clinical severity.

Results of these studies, given the resources and skills of applied scientists, demonstrate that it is possible to improve the lives of diverse youth and communities, even when they are faced with significant problems of poverty, poor educational resources, unemployment, and inadequate services or community infrastructure.

However, the fatal flaw in this model is that after the grant funding the research or demonstration project ends, or the expertise possessed by university faculty has left the community, the members of the community do not have the capacity to identify new resources to sustain the program. In addition, they may not have the skills themselves to conduct the program, especially in the manner that will enable them to both continue to improve the program and to prove to potential funders that they are effectively changing youth for the better (e.g., Jacobs, 1988; Lerner, Ostrom, & Freel, 1995).

When researchers "parachute" into and out of a community to demonstrate what "could work," and do not leave behind an infrastructure that enables the transformation of that demonstration into a set of actions that can be a continuing part of that community, community members may be worse off than they were before the demonstration project was launched. Having their hopes raised, having seen what might be possible with new skills and resources brought into their lives, they may feel more disappointed and more hopeless than before the demonstration began. Is there no alternative, then, to such a community outcome of applied science? Yes, there is. The second model of research introduced by Jensen et al. (1999), which has been rarely used and underfunded, Jensen et al. termed the outreach research. Outreach research involves research conducted in real-world community settings and is aimed both at conducting rigorous, contextual- and diversity-sensitive research and empowering the community to gain the knowledge and skills needed to keep effective, valued initiatives within the community.

The key question addressed in this model is: What programs work that are also palatable, feasible, durable, affordable, and sustainable in real-world settings? Jensen et al. (1999) concluded that the answer to this question is very few (if any), indeed. At this writing, almost 10 years after the publication of the Jensen article, the answer remains very much the same. What can be done to remedy this situation? Jensen et al. (1999) argue that the federal government must continue to move to support outreach research and new, more effective partnerships must be created between universities and communities to change the answer to many, if not most (see Eccles, 1996; McHale & Lerner, 1996).

Presented in Table 3.2 are the ideas suggested by Jensen et al. (1999) about how universities and communities can collaborate in sustaining effective youth-serving programs. Other scholars have contributed ideas about what is required to enact outreach research that empowers communities and enhances the lives of children and adolescents (e.g., Chibucos & Lerner, 1999; Eccles, 1996; Fetterman, Kaftarian, & Wandersman, 1996; Lerner & Simon, 1998; McHale & Lerner, 1996; Weinberg & Erikson, 1996; Zeldin, 1995). These ideas include a commitment by both the university and the community to learn from each other (to co-learn) about what is required to enhance the lives of particular youth; and humility on the part of the university and its faculty, so that (a) true co-learning and collaboration among equals can occur, and (b) cultural integration is achieved. Whereas the culture of the university is to care about (value) the quality of its research, the culture of the community is to care about (value) the presence in their lives of sustained, best practice programs.

TABLE 3.2 Sustaining Effective Youth-Serving Programs: Ideas for Building University–Community Collaborations

Jensen et al. (1999) point out that effective university–community collaborations in support of positive youth development should be based on several specific principles. These include:

1. An enhanced focus on the relevance of research to the actual ecology of youth (Bronfenbrenner & Morris, 2006). We have to study youth in the actual settings within which they live as opposed to contrived, albeit well-designed, laboratory-type studies.

2. Incorporating the values and needs of community collaborators within research activities (Kellogg Commission on the Future of State and Land-Grant Universities, 1999; Spanier, 1999).

3. Understanding both the intended and the unintended outcomes of an intervention program for youth and their context, and to measuring these outcomes.

4. Flexibility to fit local needs and circumstances, that is, an orientation to adjust the design or procedures of the research to the vicissitudes of the community within which the work is enacted (Jacobs, 1988).

5. Accordingly, a willingness to make modifications to research methods in order to fit the circumstances of the local community.

6. The embracing of long-term perspectives, that is, the commitment of the university to remain in the community for a time period sufficient to see the realization of community-valued developmental goals for its youth.

The vision of the outreach research model identified by Jensen et al. (1999) is to find the means to integrate these two cultures and, in so doing, provide benefits to both those conducting applied scholarship and those living in the communities where this scholarship is conducted.

Indeed, the ideas put forward about the outreach research model suggest that it is possible to conduct important, sound, and ecologically valid scholarship about youth development and provide the capacity within youth and community members to sustain valued, effective actions promoting positive development. In this way, applied developmental scientists may work to understand and serve society with program- and policy-related research and interventions.

Conclusion

Applied developmental scientists seek ways to apply their scientific expertise to promote the life chances of the individuals, social groups, and communities. The key challenge in such efforts is to generate scientifically rigorous evaluations of the usefulness of the policies and the programs and to use such information in the day-to-day operation of programs (e.g., Fetterman et al., 1996; Jacobs, 1988; Lerner, 2002). How may this challenge be addressed?

The expertise of the research and practitioner communities can provide much of the human resources needed to meet this challenge if means can be created to foster collaborations with the goal of creating empowered communities. At this writing, efforts in the United States, such as the America's Promise Alliance (APA), are aimed at precisely this sort of collaboration (America's Promise Alliance, 2007). APA is the country's largest multisector collaboration dedicated to the well-being of all young people in America (more information about APA may be found at http://americaspromise.org). Through partnering with researchers to conduct basic developmental research and evaluations of its work, the APA uses data to guide its strategy. Importantly, the APA disseminates the best practices derived from research to national partners, policy makers, and community leaders throughout the country. Based on the efforts such as those being pursued by APA, policies promoting such researcher–practitioner–community coalitions could become an integral component of a national youth and family development policy aimed at creating caring communities that possess the capacity to further the healthy development of youth and families (e.g., Kennedy, 1999; Sherrod, 1999; Spanier, 1999; Thompson, 1999; Zaff & Smerdon, 2009).

These partnerships, if facilitated and rewarded by an engaged university (Kellogg Commission on the Future of State and Land-Grant Colleges, 1999; Spanier, 1999), will enable scholars and their community collaborators to enhance social justice and contribute to civil society. As such, these collaborations will model how universities, and the applied developmental scientists working within them, may be part of a multi-institutional system changing American society by moving it in the direction of greater equity and access to democratizing resources for all its diverse citizens.

Given the enormous, indeed historically unprecedented, challenges facing the families of America and the world, perhaps especially as they strive to raise healthy and successful children capable of leading civil society productively, responsibly, and morally across the 21st century (Lerner, 2004, 2007), there is no time to lose in the development of such collaborations. Indeed, by enhancing its motivation for and capacity to engage in outreach research, the field of human development can improve upon the often-cited idea of Kurt Lewin (1943) that there is nothing as practical as a good theory. We can, through the application of developmental science, serve our world's citizens and demonstrate that there is nothing of greater value to civil society than a science devoted to using its scholarship to improve the life chances of all people.

Acknowledgments

The preparation of this chapter was supported in part by grants from the National 4-H Council and the John Templeton Foundation. I am grateful to Lawrence Gianinno, Jon Zaff, and Nicole Zarrett for their comments.

References

America's Promise Alliance. (2007). *From a meeting to a movement: Building a blueprint for action. An interim report on the Leadership Forum.* Washington, DC: Author.

Baltes, P. B., Lindenberger, U., Staudinger, U. (2006). Life span theory in developmental psychology. In W. Damon & R. M. Lerner (Eds.), *Handbook of Child Psychology: Vol. 1. Theoretical models of human development* (6th ed.; pp. 569–664). Hoboken, NJ: Wiley.

Baltes, P. B., Reese, H. W., & Nesselroade, J. R. (1977). *Life-span developmental psychology: Introduction to research methods.* Monterey, CA: Brooks/Cole.

Boyer, E. L. (1990). *Scholarship reconsidered: Priorities of the professoriate.* Princeton, NJ: The Carnegie Foundation for the Advancement of Teaching.

Bronfenbrenner, U., & Morris, P. A. (2006). The bioecological model of human development. In W. Damon & R. M. Lerner (Eds.), *Handbook of Child Psychology: Vol. 1. Theoretical models of human development* (6th ed., pp. 793–828). Hoboken, NJ: Wiley.

Chibucos, T., & Lerner, R. M. (Eds.). (1999). *Serving children and families through community-university partnerships: Success stories.* Norwell, MA: Kluwer Academic.

Collins, L. M. (2006). Analysis of longitudinal data. The integration of theoretical model, temporal design, and statistical model. *Annual Review of Psychology, 57,* 505–528.

Damon, W., & Lerner, R. M. (Eds.). (2006). *Handbook of child psychology* (6th ed.). Hoboken, NJ: Wiley.

Eccles, J. S. (1996). The power and difficulty of university-community collaboration. *Journal of Research on Adolescence, 6,* 81–86.

Elder, G. H. (1974). *Children of the Great Depression.* Chicago: University of Chicago Press.

Elder, G. H., Jr., & Shanahan, M. J. (2006). The life course and human development. In W. Damon & R. M. Lerner (Eds.), *Handbook of Child Psychology: Vol. 1. Theoretical models of human development* (6th ed., pp. 665–715). Hoboken, NJ: Wiley.

Fetterman, D. M., Kaftarian, S. J., & Wandersman, A. (Eds.). (1996). *Empowerment evaluation: Knowledge and tools for self-assessment and accountability.* Thousand Oaks, CA: Sage.

Fisher, C. B., & Lerner, R. M. (1994). Foundations of applied developmental psychology. In C. B. Fisher & R. M. Lerner (Eds.), *Applied developmental psychology* (pp. 3–20). New York: McGraw-Hill.

Fisher, C. B., & Lerner, R. M. (2005). *Applied developmental science: An encyclopedia of research, policies, and programs.* Thousand Oaks, CA: Sage.

Fisher, C. B., Murray, J. P., Dill, J. R., Hagen, J. W., Hogan, M. J., Lerner, R. M., ... Wilcox, B. (1993). The national conference on graduate education in the applications of developmental science across the life-span. *Journal of Applied Developmental Psychology, 14,* 1–10.

Garcia Coll, C., Bearer, E., & Lerner, R. M. (Eds.). (2004). *Nature and nurture: The complex interplay of genetic and environmental influences on human behavior and development.* Mahwah, NJ: Lawrence Erlbaum Associates.

Gottlieb, G., Wahlsten, D., & Lickliter, R. (2006). The significance of biology for human development: A developmental psychobiological systems view. In W. Damon & R. M. Lerner (Eds.), *Handbook of Child Psychology: Vol. 1. Theoretical models of human development* (6th ed., pp. 210–257). Hoboken, NJ: Wiley.

Graham, S. (1992). "Most of the subjects were white and middle class": Trends in published research on African Americans in selected APA journals, 1970–1989. *American Psychologist, 47*, 629–639.

Jacobs, F. (1988). The five-tiered approach to evaluation: Context and implementation. In H. B. Weiss & F. Jacobs (Eds.), *Evaluating family programs* (pp. 37–68). Hawthorne, NY: Aldine.

Jensen, P., Hoagwood, K., & Trickett, E. (1999). Ivory towers or earthen trenches?: Community collaborations to foster "real world" research. *Applied Developmental Science, 3*(4), 206–212.

Kellogg Commission on the Future of State and Land-Grant Colleges. (1999). *Returning to our roots: The engaged institution.* Washington, DC: National Association of State Universities and Land-Grant Colleges.

Kennedy, E. M. (1999). University-community partnerships: A mutually beneficial effort to aid community development and improve academic learning opportunities. *Applied Developmental Science, 3*(4), 197–198.

Lerner, R. M. (2002). *Concepts and theories of human development* (3rd ed.). Mahwah, NJ: Lawrence Erlbaum Associates.

Lerner, R. M. (2004). *Liberty: Thriving and civic engagement among America's youth.* Thousand Oaks, CA: Sage.

Lerner, R. M. (2005, September). *Promoting positive youth development: Theoretical and empirical bases.* White paper prepared for the Workshop on the Science of Adolescent Health and Development, National Research Council/Institute of Medicine. Washington, DC: National Academies of Science.

Lerner, R. M. (2006). Developmental science, developmental systems, and contemporary theories of human development. In W. Damon & R. M. Lerner (Eds.), *Handbook of Child Psychology: Vol. 1. Theoretical models of human development* (6th ed., pp. 1–17). Hoboken, NJ: Wiley.

Lerner, R. M. (2007). *The good teen: Rescuing adolescents from the myths of the storm and stress years.* New York: Crown.

Lerner, R. M., Dowling, E., & Chaudhuri, J. (2005). Methods of contextual assessment and assessing contextual methods: A developmental contextual perspective. In D. M. Teti (Ed.), *Handbook of research methods in developmental science* (pp. 183–209). Cambridge, MA: Blackwell.

Lerner, R. M., Fisher, C. B., & Weinberg, R. A. (2000). Toward a science for and of the people: Promoting civil society through the application of developmental science. *Child Development, 71*, 11–20.

Lerner, R. M., Jacobs, F., & Wertlieb, D. (Eds.). (2003). *Handbook of applied developmental science: Promoting positive child, adolescent, and family development through research, policies, and programs.* Thousand Oaks, CA: Sage.

Lerner, R. M., Ostrom, C. W., & Freel, M. A. (1995). Promoting positive youth and community development through outreach scholarship: Comments on Zeldin and Peterson. *Journal of Adolescent Research, 10,* 486–502.

Lerner, R. M., Schwartz, S. J., & Phelps, E. (2008). *Studying the processes of individual development: Theoretical problematics and methodological possibilities. Human Development, 52,* 44–68.

Lerner, R. M., & Simon, L. A. K. (Eds.). (1998). *University-community collaborations for the twenty-first century: Outreach scholarship for youth and families.* New York: Garland.

Lerner, R. M., & Steinberg, L. (Eds.). (2009). *Handbook of adolescent psychology* (3rd ed.). Hoboken, NJ: Wiley.

Lewin, K. (1943). Psychology and the process of group living. *Journal of Social Psychology, 17,* 113–131.

Lewontin, R. C. (2000). *The triple helix.* Cambridge, MA: Harvard University Press.

Little, T. D., Card, N. A., Preacher, K. J., & McConnell, E. (2009). Modeling longitudinal data from research on adolescence. In R. M. Lerner & L. Steinberg (Eds.), *Handbook of adolescent psychology* (3rd ed.). Hoboken, NJ: Wiley.

McHale, S. M., & Lerner, R. M. (1996). University-community collaborations on behalf of youth. *Journal of Research on Adolescence, 6,* 1–7.

Overton, W. F. (2006). Developmental psychology: Philosophy, concepts, methodology. In W. Damon & R. M. Lerner (Eds.), *Handbook of Child Psychology: Vol. 1. Theoretical models of human development* (6th ed., pp. 18–88). Hoboken, NJ: Wiley.

Phelps, E., Balsano, A., Fay, K., Peltz, J., Zimmerman, S., Lerner, R. M., & Lerner, J. V. (2007). Nuances in early adolescent development trajectories of positive and of problematic/risk behaviors: Findings from the 4-H Study of Positive Youth Development. *Child and Adolescent Clinics of North America, 16*(2), 473–496.

Ralston, P., Lerner, R. M., Mullis, A., Simerly, C., & Murray, J. (Eds.). (1999). *Social change, public policy and community collaboration: Training human development professionals for the twenty-first century.* Norwell, MA: Kluwer Academic.

Sherrod, L. R. (1999). "Giving child development knowledge away": Using university-community partnerships to disseminate research on children, youth, and families. *Applied Developmental Science, 3,* 228–234.

Shiner, R. L., & Caspi, A. (2008). Personality development. In W. Damon & R. M. Lerner (Eds.), *Child and adolescent development: An advanced course* (pp. 181–215). Hoboken, NJ: Wiley.

Spanier, G. B. (1999). Enhancing the quality of life: A model for the 21st century land-grant university. *Applied Developmental Science, 3,* 199–205.

Suomi, S. J. (2004). How gene-environment interactions influence emotional development in rhesus monkeys. In C. Garcia Coll, E. L. Bearer, & R. M. Lerner (Eds.), *Nature and nurture: The complex interplay of genetic and environmental influences on human behavior and development* (pp. 35–51). Mahwah, NJ: Lawrence Erlbaum Associates.

Takanishi, R. (1993). An agenda for the integration of research and policy during early adolescence. In R. M. Lerner (Ed.), *Early adolescence: Perspectives on research, policy, and intervention* (pp. 457–470). Hillsdale, NJ: Erlbaum.

Teti, D. M. (Ed.). (2005). *Handbook of research methods in developmental science.* Cambridge, MA: Blackwell.

Thelen, E., & Smith, L. B. (2006). Dynamic systems theories. In W. Damon & R. M. Lerner (Eds.), *Handbook of Child Psychology: Vol. 1. Theoretical models of human development* (6th ed., pp. 258–312). Hoboken, NJ: Wiley.

Thompson, L. (1999). Creating partnerships with government, communities, and universities to achieve results for children. *Applied Developmental Science, 3,* 213–216.

Tobach, E., & Greenberg, G. (1984). The significance of T. C. Schneirla's contribution to the concept of levels of integration. In G. Greenberg & E. Tobach (Eds.), *Behavioral evolution and integrative levels* (pp. 1–7). Hillsdale, NJ: Erlbaum.

Weinberg, R. A., & Erikson, M. F. (1996). Minnesota's Children, Youth, and Family Consortium: A university-community collaboration. *Journal of Research on Adolescence, 6*(1), 37–53.

Zaff, J., & Smerdon, B. (2009). Putting children front and center: Building coordinated social policy for America's Children. *Applied Developmental Science, 13*(3), 105–118.

Zeldin, S. (1995). Community-university collaborations for youth development: From theory to practice. *Journal of Adolescent Research, 10,* 449–469.

CHAPTER 4

Letting Your Questions Guide the Way

Framing Applied Questions in Child and Adolescent Development Research

Pamela M. Cole, PhD
The Pennsylvania State University

Introduction

Why are emotional distress and difficulties so prominent among the symptoms of mental health problems? Is it possible that emotional difficulties precede the emergence of problems like depression and conduct disorder, such that they can be detected early as a sign of risk? If so, how early can we identify emotional difficulties that signal risk? In early childhood, what is normal (a 2-year-old's tantrums) and what is a sign of atypical development? These are questions that arose as a result of my clinical work and which have motivated my research to this day. In this chapter, I reflect on this path, beginning with illustrations of some of the clinical work that stimulated my desire to study the development of emotion regulation. I offer these reflections as an example of how you might frame questions to pursue your own interests in the study of child and adolescent development and how you might consider the theoretical and conceptual frameworks that could provide the bases for your research aims and hypotheses. I note that I have not achieved all I had hoped, but I continue to be enthusiastic about progress and future directions in my area of interest. Along the way, I briefly summarize the knowledge about early childhood emotion regulation and share some of the bumps along the road, lessons learned, and new questions that need to be asked and answered.

What Is the Role of Emotions in Mental Health?

Emotion is an aspect of human functioning that has been receiving intense scientific attention. Why? There are two primary reasons. First, over the last 20 years it has become apparent that emotions play a major role in most aspects of healthy functioning, and they must be understood for a complete understanding of human behavior. We lack consensus as to the definition of emotion but many conceptualize emotions as priming action (Schutter, Hofman, & van Honk, 2008) and organizing information processing, for example, attention and memory (Craik & Turk-Brown, 2007; Jefferies, Smilek, Eich, & Enns, 2008). Emotions are also an important ingredient in social interaction and relationships; a child's social competence requires abilities to interpret others' emotional cues, to recognize one's own emotions and communicate them appropriately, and to manage them in ways that are socially acceptable (Halberstadt, Denham, & Dunsmore, 2001). A second reason that emotion research has sustained interest is the emergence of exciting new technical advances, particularly in genetics and neuroimaging, which aid our ability to describe the neurophysiological underpinnings of emotional functioning. I adopt the view that emotions are biologically prepared processes that enable us to cope with the ever-changing circumstances we face, as articulated in emotion theories that emphasize the adaptive nature of emotion (Frijda, 2007; Izard, 1991; Lazarus, 1999; Saarni, Campos, Camras, & Witherington, 2006). The developmental perspective that shares this view is the functional perspective (Barrett & Campos, 1987), in which each emotion is defined as a particular (a) *appreciation* of the significance of circumstances in relation to goals for well-being and (b) *preparedness to act* to maintain or regain well-being. Emotions, including negative emotions such as anger and shame, are normal, functional processes that allow us to recognize and deal with obstacles, losses, danger, and mistakes.

Despite the adaptive value of the capacity to be emotional, difficulties with emotion figure prominently in health-related problems, including poor sleep, obesity, heart disease, depression, and posttraumatic syndrome, to name just a few. The role of emotion in mental health problems became clear to me during my training as a clinical psychologist and, as I will explain, this led me to become interested in the development of *emotion regulation* in early childhood. Often, clinicians who are trying to alleviate symptomatic behavior encounter individuals with emotional profiles that deviate from the norm. Chronic hostility, paralyzing anxiety, lack of pleasure, unrelenting sadness, lack of remorse, mood swings, mania, recurring images of frightening events— these are among the many symptoms that define different disorders and that interfere with day-to-day functioning, relationships, and future prospects. The world philosophies and religions have always recognized the potentially problematic side of emotions, such that emotions were often regarded as irrational and undesirable. Yet the functional view asserts that emotions evolved and endured because they heighten survival, allowing us to read the meaning of circumstances for our well-being and to be ready to act quickly in those interests.

How do I link concepts within the framework of applied child and adolescent development?

The concept of emotion regulation provides a framework for integrating both the adaptive and maladaptive aspects of emotions. When well regulated, emotions serve goals for well-being in ways that are acceptable or tolerated within the sociocultural context of a person's life. That is, emotions enable us to deal with circumstances and we are equipped to modulate emotions to meet our goals within the situational and social constraints of any given set of circumstances. For instance, I can shout and quickly and forcefully move to grab my child from being hit by a car, and I can appear calm and poised despite being furious with my boss. In contrast, individuals suffering psychopathology appear emotionally dysregulated (Cole & Hall, 2008; Cole, Michel, & Teti, 1994). Poorly regulated emotional functioning—which may result from biological vulnerabilities, exposure to environmental adversities, or most likely the inter-action of these—compromise the individual's ability to achieve well-being in socially and situationally appropriate ways. This may reflect an atypical pattern of emotion regulation that arose under adverse circumstances and which becomes well estab-lished such that the individual does not change the pattern even when it compromises relationships, productive activity, and future development (Cicchetti, Ganiban, & Barnett, 1991; Cole et al., 1994). Because we lack consensus about the nature of emotion, and because we are increasingly realizing that the nervous system is inherently regulatory, it becomes difficult to understand what is being regulated and what is doing the regulation (Cole, Martin, & Dennis, 2004). Acknowledging this problem, I prefer the working definition most often cited in developmental science. Emotion regulation is defined by "intrinsic and extrinsic processes responsible for monitoring, evaluating, and modifying emotional reactions, especially their temporal and intensive features, to accomplish one's goals" (Thompson, 1994, pp. 27–28). In framing questions and decid-ing how to pursue a line of inquiry in your area of interest, a helpful and important first step is to search for gaps in the liter-ature and areas where consensus is lacking. This may provide an opportunity for you to take a unique perspective or put forward a novel approach that could potentially shift the prevailing par-adigm and allow significant advances in your field of study.

How I Became Interested in Studying the Development of Emotion Regulation

My interest in the study of early childhood development of emo-tion regulation was catalyzed by my clinical experiences at the University of Colorado Health Sciences Center (UCHSC), a stimulating and demanding internship year that forever influenced the path of my career. Prior to internship, I studied at the College of William and Mary (MA) and Penn State University (PhD). In a first-year seminar in my master's program, Dr. Deborah Hartley stated that developmental psychology was less a content area (compared to, say, cognitive psychology) and more an ori-entation to studying any aspect of psychology. This general atti-tude led me to the view that atypical development, as in the case of emerging psychopathology, cannot be understood without a firm understanding of the normal development of the processes that are affected in psychopathology. Dr. Hartley's assertion is likely the catalyst of my belief that we cannot understand child clinical psychology without examining it through the lens of a developmental approach. This led me to be interested in how the emotional development of a problem child differed from that of a typically developing child, which then helped me to frame my research questions and set the stage for clinical research and practice and, most important, their integration.

How do you trim down big ideas into feasible projects?

In support of my goal to understand childhood distress and symptoms through a developmental lens, all of my mentors allowed me to train jointly in clinical and developmental psychology; most important, they encouraged me not to do this as two separate specializations but to integrate the fields in my comprehensive exams and in my research. They saw value for clinical research in studying child psychopathology in relation to typical development and for developmental research in including children with or at risk for psychopathology in the study of individual differences. This approach gave me a broader range of questions to ask and perspectives from which to draw. The time was right for such thinking. Indeed leaders in child development research eloquently articulated and named a new approach called developmental psychopathology (Cicchetti & Cohen, 2006; Sroufe & Rutter, 1984).

I focused my graduate research on young children's cognitive self-control. Verbal self-instruction (Meichenbaum & Goodman, 1971) was a cognitive behavior therapy technique grounded in a developmental theory about how language comes to regulate behavior. Despite its developmental roots, the method was applied without regard to a child's developmental status, which perhaps explained why self-instruction was more effective in modifying motor behavior than academic performance (Cole & Kazdin, 1980). My dissertation examined resistance to distraction in young readers. I assessed the effects of verbal- and imagery-based self-instructions on second graders' ability to remember information they studied while they tried to help themselves resist distraction, a "talking" surprise jar. Both forms of self-instruction helped children resist distraction, but strategies recruiting the same cognitive domain (language, imagery) as the learning material (words, pictures) interfered with recall of material (Cole & Newcombe, 1983). That is, for young readers, talking to oneself to resist distraction interfered with word recall.

My interest in cognitive self-control, however, was transformed by my clinical internship. I sought an internship at UCHSC because of its strong tradition in developmental approaches to children's mental health (represented by scholars such as Emde, Harmon, Gaensbauer, Kempe, Pennington, and Spitz). There I learned about clinical models that took a developmental approach; these emphasized emotional development and relationships, particularly in early childhood, and the development of self-regulation. But more than what I read, my clinical experiences stimulated my interest in emotion regulation and raised more questions, some of which I would later pursue:

- Jerome, a 17-year-old, was caught sexually molesting young children. He had a flippant demeanor, with no remorse for his behavior. Did he lack a fundamental capacity to feel concern for others or anxiety about the consequences of his behavior?
- Delia, an 11-year-old, was so hard for her adoptive parents to manage that they were moving forward with relinquishing custody of her. Delia become silly and disruptive each time her therapist tried to help her deal with this situation. Was she unable to tolerate emotions associated with not only the loss of her adoptive but also her biological parents?
- What did Mark, the 12-year-old son of a mother with borderline personality disorder, feel when his mother "forgot" to pick him for a hard-earned home visit? Was it rage at his mother that caused him to throw a barbell at the head of a nurse who asked him about the call?

Looking at these problems through a developmental lens required consideration of their etiology, particularly the conditions that led to emotional difficulties; possibly each child had developed ways of coping with strong emotions that motivated or sustained their problem behaviors as well as interfered with treatment. Jerome, for instance, continued to be flippant until a day when the stringent rules of his treatment program frustrated him to the point of losing emotional control. In the aftermath of his rage, Jerome revealed that his father had sexually abused him for years, an accusation later substantiated by his father. Jerome changed emotionally after this disclosure. Abruptly, he was no longer flippant or indifferent; he became clinically depressed but also more amenable to using therapy to deal with his problems. The question arises then whether Jerome's problematic emotional profile resulted from the ways that he had regulated the intense and confusing emotions associated with being abused (being emotionally cut off) and whether this emotional profile actually contributed to his sexual misconduct.

After internship, I read everything I could on emotional development. I learned, for instance, about infant emotion production (Izard, Huebner, Risser, & Dougherty, 1980), young children's understanding of the causes of and expressions associated with different basic emotions (Barden, Zelko, Duncan, & Masters, 1980; Camras, 1980), and the role of feeling secure in predicting later competence (Matas, Arend, & Sroufe, 1978), but found little empirical work that directly addressed children's emotion regulation, the normative baseline I sought to understand in the development of problems in the clients I served. Then I read a pair of papers that inspired my first independent steps as a researcher: Carolyn Saarni's studies of children's knowledge of emotional display rules (1979) and ability to mask disappointment (1984). As often happens, I made a few modest changes in Saarni's procedures. To my surprise these changes led to the discovery that children, even as young as 3 years of age, spontaneously smiled when receiving a "disappointing" reward, that is, they seemed to attempt to regulate disappointment (Cole, 1986). Initially, journal reviewers were very skeptical (i.e., it was hard to get the work published). But persistence paid off and the paper was published and the findings—that preschool age children understand that they received a wrong, undesirable prize and still smile in the presence of the person who disappointed them but pout, frown, and mutter if alone—has been replicated in many labs. Thus, the evidence indicated that there is some ability to self-regulate negative emotions in very young children, an important building block in our ability to understand individual differences in emotion regulation and their implications for mental health and of psychopathology.

Building on Knowledge and Charting New Directions in *Your* Research

Since that time, there has been considerable progress in understanding emotional development. Summarizing early childhood development research at the turn of the century, Shonkoff and Phillips (2000) noted that science has established the fact that infants have the capacity to be emotional, that the development of self-regulation is a cornerstone of healthy development, and that some of the important developmental transitions in self-regulation occur between infancy and school age. It is now appreciated that infants' capacity to be emotional makes them sensitive to their emotional environments, both biologically and behaviorally; rather than being too immature to be affected by stress, the very young, even fetuses, are vulnerable to stress (Talge, Neal, & Glover, 2007). A new investigator could build on this knowledge to address questions about the mechanisms of transmission of risk or about which biological and environmental conditions offset risk. We know that emotionality plays a large role in biologically based individual differences in infants and that early childhood anger- or fear-proneness constitute one risk factor for later symptoms (Rothbart & Bates, 2006). Under what conditions does an anger-prone child develop conduct problems? Under what conditions does a fear-prone child avoid anxiety disorder?

We know that the manner in which a caregiver helps an infant to regulate states of pleasure and distress is central to emotional development, particularly the formation of secure attachment with caregivers, and that attachment security is a cornerstone of the ability to self-regulate, including the regulation of emotion (Sroufe, 1996). We understand that moral, social, or self-conscious emotions have their origins in toddlerhood (Kochanska, Aksan, & Koenig, 1995) and that even 2- and 3-year-olds have some basic understanding about emotion (Denham, 1998). We appreciate that the ability to regulate emotions is important for getting along with peers, complying with adults' directions, and learning new material even if it is difficult, all aspects of school readiness (Blair, 2002; Denham, 2006). What aspects of early social experience are critical to a child's becoming a secure, moral, cooperative, successful person? Does the same model of the adequate or optimal early experience apply to children from diverse backgrounds? What if your mother is overseas in the military? What if you are growing up in an unsafe neighborhood? Why do some children seem so resilient in the face of adverse experiences? Clearly, our models are insufficient because the role of caregiving and experience in development remain a mystery in so many respects.

Broadly, we are learning how neurobiology supports the ability to be emotional and to regulate emotion, in large part because of advances in the study of the human nervous system and of how genetic processes influence brain development. In regard to the development of psychopathology, we generally understand that heightened negative emotion, whether assessed as a temperamental trait or as a response to a specific situation, is a risk factor for later symptoms and disorders. Moreover, we know that the processing of information about others' emotions, measured as a behavioral or biological response, is atypical in individuals with psychiatric diagnoses. So, why then, do we lack precision in predicting which infant, child, or youth is at risk for specific disorders? What pieces of information could be added to the models and their tests that would increase the sensitivity of early screening for risk? Furthermore, we appreciate now that both the autonomic and central nervous system circuitries involve inherent regulatory features although we know less about how these specifically map onto behavioral processes over the course of development. How does environmental input, for example, influence developing neurocircuitry in the brain in ways that foster healthy emotional development, even in children with genetic risk (e.g., offspring of parents with disorders)?

Despite all that has been learned, there remains much to explain if we are to address the serious emotional difficulties of children and youth like those I met on my internship. It has been established that children who are more emotionally negative, and perhaps those who are less emotionally positive, are at risk for later psychological problems. This is progress because it increases our ability to understand how normal processes develop atypically such that they come to underlie formal disorder. Yet, to date, the findings are quite general and lack sufficient specificity as to which characteristics of emotional functioning are uniquely associated with the development of particular symptom patterns (Cole & Hall, 2008). To accomplish that level of specificity, we need to know which individual differences represent normal variations among typically developing children, which signal risk but not the presence of disorder, and which represent symptoms of an emerging disorder (Cole, Luby, & Sullivan, 2008). Each of these matters must also be considered in terms of the developing child and optimal times for intervention, a critical question if we hope to improve our ability to use science to prevent disorders. Finally, let's consider serious, chronic mental health problems such as personality disorders, which are among the most disabling and difficult to treat problems. Theories suggest that these involve specific types of emotional difficulties, as I have often seen in my clinical practice. Furthermore, theories indicate that personality disorders have their origins in early childhood, perhaps as a result of adverse environments and biological vulnerabilities. A large gap in our knowledge base is the link between early childhood emotional development and later emerging personality disorders. What might we see in a young child that would presage the child's risk for developing a personality disorder in late adolescence or early adulthood? Building on our knowledge of the emotional profile (intense emotional reactivity, feelings of abandonment, unpredictable mood changes) and psychological histories (high prevalence of child maltreatment) of women with borderline personality disorder, what pattern of emotional functioning might we see in a maltreated 4-year-old, for example, that would forecast the later development of borderline personality disorder symptoms? Jerome, the 17-year-old introduced earlier in this chapter, was diagnosed with conduct disorder (due to his criminal molestation of younger children) and narcissistic personality disorder (e.g., due to his sense of entitlement and exploitation of others). In hindsight, his history of father–son incest, which began when Jerome was 6 years old, may have played a contributing role to his later antisocial behavior. Did he begin to cut off emotionally as a means of dealing with this overwhelming experience? Were there signs of this when he was 6 or 7 years old? When did he begin to engage in misbehavior without regret and indifference to punishment? If we wished to study his emotional profile and how it changed over time, how would we measure the most clinically relevant aspects of his emotional functioning? The more we learn, the more complex the questions we need to figure out.

It may be that we do not yet have an adequate description of the early development of emotion regulation to detect the roots of emotional dysfunction. After discovering that children as young as 3 and 4 years of age spontaneously attempt to manage disappointment, I pursued the possibility that symptomatic preschool age children, specifically children whose parents and preschool teachers found "hard to manage," differed from their typically developing counterparts in their ability to regulate frustration and disappointment. Supported by the National Institute of Mental Health (NIMH), we learned that preschoolage children with symptoms of oppositional defiant disorder (e.g., angrily reactive, argumentative, noncompliant) did not regulate frustration and disappointment as well as children their age who are not symptomatic (Cole, Teti, & Zahn-Waxler, 2003; Cole, Zahn-Waxler, Fox, Usher, & Welsh, 1996; Cole, Zahn-Waxler, & Smith, 1994; Denham et al., 2000; Zahn-Waxler et al., 1994; Zahn-Waxler, Cole, Welsh, & Fox, 1995). In conjunction with federally sponsored studies in other labs, it became increasingly clear that early difficulties regulating negative emotions are a risk factor for behavior disorders. Yet, childhood depression and anxiety are also associated with heightened negative emotion, leaving open the question of whether there are specific emotional profiles that forecast risk for different forms of psychopathology. Moreover, it was clear that the typically developing preschoolage children had already acquired skills such that they were too "old" for us to study the contributing influences to their ability to regulate negative emotion. The research needed to include ages prior to age 4 years. So, if you are making your first foray into the study of child and adolescent development, it is essential for you to have on your research team a collaborator who has expertise in the specific developmental period you wish to study.

What are tips for writing concise applied research questions while still considering the many factors that often impinge upon an applied study?

Again supported by the NIMH, we have conducted a longitudinal study with the goal of understanding what precisely develops in the development of emotion regulation and what some of the contributing influences are to those specific changes. Generally, we knew that children's negative emotion episodes declined between the terrible twos and the time children enter school. But we did not know precisely why—information that may be critical for effective prevention and clinical intervention.

Moreover, during this same period of improved emotional behavior, there is rapid language development, it is assumed that language aids the regulation of emotion (we tell children "use your words"), and children with behavior problems are more likely to have language delays and children with language delays are more likely to have behavior problems—all of these perspectives led us to appreciate that we know very little about how language development contributes to the development of emotion regulation in this age period.

In the literature there were four disparate lines of work that argue for the role of language in the development of emotion regulation. First, there is a higher rate of behavior problems among children with language delays (Baker & Cantwell, 1975). Second, teaching typically developing children to talk about emotions seems to promote socioemotional competence (for review, see Denham, 1998). Third, effective prevention programs teach children to regulate anger by talking about their feelings (e.g., Domitrovich, Cortes, & Greenberg, 2007). Fourth, language and emotion systems are not automatically integrated; very young children do not express emotion simultaneously with speaking during early language acquisition (Bloom, 1993). Two of my students, Laura Armstrong and Caroline Pemberton, and I felt that this literature argued for a role for language in the development of emotion regulation but we could not find studies that actually demonstrated the mechanisms by which language enhanced emotion regulation We therefore tried to articulate our own thoughts about this, which became a chapter (Cole, Armstrong, & Pemberton, 2010). We argued that language provides a child with three tools that support self-regulation of emotion: (1) an alternative means of communicating needs, (2) a means of conceptualizing or "objectifying" experience that aids reflecting on events and planning behavior, and (3) a means of regulating behavior through self-directed speech. Yet, all of these are hypotheses that require testing.

In our work, we are following 120 children from age 18 months, when the terrible twos are underway, until they are 48 months old. We observe them at home and in our Child Study Center, asking (1) what are the behavioral changes that constitute improvements in self-regulation of anger between the toddler and preschool years, (2) to what degree do the rapid advances in language during this same developmental period contribute to the emergence of effective self-regulation of emotion, (3) to what degree do links between language development and emotion regulation depend on a parent's ability to harness child language into the service of emotion regulation, and (4) to what degree do stressors, such as family economic strain, marital conflict, daily hassles and major life events, compromise the integration of language skills into emotion regulation?

We recently completed this extensive data collection, and we are slowly digging out of the mound of information we have and answering our questions. The mound is huge because of the level of analysis we chose—we have extensive natural speech samples from family discourse during home visits (and now we see why so much language development research has been based on relatively small samples!) and so we have been transcribing family discourse for years and are still not finished. In addition, we generated hours of video records of children during challenging and pleasurable activities in our lab. Each procedure provides us an opportunity to conduct microanalytic assessments of children's emotion expressions, their behaviors, and the behaviors of their mothers. Our overall ratings of children's emotion regulation were completed relatively quickly but the detailed moment-by-moment assessment of the dynamic patterns involving children's emotion expressions and their associated behaviors has also taken years to complete. Why, you ask, did we put ourselves through this agony? Well, we ask ourselves that question often, but here's the catch. Despite the labor, we are excited to see we are getting closer to describing the nature of developmental changes and the mechanisms by which these changes occur. Indeed, a preliminary finding is that the degree to which a child gets angry at age 18 months predicts the child's language ability at 24 months, and child language ability at 24 months predicts child self-regulation of anger at later ages.

Based on our thinking about the role of the rapid growth in language development in this period, we propose that parents who capitalize on children's emerging language skills to encourage child self-regulation of emotion will have children who more effectively self-regulate in frustrating situations. It was exactly Jason's third birthday when he visited the lab. When a pair of puppets needed his help so they could stop being angry, Jason puzzled for a bit and then said, "When I'm cranky, I take a nap." Does Jason's ability to articulate a meaningful way of dealing with anger index an ability to deploy language when he has to regulate his own emotions? We hope that our mounds of family discourse transcripts and observations of children's self-regulatory attempts in quasi-naturalistic lab situations will reveal the mechanisms by which child language comes to serve emotion regulation.

We are excited about our family observation data for two additional reasons. First, the home visit data include fathers as well as mothers. Now, here's another bump on our road. Fathers tend to be a bit more reluctant than mothers to participate in research, and yet their inclusion is critical to our complete understanding of child development. However, we have more data from mothers than fathers, a missing data problem that reduces the power to detect effects. Still, we tell ourselves, we have more than 100 participating fathers and there may be appropriate ways to handle the problem; the cup is half full. Another challenge associated with our home visits is that they were scheduled for the convenience of the family, which surely helped our ability to retain over 90% of the families over 30 months of the child's life, but home visits were both relatively naturalistic and therefore the conditions highly varied. This introduces "noise" in the data because many varying factors influence our opportunities to observe certain behaviors and because the transcripts are not all equally clear. The TV is blaring, friends are over, the child is playing outside—not only does this make it more challenging to compare data across cases but the transcribers must be very patient. Still, the early data clearly indicate that 18-month-olds have many emotionally negative episodes during the visits, providing ample opportunity to understand how parental responses to child distress contribute to the later development of effective self-regulation of emotion. Still, it is worth it. We are finding that early parenting practices, such as elaborated discourse about a child's experience and structuring of child language when a child is upset, contribute to children's understanding of regulatory strategies at later ages (Pemberton, Armstrong, & Cole, 2009).

Another reason we are eager about our data is that our families represent a less often studied demographic group: rural and semirural economically strained families. We chose to study these particular families because they are representative of over 80% of the families we serve in the Child and Adolescent Service of our Penn State Psychological Clinic. In the clinic, we administer evidence-based interventions but must acknowledge that these were developed with more advantaged families, who were relatively well educated and had more financial resources. It is well established that socioeconomic status is related to both the amount of language input a child receives at home and the child's language abilities (Hart & Risley, 1995). Moreover, there is considerable reason to assume that cultural and subcultural influences affect emotion socialization and the relations between emotional functioning and risk (Cole & Tan, 2006). Evidence-based interventions for treating emotional difficulties or prevention efforts to promote emotional competence emphasize *talking about feelings*, but in many of our clinic families this is not as natural as the interventions might assume. Thus we have a unique opportunity to study the contributions of language development in children who are growing up in homes that tend to talk less than those of children in the majority of child development studies. We worked very hard to recruit our families, who were less likely to volunteer to participate in advertised research. First, with the help of the Geographical Information Systems unit of our Population Research Institute, we identified census tracts in towns that were, on average, about half an hour away from the university and were relatively dense with households in our income range and with young children. These areas became our recruitment hubs. Next, we spent hours in these towns, educating ourselves about the towns' histories and their oral traditions, an activity that made the graduate students question whether they were to be anthropologists or psychologists.

How do you choose your sample?

Once knowledgeable about the communities, we met with local clergy, educators, politicians, and pediatric care staff to describe our study and gain visibility for our project. Then, we sent undergraduates into the libraries to research community birth announcements, which we cross-referenced with our census tract data and then, finally, we mailed letters to homes we thought would be eligible, inviting them to participate in our study. In the end it took us 2 years to recruit 124 eligible families. Although we are just beginning to process our findings, it appears that the participating families, as a group, engage in less verbal exchanges with their young children, and that the children are less verbal than the families and children described in much of the child development literature, and consistently with evidence reported by Hart and Risley (1995) who studied 42 families with varying socioeconomic status.

Conclusion

Now, you may ask, what happened to our interest in risk for psychopathology? Sometimes what seems a simple first step takes a lifetime to complete. We are just designing our next study that will examine the same developmental processes in families where there is risk for psychopathology. By knowing the specific abilities that children are acquiring between ages 24 and 48 months, we will examine the processes in families in which both economic and emotional resources are strained. Our data suggest that it requires considerable parental patience, mindfulness, and creativity to help children learn to self-regulate, a task that is made more difficult when there is stress, particularly if it affects a parent's ability to regulate his or her own emotions in the presence of the child. We hope to further understanding of the child's emotional environment as a mechanism by which risk is conferred. We will be wiser about our methods as well, having learned that we need to improve our recording of natural speech and transcribe data more quickly. We will also make sure that we have far better recordings of young children's speech when they are in the lab so that we can better understand the very interesting things that they say to themselves.

I wrote this chapter during a semester when I was also supervising child clinical students in a practicum. The four graduate students are providing therapy services to about 15 families. One adolescent client lacks a supportive, guiding family and describes herself as emotionally strong and yet, when she is stressed, she runs away to get emotional relief, interfering with her ability to secure a safe and successful future. A young boy has intense temper tantrums 10 times a day every day. A boy in middle school has been engaged in inappropriate sexual behavior with peers, but he feels "sleepy" when the topic comes up in therapy. We have learned so much, and yet there is so much more to learn.

References

Baker, L., & Cantwell, D. P. (1975). Psychiatric and learning disorders in children with speech and language disorders: A critical review. *Advances in Learning and Behavioral Disabilities, 4,* 1–28.

Barden, R. C., Zelko, F. A., Duncan, S. W., & Masters, J. C. (1980). Children's consensual knowledge about the experiential determinants of emotion. *Journal of Personality and Social Psychology, 39,* 968–976.

Barrett, K. C., & Campos, J. J. (1987). Perspectives on emotional development II: A functionalist approach to emotions. In J. D. Osofsky (Ed.), *Handbook of infant development* (2nd ed., pp. 555–578). Oxford, England: Wiley.

Blair, C. B. (2002). School readiness: Integrating cognition and emotion in a neurobiological conceptualization of children's functioning at school entry. *American Psychologist, 57,* 111–127.

Bloom, L. (1993). *Language development from two to three.* New York: Cambridge.

Camras, L. A. (1980). Children's understanding of facial expressions used during conflict encounters. *Child Development, 51,* 879–885.

Cicchetti, D., & Cohen, D. J. (Eds.). (2006). *Developmental psychopathology: Volumes 1–3.* Hoboken, NJ: Wiley.

Cicchetti, D., Ganiban, J., & Barnett, D. (1991). Contributions from the study of high risk populations to understanding the development of emotion regulation. In J. Garber & K. A. Dodge (Eds.), *The development of emotion regulation and dysregulation* (pp. 15–48). New York: Cambridge University Press.

Cole, P. M. (1986). Children's spontaneous control of facial expression. *Child Development, 57,* 1309–1321.

Cole, P. M., Armstrong, L. M., & Pemberton, C. K. (2010). The role of language in the development of emotion regulation. In S. D. Calkins & M. A. Bell (Eds.), *Child development at the interface of emotion and cognition.* Washington, DC: American Psychological Association.

Cole, P. M., & Hall, S. E. (2008). Emotion dysregulation as a risk factor for psychopathology. In T. Beauchaine & S. Hinshaw (Eds.), *Developmental psychopathology* (pp. 265–298). Hoboken, NJ: Wiley.

Cole, P. M., & Kazdin, A. E. (1980). Critical issues in self-instruction training with children. *Child Behavior Therapy, 2,* 1–23.

Cole, P. M., Luby, J., & Sullivan, M. W. (2008). Emotions and the development of early childhood depression: Bridging the gap. *Child Development Perspectives, 2*(3), 141–148.

Cole, P. M., Martin, S. E., & Dennis, T. A. (2004). Emotion regulation as a scientific construct: Methodological challenges and directions for child development research. *Child Development, 75,* 317–333.

Cole, P. M., Michel, M. K., & Teti, L. O. (1994). The development of emotion regulation and dysregulation: A clinical perspective. *Monographs of the Society for Research in Child Development, 59*(2–3), 73–100.

Cole, P. M., & Newcombe, N. (1983). Interference effects of children's verbal and imaginal strategies for resistance to distraction on verbal and visual recognition memory. *Child Development, 54,* 42–50.

Cole, P. M., & Tan, P. Z. (2006). Emotion socialization from a cultural perspective. In J. Grusec & P. Hastings (Eds.), *Handbook of socialization* (pp. 516–542). New York: Guilford.

Cole, P. M., Teti, L. O., & Zahn-Waxler, C. (2003). Mutual emotion regulation and the stability of conduct problems between preschool and early school age. *Development and Psychopathology, 15,* 1–18.

Cole, P. M., Zahn-Waxler, C., Fox, N. A., Usher, B. A., & Welsh, J. D. (1996). Individual differences in emotion regulation and behavior problems in preschool children. *Journal of Abnormal Psychology, 105,* 518–529.

Cole, P. M., Zahn-Waxler, C., & Smith, K. D. (1994). Expressive control during a disappointment: Variations related to preschoolers' behavior problems. *Developmental Psychology, 30,* 835–846.

Craik, F. I. M., & Turk-Brown, N. B. (2007). The effects of attention and emotion on memory for context. In J. S. Naime (Ed.), *The foundations of remembering: Essays in honor of Henry L. Roediger, III* (pp. 159–170). New York: Psychology Press.

Denham, S. A. (1998). *Emotional development in young children.* New York: Guilford.

Denham, S. A. (2006). Social-emotional competence as support for school readiness: What is it and how do we assess it? *Early Education and Development, 17,* 57–89.

Denham, S. A., Workman, E., Cole, P. M., Weissbrod, C., Workman, E., Kendziora, K. T., & Zahn-Waxler, C. (2000). Prediction of externalizing behavior problems from early to middle childhood: The role of parental socialization and emotion expression. *Development and Psychopathology, 12,* 23–45.

Domitrovich, C. E., Cortes, R. C., & Greenberg, M. T. (2007). Improving young children's social and emotional competence: A randomized trial of the preschool "*PATHS*" curriculum. *Journal of Primary Prevention, 28,* 67–91.

Frijda, N. (2007). *The laws of emotion.* Mahwah, NJ: Erlbaum.

Halberstadt, A. G., Denham, S. A., & Dunsmore, J. C. (2001). Affective social competence. *Social Development, 10,* 79–119.

Hart, B., & Risley, T. R. (1995). *Meaningful differences in the everyday experience of young American children.* Baltimore: Brookes.

Izard, C. E. (1991). *The psychology of emotions.* New York: Plenum.

Izard, C. E., Huebner, R. R., Risser, D., & Dougherty, L. (1980). The young infant's ability to produce discrete emotions. *Developmental Psychology, 16,* 132–140.

Jefferies, L. N., Smilek, D., Eich, E., & Enns, J. T. (2008). Emotional valence and arousal interact in attentional control. *Psychological Science, 19*, 290–295.

Kochanska, G., Aksan, N., & Koenig, A. L. (1995). A longitudinal study of the roots of preschoolers' conscience: Committed compliance and emerging internalization. *Child Development, 66*, 1752–1769.

Lazarus, R. S. (1999). *Stress and emotion: A new synthesis*. New York: Springer.

Matas, L., Arend, R. A., & Sroufe, L. A. (1978). Continuity of adaptation in the second year: The relationship between attachment and later competence. *Child Development, 49*, 547–566.

Meichenbaum, D. H., & Goodman, J. (1971). Training impulsive children to talk to themselves: A means of developing self-control. *Journal of Abnormal Psychology, 77*, 115–126.

Pemberton, C. K., Armstrong, L. M., & Cole, P. M. (April, 2009). *Preschool age understanding of anger regulation: Contributions of toddler language ability and parent-child interaction*. Paper presented at the Biennial Meeting of the Society for Research in Child Development, Denver, CO.

Rothbart, M. K., & Bates, J. E. (2006). Temperament. In N. Eisenberg, W. Damon, & R. M. Lerner (Eds.), *Handbook of child psychology: Vol. 3. Social, emotional, and personality development* (6th ed., pp. 99–166). Hoboken, NJ: Wiley.

Saarni, C. (1979). Children's understanding of display rules for expressive behavior. *Developmental Psychology, 15*, 424–429.

Saarni, C. (1984). An observational study of children's attempts to monitor their expressive behavior. *Child Development, 55*, 1504–1513.

Saarni, C., Campos, J. J., Camras, L. A., & Witherington, D. (2006). Emotional development: Action, communication, and understanding. In N. Eisenberg, W. Damon, & R. M. Lerner (Eds.), *Handbook of child psychology: Vol. 3. Social, emotional, and personality development* (6th ed., pp. 226–299). Hoboken, NJ: Wiley.

Schutter, D. J. L. G., Hofman, D., & van Honk, J. (2008). Fearful faces selectively increase corticospinal motor tract excitability: A transcranial magnetic stimulation study. *Psychophysiology, 45*, 345–348.

Shonkoff, J. P., & Phillips, D. A. (Eds.). (2000). *From neurons to neighborhoods: The science of early childhood development*. Washington, DC: National Academy Press.

Sroufe, L. A. (1996). *Emotional development: The organization of the early years*. New York: Cambridge University Press.

Sroufe, L. A., & Rutter, M. (1984). The domain of developmental psychopathology. *Child Development, 55*, 17–29.

Talge, N. M., Neal, C., & Glover, V. (2007). Antenatal maternal stress and long-term effects on child neurodevelopment: How and why? *Journal of Child Psychology and Psychiatry, 48*, 245–261.

Thompson, R. A. (1994). Emotion regulation: A theme in search of definition. *Monographs of the Society for Research in Child Development*, *59*(2–3), 25–52.

Zahn-Waxler, C., Cole, P. M., Richardson, D. T., Friedman, R. J., Michel, M. K., & Belouad, F. (1994). Social problem solving in disruptive preschool children: Reactions to hypothetical situations of conflict and distress. *Merrill-Palmer Quarterly, 40*, 98–119.

Zahn-Waxler, C., Cole, P. M., Welsh, J. D., & Fox, N. A. (1995). Psychophysiological correlates of empathy and prosocial behaviors in preschool children with behavior problems. *Development and Psychopathology, 7*, 27–48.

SECTION **II**

CHALLENGES AND ISSUES CONDUCTING APPLIED RESEARCH ON CHILD AND ADOLESCENT DEVELOPMENT

CHAPTER 5

Designing Applied Studies for Special Populations

Establishing and Maintaining Trust in Research Relationships

Paul Spicer, PhD
University of Oklahoma

Introduction

In this chapter I explore my growing involvement with the philosophy and practice of community engagement in research, both generally, in the context of debates about research in American Indian and Alaska Native communities, and specifically in my applied work on child and adolescent development. Although my experiences are derived from my work in American Indian and Alaska Native communities, I argue that the lessons I have learned have more general implications for all applied developmental research, especially in communities of color in the United States that so often have felt betrayed by the research enterprise. By detailing ways of establishing more equitable distributions of power and responsibility in research, I hope to show how scholars can design studies that will work in communities that have not previously been involved in the articulation of developmental science.

I did not always identify as an applied researcher. Indeed, as it became clear that my career would center on health and human development in American Indian and Alaska Native communities, there was a time that I actively resisted the label of applied anthropologist, which seemed to imply that my work would never advance method and theory in anthropology, that I was a mere technician just applying the discoveries of my colleagues. I became even more aware of this potentially marginal role in anthropology when I took my first faculty position in academic medicine, which seemed to draw me even more into the world of application and away from discovery. As I started down the road of applied research, however, it became clear to me that, from the perspective of American Indian communities, the hierarchy of research was actually reversed: people and programs struggling to address the myriad social and medical problems that continue to plague all too many American Indian and Alaska Native communities saw little or no value in basic research. In fact, many in the tribal communities I visited argued that while they had been researched to death, they were dying at rates greater than ever. I recall this critique most vividly in the context of debates I sponsored with funds from the program on Ethical, Legal, and Social Implications (ELSI) research at the National Institutes of Health on the possible value of genetics to American Indian and Alaska Native people. Participants in these discussions pointed out that decades of research on diabetes had done nothing to ameliorate the disease; in fact its prevalence had dramatically increased over the same period that it had been most intensively studied.

Observations like this forced me to reevaluate my values as a researcher and I began to engage in dialogue with community members about what kinds of studies they felt might be of value and then to work with them to actually conduct this research. In the process, the way I saw myself as a scholar also changed. Rather than seeing myself as a technician, I discovered that a wealth of some of the most important questions in all of developmental science opened up in new and intriguing ways as I was forced to articulate knowledge that might matter to native communities. And far from simply applying the lessons of the true innovators in our fields, I discovered that, in many cases, these scholars were silent on very crucial questions about how their basic discoveries might be translated into interventions that had a demonstrable impact.

In the time since I began this journey, there have been numerous changes in how we see research and our accountability to our diverse publics. This includes the rise of community-based participatory research in public health, the priority of translational research in medicine, and emerging scholarship on dissemination and implementation more generally. After situating some of these trends in science in the American Indian and Alaska Native context, with specific reference to the emergence of a tribal participatory research (Fisher & Ball, 2003), I focus on a relatively simple set of techniques for engaging publics, often derived from my home discipline of anthropology, that can overcome many of the difficulties that researchers encounter when attempting to design studies in communities who have multiple reasons to distrust us. I focus, specifically, on my experiences in American Indian and Alaska Native communities, but some of my more recent inquiry into trust and trustworthiness in other ethnic communities, also funded by the ELSI program, suggests that American Indian and Alaska Native experiences are by no means unique with regard either to their grievances about research or the ways in which these can be addressed in the ways I outline here.

Applied Research in American Indian and Alaska Native Communities

American Indian and Alaska Native concerns about research have a long history. Writing nearly four decades ago, Vine Deloria, Jr., (1969) noted the problematic nature of relationships between American Indian people and the kind of researchers they most commonly encountered—anthropologists. American Indian and Alaska Native communities thus have a very long history of thinking about their relationships with researchers in the context of colonial regimes of power, and they have a well-documented set of grievances, including marginal involvement in study design and execution, little if any input into the interpretation and dissemination of results, and a general sense of betrayed trust as researchers have left communities once they have acquired their data with no continuing community engagement (Christopher, 2005; Manson, Garoutte, Goins, & Henderson, 2004; Norton & Manson, 1996; Wax, 1991).

Community-based participatory research (Burhansstipanov, Christopher, & Schumacher, 2005; Wallerstein & Duran, 2006), and the related formulation of tribal participatory research (Fisher & Ball, 2003), have been offered as remedies to many of these problems. These approaches seek to rebalance power within the research enterprise by including community expertise in all phases of the study, recognizing that community expertise is as, if not more, valuable than that of the scientist. Accounts of these processes in tribal communities have proliferated in recent years, and general consensus on both principles and practices is by now reasonably clear.

An early formulation of tribal research processes, developed in the context of research on environmental health among the Akwesasne Mohawk, emphasized the key role of three values: respect, equity, and empowerment, which gave shape to multiple aspects of research design, including communication strategies, the gathering of information, the establishment of the research agenda and parameters for the study, the exchange of knowledge, the negotiation and establishment of roles, the resolution of differences, and the gaining of acceptance and trust (Santiago-Rivera, Morse, Hunt, & Lickers, 1998). In Fisher and Ball's (2003) articulation of tribal participatory research, four key components converge to ensure effective tribal participation in research: tribal oversight, facilitation of discussions, community staffing, and the development of culturally specific intervention and assessment. One of the most intriguing and thorough uses of these approaches is that offered by Mohatt and his colleagues (2004), who describe an ongoing and comprehensive campus–community partnership for research to inform alcohol prevention in Alaska. Most notable is an emphasis on strategies for jointly articulated knowledge formation, which have led to important insights in all phases of the research. As they note: "It is not enough 'to involve participants' or 'to create forums for participation.' It is not enough to 'create a research advisory board.' Deeper levels of inquiry become possible when community representatives with differentiated roles and expertise reciprocally share the responsibility for inquiry with the researchers" (Mohatt et al., 2004, p. 272). In a related observation, Salois, Holkup, Tripp-Reimer, and Weinert (2006) emphasize the spiritual dimensions of the principles governing their tribal research, arguing that their study was structured by what they call a "spiritual covenant" to uphold the fundamental values of reciprocity, harmony, respect, and cultural humility in all aspects of their research program.

Work by Canadian scholars has been especially influential in the articulation of these policies and practices. Jacklin and Kinoshameg (2008) have articulated a set of eight values that have shaped their work: partnership, empowerment, community control, mutual benefit, holism, action, communication, and respect, which gave specific shape to survey design, study advertising, local staffing, sampling, interviewing, advocacy, and dissemination strategies. A commitment to these processes is also articulated by Ball and Jaynst (2008), who focus on the role of trust in the research relationship, the recording of agreements in memoranda of understanding, the development of campus–community teams with mutual capacity building, the thorough incorporation of indigenous perspectives in study design and analysis, and a commitment to community involvement in dissemination and applications of the knowledge derived from this work. Most notable, in the Canadian context, has been the promulgation of explicit guidance on the conduct of research among Aboriginal people by the Canadian Institutes of Health Research (2007)—a step that has, to date, not been taken by the U.S. National Institutes of Health.

How do applied researchers establish validity for methods that are designed in response to specific community contexts?

Although there certainly are issues that remain to be resolved, especially those that arise because of different orientations toward knowledge and practice in indigenous communities and the academy (Chino & DeBruyn, 2006; Cochran et al., 2008), broad consensus appears to have emerged concerning the need for shared power and responsibility in research in order to address questions of paramount concern in American Indian and Alaska Native communities. In what follows I want to focus on five lessons that have emerged in my own efforts to apply these insights into research in early childhood intervention, which is often listed as one of the fundamental priorities for research and program development in tribal communities.

Engaging Communities to Design Research in Applied Developmental Science

In discussing my particular approach to these requirements of research design in American Indian and Alaska Native communities, I begin with what I think is the most fundamental commitment that researchers and communities can make to each other: an agreement to work toward addressing an agreed upon problem. Without that, it is unlikely that any of the additional steps

I describe here will occur. I begin, then, with what I call a commitment to intervention, before turning to community engagement, local ownership, joint authorship, and new applications, which I offer as partial solutions to the challenges of designing research in special populations.

How can a researcher create an open and meaningful dialogue with people in the community about ways research can meet the needs of children?

A Commitment to Intervention

In a context in which people feel betrayed by research that has only benefited researchers, academics with an interest in articulating developmental research will not even be able to start a dialogue without a demonstrable commitment to work with communities on issues of paramount concern to them. I have characterized this as a commitment to intervention, but I do not mean to imply that there is no place for descriptive work or that all research must centrally involve a particular intervention model. Indeed, in my experience many American Indian and Alaska Native communities actually resent a leap to intervention if that presumes that an academic investigator knows what is wrong and how to fix it even more than they resent the idea that a researcher would conduct a study simply to resolve a debate in the literature. Such an approach runs counter to almost every tenet of participatory research reviewed earlier. Accordingly, researchers with an interest in pursuing applied developmental science in American Indian and Alaska Native communities must walk a fine line between acknowledging that problems exist and presuming either a full understanding of what these problems are or what the solutions might be. A commitment to intervention does not, indeed cannot, imply a rush to intervention. Rather, it simply means that all research must be building toward solutions to the problems of concern in communities. Without this fundamental orientation one simply cannot design or sustain meaningful programs of research in communities who feel they have gained little from their participation in previous research. At the same time, one cannot possibly hope to demonstrate an openness to the concerns of communities if one already knows what is wrong and what to do about it. Indeed, communities appreciate, and may even request, basic descriptive inquiry in advance of the development of an intervention to better identify targets of intervention.

With funds from the program in the Science and Ecology of Early Development from the National Institute of Child Health and Human Development, my colleagues and I have just completed basic descriptive research on the patterns and correlates of development over the first three years of life in the participating tribe. This research was designed to examine the ways in which the stresses of reservation life complicate parent–child interaction, as mediated through parental mental health and substance abuse problems, and compromise infant development. We articulated this research agenda jointly with partners from community service providers in the tribe, and this project built directly upon previous descriptive work we had done on the prevalence of mental health disorders in the same community (Beals, Manson, Mitchell, & Spicer, 2003). We identified variables that would inform intervention from previous pilot work in the same community (Sarche, Croy, Big Crow, Mitchell, & Spicer, 2009), but this study was never designed to directly develop an intervention. Nevertheless, it enjoyed broad-based support from the community because of the dearth of information they had to guide intervention development, which was a problem *they* had long recognized.

We have just now received funding for the next phase of this research, which will involve using the results from this descriptive research to identify intervention targets and to develop new intervention models. We expect to end this exploratory developmental grant with an intervention manual, which we will then test in a randomized controlled trial. Our experience with this tribe underscores its strong commitment to the best possible science, including randomized controlled trials, if this work addresses core concerns of the tribe in ways that are consonant with its ways of knowing and intervening in the world.

Our commitment to intervention is very long term and deliberate in this context. We began with basic descriptive work because we needed to identify targets for intervention. We have now identified several of those targets and are moving to consider what interventions make the most sense. Only after completing that work will we feel it is time to test what we have jointly created. All throughout this research both academic and community members of our teams have kept oriented to addressing the needs of young children and families and have remained committed to conducting the strongest possible science. But doing so has required constant dialogue between academic and community partners, and it is these processes to which I now turn, for without a joint understanding of the questions and the proper approach to answering them, all the commitment to intervention in the world will not make a bit of difference.

Although the experience I describe here derives from very specific experiences in American Indian communities, the lessons that emerge are obviously much more generally applicable. Research in any disadvantaged community will run into considerable difficulty if the investigator does not show a commitment to intervention. The concerns expressed by members of American Indian and Alaska Native communities are by no means unique to them. Our discussions on questions of trust in biomedical research in Colorado communities of color, which builds on our discussions of these issues in American Indian communities, underscore a very similar set of concerns regarding investigators who are motivated only by their own gain, and whose primary interest is in describing rather than addressing problems. Thus, the lessons that emerge from my work on infant development in an American Indian community are likely much more generally applicable: Disadvantaged communities have a history of exploitation, which colors their openness to research and the only sure way to break this cycle is to forge an authentic partnership to generate knowledge that offers some hope for addressing some troubling aspect of their lives. To do this, however, requires that we know how to engage with community members who may share our interests.

Community Engagement

Work in American Indian and Alaska Native communities is unique in that research within tribal jurisdictions requires the authorization of the tribal government. Although the specifics of these processes vary by tribe, with a growing number of tribes constituting their own research review boards, researchers working in American Indian and Alaska Native communities have long known that they needed the consent of tribal governments to conduct their research. But researchers have also known that such official approvals are no substitute for meaningful community engagement in research. Indeed, tribal councils have multiple competing priorities and research is generally quite low on their agendas, so a much broader set of community discussions are indicated in the design phases of any study if one truly wants it to be shaped by community perspectives. My colleague, Morris Foster, has articulated a process that he refers to as community consultation, by which he means a careful ethnographic attempt to determine who the key constituencies for any particular inquiry are coupled with a conscientious attempt to enter into dialogue with them on core aspects of the research design (Foster, Eisenbraun, & Carter, 1997). These processes require an ethnographic sensitivity to local community forms and an openness to discovering whom the key constituencies in a community may be. As such, these approaches apply equally well to any community that an investigator may choose to engage.

Standard techniques for community engagement include the formation of community advisory boards or steering committees and the elicitation of feedback from key stakeholders using focus groups, but what I want to emphasize here is the spirit with which we pursue these dialogues in our work, for without an openness and genuine humility, these can degenerate into mere tokens of inclusion, leaving the research irrelevant and the community yet again disappointed. Several of the articulations of participatory research emphasize the spirit of collaboration that should pervade efforts to engage community members in the design of a study and, in particular, the need for openness regarding diverse perspectives. This is essential if these efforts are to succeed, but it is also important to bear in mind that openness and collaboration are two-way streets. Early in my career, when faced with the intensity of people's anger toward research, my initial impulse was simply to shut up and listen. Indeed, one of the few compliments I remember receiving in my early efforts to foster discussions about genetic research in American Indian and Alaska Native communities was that I sure "knew how to take" the very severe criticism that was flying all about the forum. And please do not misunderstand: knowing how to react to such criticism in a nondefensive manner is an essential skill as one begins to probe the depths of the ways that past research has failed communities. But this cannot excuse us from an honest accounting of ourselves and our own needs as scientists. Honest and sincere community engagement requires openness on both sides of the dialogue. As I have indicated, in our own work in infant development, we have made clear to community partners from the beginning that we want to work with them to develop interventions that respond to the needs as they see them, in ways that they are proud of, but that if we (as a team) want to change policy and practice for their children, then we also need to conduct this work in the ways that the best developmental science demands. They are, of course, free to stop this research at any time, but the trust we have built over the years, based on honest sharing of perspectives on both sides of the partnership, suggests to me that we will, in the end, see this effort through to the actual testing of an intervention in a randomized controlled trial.

A commitment to the forms of community engagement is essential, which means that investigators must select community partners in a deliberate manner to ensure that they represent a broad range of community perspectives and experiences and must provide appropriate fora for discussions. But getting the right people to the right venues is only the first part of the task. Sincere and legitimate community engagement requires a very difficult balance for researchers between listening to, respecting, and acting upon community perspectives, on the one hand, while remaining true, as well, to their own personal identity and values as scientists. If one is careful about these ongoing discussions, then the result can be profound in the creation of a truly hybrid research enterprise, which builds community capacity for research at the same time that it develops an investigator's program of research in ways I describe next.

Local Ownership

Many of the aforementioned models of participatory research reviewed have local research assistants as centerpieces and, in the context of a particular study, this is a crucial step. But this is only one step on the way to building the infrastructure for a truly community-based participatory research program. More important still is a commitment to local research leadership and to the infrastructures of research that outlast any particular project. This is how universities have long operated, and this is a model of local economic development in which many tribal communities are increasingly interested. My work at the American Indian and

Alaska Native programs at the University of Colorado, where I was a faculty member for 13 years, was greatly facilitated by the creation of permanent field offices in several partner tribal communities. These field offices had several different staff positions and a genuine research career was possible as people moved from research assistants hired on specific projects, to supervisory responsibilities, to overall authority across all projects in the field office. These offices provided valuable resources for projects, but they also had another impact: they created a local research workforce that had in-depth familiarity with the concerns of the community and, at the same time, had grown to understand the needs of researchers. These community-based researchers achieved, in reverse, what we as university-based researchers had achieved: a perspective that blended community and campus. But while our perspective continued to privilege the concerns of our campus, theirs continued to privilege that of the community, which gave the community ownership of the research in a much more significant way than would have been possible had we simply employed local people to run the projects. Indeed, as these relationships evolved, many ideas for projects originated from the field offices, which became resources not only to our faculty and staff, but also to their communities, who had begun, at the time I relocated to the University of Oklahoma, to come to our field staff with ideas for projects that our faculty then wrote grants to try and fund.

Although this recommendation emerges from a relatively mature field operation, and no new investigator can create such an infrastructure with their first grant, the creation of community-based researchers is part and parcel of a long-term commitment to intervention and engagement in specific communities. And it is the process of seeking and developing these partners, rather than the specific trappings of a field office with a high-speed internet connection, that truly matters. Indeed, depending on the circumstances where one works, a field office with a large staff may never be practical, but an investment in the development of community-based researchers is something that legitimate community-based research can never do without. For without these kinds of partners, one can rest assured that his or her research will never be derived from a full dialogue between the campus and the community since no matter how savvy researchers may become, unless they become community members they will never appreciate those perspectives in the way that community-based researchers will. And it is for this reason that, in addition to the creation of community-based researchers, I also recommend the development of local coauthors.

Joint Authorship

Many tribes now require either review or approval of manuscripts and presentations arising from research in their jurisdictions or with their tribal members. Although these processes do succeed in establishing tribal authority over the dissemination of research findings, and ensure that egregious representations of communities and their problems are reworked before they ever see the light of day, these processes have the potential, always, to either be or become adversarial, especially when the community claims authority over what is published. My own hope is that these processes have been a necessary step on the way to ensuring genuine community participation in the analysis, interpretation, and dissemination of results. As noted, American Indian and Alaska Native communities have often felt betrayed by researchers either because they never hear what the results of a study were or because they do not agree with the way the results were interpreted or presented. Thus, tribal control over research dissemination has been a logical and appropriate protection to pursue. My colleagues and I have worked under these review procedures for a decade and have never been censored. Indeed, as these processes have evolved they have moved, naturally, to more collaborative participation in the dissemination of the research, with community review often adding or clarifying aspects of the research that would otherwise have been unarticulated or left poorly explained. And as my own team has moved more explicitly to formal coauthorship, these gains have multiplied. One of the best examples of this is the paper on which my colleague Michelle Sarche was lead author, which presents the results of some of our earlier infancy research in terms that were derived directly from discussions with our tribal field office staff who participated as coauthors and who emphasized throughout these discussions the need to stay focused on independent variables that were amenable to intervention (Sarche et al., 2009). Indeed, because of their insistence on these points we were persuaded to include a measure of American Indian identity that had previously disappointed us, and we were pleasantly surprised when we discovered that the strength of a mother's American

Indian identification was correlated with multiple aspects of her children's development—a finding that gave us additional momentum as we worked toward interventions that would strengthen the cultural attachments of American Indian parents.

Readers will no doubt have noticed that this piece is single-authored, which may strike many as inconsistent with the principles I am describing here. Indeed, were this a dissemination of the results of our study, I would certainly have jointly authored the piece with at least one community author and, were this intended to be a complete account of community-based research in American Indian and Alaska Native communities, balance would have dictated that this chapter reflect consensus between myself and my community partners. But this piece is neither a dissemination of the findings from my research, nor does it reflect any kind of consensus statement of procedures in the communities where I work. Instead, in keeping with spirit of this volume, it is intended simply to represent my reflections on an evolving practice in applied developmental science in disadvantaged communities and is offered only as points of departure for new researchers in applied developmental science who seek to draw on my experiences in seeking to jointly articulate knowledge in the developmental sciences, which I now close by considering the ways in which knowledge derived from these processes feeds into the evolution of a program of community-based research.

New Applications

Although the processes outlined so far ensure that studies are designed, conducted, and disseminated in collaboration with community partners, none of these close the loop opened by the initial commitment to intervention. The knowledge generated from studies designed through processes of community engagement in study design, local ownership of the research infrastructure, and joint authorship of study reports will do nothing to address the problems that gave rise to the inquiry without the generation of new applications. My label for this process is deliberately ambiguous, designed to recognize both new applications of the knowledge derived from a particular study to a particular problem (as in the earlier example of American Indian identity), and the development of new grant applications to support additional work that builds upon previous studies (as in the move we

have made from basic descriptive work to intervention development). Were we to stop our community-based research simply
at the production of jointly authored reports, we would actually
have failed to honor the commitment to intervention with which
we began, for a commitment to intervention requires the application of research, both in using the knowledge derived from
research to improve policy and practice, and in creating new
projects that build upon earlier work. Thus, new applications
bring us right back to where we began, with our commitment to
generate knowledge that would be of use in guiding intervention,
which we have arrived at through the engagement of community
partners in both the conduct of research and the articulation of
the knowledge derived from it. Before closing with some general observations on the implications of these practices, I want to
turn, first, to three questions I am often asked. Although I have
tried to anticipate these in the preceding discussion, I now want
to explicitly address them.

Frequently Asked Questions

Perhaps the question most frequently asked when I present these
approaches concerns the perception that one's research cannot be
guided by communities at the same time that one is committed
to hypothesis testing, state-of-the-art measurement strategies,
and careful research design. Although it is true that communities
do not generally share scientists' concerns about these issues, and
often lose patience with the deliberate pace of research when the
need for services is so often obvious, I have always been able to
find workable compromises in my studies that allow us to address
both community concerns and the requirements of developmental
science. Indeed, my colleagues and I have increasingly been told
that communities want the highest quality research on issues of
concern to them since they recognize that their ability to advocate
for policies and practices is limited without this kind of evidence,
which means that my community partners are often now the first
to advocate for randomized controlled trials of the interventions
they believe in.

Another question I am often asked is the extent to which
the lessons derived from tribal communities, with formal governments, apply to communities without such structures. In the
earlier sections I pointed to more general applications of these

processes, even though they have been derived from specific tribal contexts. Indeed, even when one does have a tribal council with which to work, sincere community engagement often requires work with other members of the community who may have interests that are more directly germane to the project. Of course one cannot use community engagement to bypass work with the tribal council, but the fact that such additional work is required even when a tribal council exists underscores my broader guidance. The point is not to simply get authorization to do a study, but rather to engage in a meaningful dialogue about what kinds of study should be done with interested community partners. And this can and should be done in any community where one seeks to develop a program of research.

A related question, then, is how one knows that a particular community engagement has been adequate. One could imagine a situation where community engagement around a particular study never concludes and the study is never started. There may, in fact, be situations where this actually does occur, for example, when one hopes to conduct research on a topic that is simply too controversial in that community at that time. In those cases, one could consult with every member of the community and still not arrive at a conclusion about how to proceed. In these cases, I would argue that a failure to arrive at agreements around study design signals that the time is simply not right to conduct that study. In my experience, however, this has not ever occurred. Achieving agreement has not always been easy, for example, in deciding on appropriate cognitive assessments for American Indian children. But we have always been able to satisfy ourselves that we have heard from those representing major divergent perspectives in the community and have been able to use that information to craft an appropriate design. Although qualitative research lacks precise numerical criteria for sample-size calculations, a commitment to seeking out diverse perspectives in community engagement, coupled with the notion of saturation, the point at which perspectives no longer diverge, provides important guidance on when an investigator has reached a reasonable stopping point for a particular phase of community engagement. Once one is at that point, and satisfied that the sampling used to tap into diverse constituencies in the community consultation was well implemented, it is generally safe to proceed with confidence on the agreed upon design.

Finally, researchers who are just beginning their research careers may well ask how they can possibly take all of these steps at the beginning of their careers when they are under such pressure to define themselves as researchers. Throughout my recommendations I have tried to emphasize the principles that are much more central to this work than any particular instantiation of them, and I made this point explicitly in my discussion of field offices staffed by community-based researchers, which probably require funding for large data collections to sustain. But this question also goes to the heart of who we want to be as researchers. In the current era, numerous opportunities for funding community-based participatory research exist and, as my own career makes clear, progress in an academic career is not at all incompatible with these processes I have outlined here. Indeed, my academic career in American Indian and Alaska Native research would, quite simply, have been impossible without these processes. Thus, from my perspective, far from getting in the way of one's development as a researcher, these processes, and one's commitment to them both in the short and the long term, is central to being able to work effectively in partnership with communities who have every reason to mistrust research and researchers. In my experience, there has been absolutely no doubt that this is, quite simply, the only way to do my work.

Conclusion

Researchers who seek to develop projects in special populations need to pay particular attention to the ways in which they have been only minimally involved in deliberations about science in the past (even the very recent past). Many of the challenges that researchers confront in designing studies for these populations have to do with the lack of trust that this neglect (and in some cases abuse) has generated. The techniques I have outlined here are all fundamentally designed to increase trust in the research relationship by demonstrating researchers' commitments to the communities where they seek to conduct their studies. Although none of these is easy, and all require compromises, these techniques build the trust in the research relationship that is so central to ensuring that the work that matters most reaches these communities, which is at the heart of all of the best work in applied developmental science.

Questions, Additional Considerations, and Research Resources

Beyond the citations reported here, students interested in learning more about these techniques, especially as they have evolved more generally, should consider joining the listservs of the Campus-Community Partnerships for Health (CCPH), which provides access to the vibrant and growing community working in these ways and whose discussions quite often relate directly to applied developmental science. These can be accessed at the CCPH Web site: www.ccph.info/. One of the best resources to appear on these processes in recent years is a volume edited by Minkler and Wallerstein (2008), which has recently appeared in a second edition. Also of interest to students will be the recent review of community-based participatory research that has been published by the Agency for Health Care Research and Quality and is available on the agency's Web site (www.ahrq.gov; Viswanathan et al., 2004). Although funding opportunities often change, there appears to be a substantial commitment to such community-based approaches at the National Institutes of Health and the Centers for Disease Control and Prevention, so new investigators would be well served to monitor these opportunities closely. The monthly Washington Update of the Society for Research on Child Development provides an excellent overview of these opportunities and is available at www.srcd.org.

Acknowledgments

The research reported here has been supported by grants from the Administration on Children and Families: 90-YF-0021 (Mitchell, PI) and 90-YF-0053 (Spicer, PI) and the National Institutes of Health: EH 10830 (Spicer, PI), HG 003891 (Spicer, PI), and HD 42760 (Spicer, PI).

References

Ball, J., & Janyst, P. (2008). Enacting research ethics in partnerships with indigenous communities in Canada: "Do it in a good way." *Journal of Empirical Research on Human Research Ethics, 3*, 33–51.

Beals, J., Manson, S. M., Mitchell, C. M., & Spicer, P. (2003). Cultural specificity and comparison in psychiatric epidemiology: Walking the tightrope in American Indian research. *Culture, Medicine, and Psychiatry, 27*(3), 259–289.

Burhansstipanov, L., Christopher, S., & Schumacher, S. A. (2005). Lessons learned from community-based participatory research in Indian country. *Cancer Control, 12*(Suppl. 2), 70–76.

Canadian Institutes of Health Research. (2007). *CIHR guidelines for health research involving aboriginal people.* Ottawa: Canadian Institutes of Health Research.

Chino, M., & DeBruyn, L. (2006). Building true capacity: Indigenous models for indigenous communities. *American Journal of Public Health, 96,* 596–599.

Christopher, S. (2005). Recommendations for conducting successful research with Native Americans. *Journal of Cancer Education, 20*(Suppl. 1), 47–51.

Cochran, P. A., Marshall, C. A., Garcia-Downing, C., Kendall, E., Cook, D., McCubbin, L., & Gover, R. M. S. (2008). Indigenous ways of knowing: Implications for participatory research and community. *American Journal of Public Health, 98*(1), 22–27.

Deloria, V. (1969). *Custer died for your sins: An Indian manifesto.* New York: Macmillan.

Fisher, P. A., & Ball, T. J. (2003). Tribal participatory research: Mechanisms of a collaborative model. *American Journal of Community Psychology, 32,* 207–216.

Foster, M. W., Eisenbraun, A. J., & Carter, T. H. (1997). Communal discourse as a supplement to informed consent for genetic research. *Nature Genetics, 17*(3), 277–279.

Jacklin, K., & Kinoshameg, P. (2008). Developing a participatory aboriginal health research project: "Only if it's going to mean something." *Journal of Empirical Research on Human Research Ethics, 3,* 53–68.

Manson, S. M., Garoutte, E., Goins, R. T., & Henderson, P. N. (2004). Access, relevance, and control in the research process: Lessons from Indian country. *Journal of Aging and Health, 16,* 58s–77s.

Minkler, M., & Wallerstein, N. (Eds.). (2008). *Community-based participatory research for health.* San Francisco: Jossey-Bass.

Mohatt, G. V., Hazel, K. L., Allen, J., Stachelrodt, M., Hensel, C., & Fath, R. (2004). Unheard Alaska: Culturally anchored participatory action research on sobriety with Alaska Natives. *American Journal of Community Psychology, 33*(3–4), 263–273.

Norton, I. M., & Manson, S. M. (1996). Research in American Indian and Alaska Native communities: Navigating the universe of cultural values and process. *Journal of Consulting and Clinical Psychology, 64,* 856–860.

Salois, E. M., Holkup, P. A., Tripp-Reimer, T., & Weinert, C. (2006). Research as spiritual covenant. *Western Journal of Nursing Research, 28*(5), 505–524; discussion 561–563.

Santiago-Rivera, A. L., Morse, G. S., Hunt, A., & Lickers, H. (1998). Building a community-based research partnership: Lessons from the Mohawk Nation of Akwesasne. *Journal of Community Psychology, 26*, 163–174.

Sarche, M. C., Croy, C. D., Big Crow, C. K., Mitchell, C. M., & Spicer, P. (2009). Maternal correlates of 2-year-old American Indian children's social-emotional development in a Northern Plains tribe. *Infant Mental Health Journal, 30*(4), 321–340.

Viswanathan, M., Ammerman, A., Eng, E., Gartlehner, G., Lohr, K. N., Griffith, D., ... Whitener, L. (2004). *Community-based participatory research: Assessing the evidence.* Rockville, MD: Agency for Healthcare Research and Quality.

Wallerstein, N. B., & Duran, B. (2006). Using community-based participatory research to address health disparities. *Health Promotion Practice, 7*(3), 312–323.

Wax, M. L. (1991). The ethics of research in American Indian communities. *American Indian Quarterly, 15*, 431–456.

CHAPTER 6

Challenges and Issues in Designing Applied Research

Robert B. McCall, PhD, and Christina J. Groark, PhD
University of Pittsburgh Office of Child Development

Introduction

Applied research in child development may be defined as the utilization of behavioral and social science theory and data to describe, explain, and optimize the course of child and adolescent development and to enhance the key settings within which young people develop (e.g., families, schools, after-school programs, community social service settings, or health settings). In more common parlance, it deals directly with how we bring "science to life for the benefit of children, youth, and families."

Conceptually, one can imagine a continuum of scientific activities beginning on the left with *basic* or *foundational research*, the focus of which is usually the study of cause and effect between basic theoretical constructs on the one hand and fundamental and broad-based outcomes on the other.

Moving to the right on the continuum, one can imagine *relevant research*, in which the questions posed are usually grounded in theory and have some relevance to practice. For example, much of the literature of the effects of television violence on children's behavior is "relevant to" but has not prescribed what actions the television industry, policy makers, or parents should take to minimize the potential undesirable consequences of children viewing a steady diet of violent programming.

Moving further to the right is *applied research*, in which the questions posed and answers derived from the studies have rather direct implications for what might be done in practice. The classic intervention demonstration project is a good example, in which an intervention is tried out under relatively controlled conditions to determine if it produces a specific desirable outcome; if so, presumably the intervention might be considered for more widespread implementation in communities conducted by practice professionals whose role in society is to deliver such services (e.g., social workers, teachers, nurses, paraprofessionals, early care and education caregivers, etc.).

At the far right on the continuum is *practice research*, which consists of studies of phenomena and interventions as they naturally occur in society with the aim of understanding how things work and could be improved. For example, after a new early care and education curriculum is demonstrated by specially trained teachers perhaps in a lab school to produce positive outcomes, it is desirable to "bring the intervention to scale" in communities where it will be implemented by staff who typically deliver such services in society. Most research on the right side of the continuum is applied research, but much of what this chapter deals with are the issues and challenges of practice research, much of which consists of *program evaluation*.

Main Themes

This chapter has several main themes:

- *Applied and certainly practice research methodology has some unique challenges.* Although applied and practiced research methods include elements of basic research methodology, they also face unique challenges and therefore require some unique approaches.
- *The gold standards of basic research methodology have certain limitations when used in applied and especially practice contexts.* Because gold standard methodology is often viewed as the ideal, applied and practice researchers may confront reviewers of grants and articles and tenure review committees who view applied and practice research as inferior and methodologically inadequate. Whereas the methodological criterion for basic research is "methodological perfection," the criterion for applied and practice research may be "best obtainable,"

and for practitioners and policy makers who need to make decisions today the criterion may be "best available."

■ *More than one approach is likely necessary in applied and practice research.* By definition, most practice research is conducted in the field, which is an imperfect laboratory, and any single study is likely to have one or more serious methodological limitations. Consequently, several different studies using different methodologies may need to be conducted before results converge on a conclusion that can be persuasively supported.

Much of what is presented in the following is based on our personal professional experience. Robert McCall has spent 40 years conducting basic, relevant, applied, and practice research, and he has seen social and behavioral research evolve from a near total preoccupation with basic research and the experimental method to a discipline that is much broader and more receptive to applied and practice research and the methods appropriate to its pursuit. Christina Groark has had an extensive career in services and policy development with respect to children and families, especially in the development and implementation of new service programs conducted in the community by service professionals. She is well aware of the importance of motivating and organizing policy makers and service professionals to implement a new program smoothly and effectively.

As codirectors of the University of Pittsburgh Office of Child Development, one of the most comprehensive and applied university centers devoted to the welfare of children and families, we have collaborated for two decades with policy makers and community professionals to create and implement new service programs and evaluations in community settings. Most recently, we have collaborated with colleagues in Russia and Latin America to create intervention programs that comprehensively change the entire operation of an orphanage to increase the warm, sensitive, and responsive caregiver–child interactions by fewer and more stable caregivers in a more family-like, rather than institutional, atmosphere. As a result, the development of infants and young children has been substantially improved in every behavioral and physical domain assessed (St. Petersburg–USA Orphanage Research Team, 2008). Much of what follows rests on this foundation of experience.

A Brief, Personally Interpreted, Methodological History

It helps to understand how social and behavioral science, especially psychology, came to emphasize basic research and the traditional gold standard methodology (see next section; Groark & McCall, 2005). In 1945, Vannevor Bush argued for a "social contract" between science and society based on the assertion that all scientific knowledge is potentially useful, at least someday, implemented by someone, for some purpose. Thus, scientists should be guided by their curiosity to study phenomena of conceptual and theoretical interest, with the assumption that it may be useful someday in some way.

In the next few decades, psychology and other behavioral disciplines were trying to establish a scientific identity; they wanted to be "sciences" like chemistry and physics. To counter these accusations that they were not a science and their empiricism was "soft" or worse and to establish scientific credibility, they adopted research methodologies that were analogous to those in the "hard" disciplines, such as theory-driven research, random assignment of subjects to conditions, uniform treatment administration, automated or blind assessments, and statistical analysis of data (see later). These gold standards were used to pursue general cause–effect laws of behavior that were presumed to explain most behavior in most contexts, so studies of gender, individual differences, context, or procedures were presumed to be unnecessary. At the same time, government was willing to fund basic behavioral research, so the confluence of these historical, social, and economic themes was that basic research and the gold standard methodologies became the coin of the behavioral academic realm. Indeed, this value system became the criteria for judging grants, publications, and academic tenure.

However, after the principles of basic learning were articulated (e.g., reinforcement, generalization, discrimination, extinction, etc.), general cause and effect principles of behavior became more elusive; cause–effect phenomena often seemed to be qualified by "nuisance factors" such as gender, individual differences, minor procedural variations, wording of instructions, particular stimuli and contexts, one versus another outcome measures—indeed, every aspect of the research process. Moreover, Bush's social contract began to wear thin in the halls of Congress, which demanded more relevancy, application, and practical value for their behavioral research dollar.

The net result of these themes has been that behavior scientists now study a great deal more complicated phenomena and more applied and practice topics. But while these issues present new challenges and often require different methodologies, the value for, and often insistence upon, traditional gold standard methods persists and is often invoked—to an inappropriate extent (in the authors' opinions)—as criteria for judging applied and especially practice research.

Benefits and Limitations of Gold Standard Methodology for Applied and Practice Research

The gold standard methods were developed to primarily demonstrate, as unequivocally as possible, cause-and-effect relations between some independent variable X and some dependent variable Y. This criterion is called *internal validity*. Applied and practiced research are certainly concerned with internal validity; for example, *can* curriculum X be demonstrated to produce better school readiness skill Y? But they often have an additional concern called *external validity*: *Does* curriculum X produce school readiness skill Y in naturalistic conditions (e.g., when curriculum X is implemented by teachers for students in schools that are typical of a given community)? Logically, it is difficult to obtain external validity without internal validity, but it is possible to have internal validity without a great deal of external validity. Experimental interventions, for example, may be demonstrated to be effective under random assignment and carefully controlled conditions but are difficult to implement successfully in community contexts. Also, the better a method is at demonstrating internal validity, the poorer it tends to be at demonstrating external validity and the reverse.

What follows is a brief discussion of the merits and limitations of several gold standards when implemented in applied and practice research. Please note that what follows is not an argument against the gold standards; it is a discussion of their assets and especially their limitations, which are often ignored, when used in applied and practice research contexts. Research methods are tools, such as a hammer and saw, each of which is better suited for one than another purpose (for more complete discussion, see McCall & Green, 2004).

Experiments are considered a "gold standard" by many but seem impractical for some areas of research. What is the best research design to approach my research questions? Is a theory-based evaluation appropriate?

Theory-Driven Research

Standard: Research should be guided by and contribute to theory. Theory usually refers to a network of interrelated causal principles (e.g., learning theory, psychoanalytical theory), but it can also refer to a single causal principle.

Benefits

Theory describes causes and effects, it usually applies to many different circumstances, it predicts to unstudied new circumstances, it explains and makes phenomena understandable, and to some (Weiss, 1995) there is "nothing so practical as a good theory." For example, a single theoretical principle is that adolescents who perceive that they have a realistic chance at a successful and fulfilling future are less likely to engage in adolescent problem behavior (e.g., excessive alcohol and drug use, risky sexual behavior, poor school performance, antisocial and criminal behavior). This principle predicts that if low-income adolescents are guaranteed college tuition, they will do better in high school and engage in less problem behavior. The principle makes understandable why guaranteeing tuition has this effect, and there are many other ways to providing a realistic future that fall under the principle. Theory is so standard that it is difficult to get a grant approved or an article accepted without providing a theoretical context for the question to be studied.

Limitations

Not all research that is of applied and practical value has a theoretical context. Applied research often focuses on the detection and description of certain problems or circumstances that have important behavioral and financial consequences for individuals in society. Topics may be studied, not for their theoretical relevance, but because of their personal and social costs. It is useful to know whether school dropout rates are increasing or decreasing, which groups of people have high dropout rates, and what school circumstances and other parameters are associated with high dropout rates. This information can help target attention and resources to deal with the problem and perhaps eventually to contribute to theoretical explanations.

Also, some social programs are implemented for political, philosophical, or religious reasons, such as abstinency programs to prevent unwanted pregnancy among teenagers. Nevertheless, it is important to know whether such programs indeed lower teenage pregnancy rates, regardless of whether there are theories about how or why.

Agreed, it is always helpful to know the causal mechanisms that make an intervention successful, because such information tells you what can and cannot be changed to fit the program to local circumstances. *Program evaluation* is primarily oriented at determining whether an intervention is faithfully implemented and produces the intended outcomes, whereas *program evaluation research* is aimed additionally at discovering crucial characteristics and possible mechanisms that produce those benefits.

Note that the absence of theory does not justify "random research." There needs to be a rationale for implementing and evaluating an intervention and for why it should be effective, but that rationale may be economic (large amounts of money are already invested in the program) or human and societal costs involved.

Random Assignment

Standard: Participants should be randomly assigned to experimental/treatment versus control/comparison groups.

Benefits

Random assignment is perhaps the shiniest of the gold standards, because randomizing participants to treatment groups randomizes subject characteristics and self-selection factors across experimental conditions, thereby contributing strongly to the internal validity of cause and effect. Further, a double-blind design with a placebo condition in which neither the participants nor the data collectors are aware of which participant is in which group provides a further check on participant as well as observer biases. Drug trials are the classic example, but note that participant commitment to the intervention is not required.

Limitations

Sometimes participants cannot be randomly assigned to certain conditions. Children cannot be randomly assigned to divorced versus widowed single mothers, for example, or to father absent versus present families. Further, when behavioral interventions are involved, it is difficult to prevent participants from knowing which treatment group they are in, in which case double-blind (and even single-blind) studies are impossible. Finally, in contrast to most drug trials, participant engagement and commitment to the intervention may be crucial to its success, and people may drop out of interventions because they do not like it and those in the comparison group may obtain the same or a similar intervention on their own (see "Intent to Treat (ITT) Analysis" section). Or participants may remain in their assigned group, but be disappointed they were not in the other ("reactive disappointment"), which can dilute the effectiveness of the treatment.

These kinds of problems are common in practice research. For example, low-income families with a newborn child were randomly assigned to the Comprehensive Child Development Program treatment versus the control groups, but ethnographers discovered that control subjects benefited from the information and services provided to their treated friend or relative (McAllister, 1993). Further, schools were randomly assigned to Comer's School Development Program (Comer, 1988; Comer, Haynes, Joyner, & Ben-Avie, 1996; Joyner, Comer, & Ben-Avie, 2004) and to a no-treatment comparison group. But in one evaluation (Millsap et al., 2000), there was little difference between the two groups, primarily because some schools in the treatment group did not implement the treatment very vigorously and some schools in the comparison group implemented elements of the program on their own. However, positive correlations were found within both groups between the extent to which a school implemented the principles and the beneficial outcomes. Do we conclude that the program did not work because there was no difference between the randomly assigned group means or that it did work because schools that chose to vigorously implement it produced better results? (See "Intent to Treat (ITT) Analysis" section.)

It is also sometimes said that random assignment produces the maximum treatment effect size, but this is not necessarily the case. In the Comer example, the randomly assigned treatment effect was nearly zero, but the correlational results suggest if schools were allowed to choose which approach they wanted, the treatment effect for the Comer program would have been much larger.

Nevertheless, the primary advantage of random assignment is that it minimizes the effect of subject characteristics, especially those correlated with self-selection into treatment groups. So in the Comer study, it is fair to ask whether *any* program that schools have faith in and commitment to implement would have the same benefits. Other programs may be much cheaper and easier to implement and produce some or even more benefits.

What are good models for randomized control trials (RCTs) within a nonmedical, applied context such as education?

Strategies

One approach to the random assignment problem is to use a design that includes both random assignment and self-selection. For example, suppose one wanted to know whether mediated custody arrangements produce better child adjustment to divorce than court-ordered arrangements. In this case it is obvious that the divorcing parents need to be committed to the decision process, and some parents are likely to do better under mediation and others under court orders. So have one condition that randomly assigns couples to the two arrangements whereas in another condition parents are allowed to choose, then measure in both groups as many characteristics of couples that are likely to predict (i.e., correlate with) a couple's self-selected choice and validate these predictors within the self-selection group. This design can assess directly the effect of self-selection and participant commitment by comparing that condition with random assignment. The random assignment provides the opportunity for internal validity support, and the self-selection condition may mimic what will be offered to couples in the future (i.e., external validity). This example also illustrates that when services are offered on a routine basis within the community, participants are rarely, if ever, randomly assigned (except, perhaps, for certain court-ordered interventions). A random assignment study may provide internal validity but very limited external validity, since one may be uncertain about the generality of results from a random assignment study to community conditions in which participants choose whether and which service to partake.

Uniform Treatment

Standard: Uniform treatment implementation in which the experimenter controls the treatment versus no treatment experience of participants and each participant in the treatment group is administered the same treatment.

Benefits

Uniform treatment permits the researcher to know exactly what treatment versus control conditions produced the observed results, it reduces error variance otherwise associated with variability in treatment implementation conditions, and it permits replication of the treatment or intervention.

Limitations

The uniform treatment strategy assumes that one intervention fits all. But some treatments are deliberately not uniform, such as family support services that are tailored to the specific needs of each individual family. Further, it is sometimes difficult to prevent service providers from tailoring a treatment to fit participant characteristics and circumstances, which is a hallmark of good treatment practice. Also, participants in interventions and especially control groups cannot practically or ethically be prevented from seeking a variety of treatments on their own, including control participants who obtain elements of the experimental treatment or other services that may compete, supplement, or interfere with the experimental versus control effects.

Strategies

An approach to dealing with these complexities is to measure the aspects of the intended as well as unintended treatment activities and services in both treatment and comparison groups. Assuming such measurements are at the individual level, hierarchical linear modeling (Bryk & Raudenbush, 1992) can be used to test the randomly assigned treatment versus comparison group difference and the treatment implementation characteristics reflected in the participant level variables imbedded within those groups.

Quantitative Measurement and Statistical Analysis

Standard: Measure independent and dependent variables quantitatively and analyze the data statistically.

Benefits

The quantitative measurement strategy allows the researcher to distinguish and quantify characteristics of the treatment and treatment effects and to make judgments that distinguish estimated treatment effects from random variation. It also allows the researcher to communicate in quantitative terms the extent of reliability and validity in measures and the treatment effects.

Limitations

Quantitative measurement assumes we know what and how to measure before starting the study. When studying new phenomena, this may not be the case. Of course, we have hypotheses and guesses, but sometimes those are incorrect (e.g., searching for lasting IQ gains as a result of early care and education programs rather than school achievement and antisocial behavior; McCall, Larsen, & Ingram, 2003). Datta (1994) suggested that rather than dropping a fishing line with a worm into an unknown lake trying to catch a new species of fish, one needs to first send a scuba diver to observe where fish congregate and what they eat. Further, some phenomena may be difficult to quantify, and qualitative, perhaps ethnographic, descriptions might be more informative, such as when studying how gangs are started, maintain order and cohesiveness, promote member loyalty, and maintain lines of authority; or the process of community service systems change. Although the debate has quieted down, the quantitative–qualitative discussions of past decades may be instructive (Reichardt & Rallis, 1994).

Further, many statistical techniques commonly used by psychologists may be less appropriate for research in which practitioners and policy makers are an important audience. For example, averages mask extreme cases, but extreme cases are often the focus of services and justify financial appropriations. Also, effect sizes expressed in terms of percent variance are less useful to policy makers than statistics that communicate the rate of service needs reduced by the treatment and cost savings (see Scott, Mason, & Chapman, 1999).

Strategies

Ethnography might be more descriptive, especially when studying new and complex phenomena, both for the purpose of generating hypotheses as well as obtaining initial answers. Originally developed to study single cultures ($n = 1$), ethnography can also be used to study subcultures within a society, and modern ethnographic and conventional statistical procedures can be used jointly in single studies. Also, qualitative procedures can often explain results. For example, a program aimed at providing services for teenage mothers who had drug and alcohol problems found that the average age of participants was 26 years, not the intended

16 to 18. Simply asking the service staff why this was the case produced the hypothesis that teenagers do not believe they have a problem because so many of their friends also use drugs and alcohol, whereas 26-year-old unmarried mothers have come to realize they have a substance abuse problem and are not being good parents. The service organization then used the 26-year-olds to counsel the teenagers to participate in the service program.

Conclusion

The gold standard methodologies are ideally suited for basic research and demonstration projects in which high internal validity of cause and effect is desired. They have many advantages that are just as necessary in applied research, but they also have limitations that become more prominent when these methods are used in applied and practice contexts. Consequently, other methodologies are also needed as complements or sometimes necessary substitutes, which attempt to handle the challenges of applied research but in turn have their own limitations. Conclusions of internal and external validity can be inferred from converging evidence from a set of studies, each of which has complementary assets and limitations.

Issues in Working in the Community

Academic–Community Collaborations

Applied and especially practice research often require that the study be conducted in community contexts (e.g., human service agencies operating in the community, schools, hospitals, early care and education facilities). These organizations and their directors and staff have different values, purposes, procedures, regulatory constraints, constituencies, and performance criteria than do researchers (Groark & McCall, 1993, 1996). Further, "community professionals" (e.g., agency directors, teachers, physicians) and researchers may possess some degree of distrust, lack of respect, and diminished value for the other group and its activities. Whereas the researcher may control the funding for the research project, the community professionals control everything that happens in their organizations and institutions; researchers must recognize that many practice studies are conducted in the community's "stadium," need to be conducted with them as major players, and operate by their rules.

Consequently, special efforts—and attitudes—may be needed to create and maintain an effective collaborative group of researchers and community professionals to conduct a mutually beneficial project. Collaborations may be difficult for academics and some community professionals as well, because they inevitably involve diminished control by each individual member of the collaboration as well as require compromises that may rub coarsely against traditional standards and values. Researchers considering a collaboration with community professionals may want to consult suggestions on how to create and operate successful research–community collaborations (e.g., Groark & McCall, 1993, 1996, 2005, 2008).

Project Creation

Usually, field projects need to be created collaboratively between researchers and community professionals, although there are some exceptions.

Evidence-Based Programs

Sometimes the state or local funders (e.g., Department of Welfare; Department of Children and Youth Services; local foundations) identify a service program that has been demonstrated to be successful, usually in applied research demonstrations but sometimes more broadly (e.g., Nurse–Family Partnership; Olds et al., 1999; Olds & Kitzman, 1993), and want it implemented locally. Indeed, some policy makers and funders subscribe to a narrow definition of "evidence-based programming," which largely consists of attempting to replicate locally service programs demonstrated elsewhere to be successful (Groark & McCall, 2005, 2008; McCall, Groark, & Nelkin, 2004). But such a strategy makes several implicit assumptions (Groark & McCall, 2005; McCall et al., 2004; McCall, 2009), namely, that sufficient evidence with reasonable internal and external validity information is available, the program itself is packaged so others can implement it, others in fact implement it faithfully, and it matches local needs and resources. Although policy makers and funders can encourage with financial resources the adoption of a specific service program or intervention, there is no guarantee that the community professionals have the same motivation, commitment, and skills as the creators of the program; that the original program is not modified to fit local participants, circumstances, and budgets and such modifications may harm its effectiveness; or that the program is faithfully or effectively implemented.

Indeed, implementation of programs is exceedingly crucial to their success but a process that is relatively unstudied and therefore without evidence-based procedures (Fixsen, Naoom, Blase, Friedman, & Wallace, 2005; McCall, 2009).

Collaboratively Creating Programs Based on Evidence

Even if an evidence-based program is in hand, collaborative planning with the community will be necessary (Groark & McCall, 2008; McCall, 2009) especially if a researcher (as opposed to a policy maker who has influence over community organizations) has an intervention in mind or no well-articulated and demonstrated service program or intervention is available. It is unlikely that a researcher can successfully "drop" a preplanned intervention or program into a community organization without going through some process designed to engage the community professionals, convince them of the merit for them of the proposed project, and garner their commitment and cooperation to implement it and to cooperate with the evaluation, which is often costly in time and in convenience to them. Instead, researchers and community professionals should collaboratively identify needs and create an intervention together, perhaps using a logic model approach (Armstrong & Barsion, 2006; Axford, Berry, & Little, 2006; W. K. Kellogg Foundation, 1998, 2000), which has been packaged in different ways, for example, pathways mapping (Schorr, 2003) and getting to outcomes (Wandersman, Imm, Chinman, & Kaftarian, 1999, 2000; Strategic planning and evaluation www.rand.org/pubs/technical_reports/TR370/; Fisher, Imm, Chinman, & Wandersman, 2006). These different versions of a logic model simply provide a structure consisting of a set of questions that the collaborators need to answer on the way to developing an appropriate program with measures of implementation and outcome that is consistent with research evidence and best practices. Sometimes a knowledgeable but independent facilitator is helpful in conducting the process, which may take one or two sessions or repeated sessions over several months. Although there is no research on the outcome effectiveness of logic models, the intended result is the creation of a program that meets local needs, can be implemented with local personnel and financial resources, has the commitment and enthusiasm of all of the major stakeholders, embodies evidence-based principles, and includes a monitoring and evaluation plan (which may be a researcher's primary interest and responsibility).

Other Issues in Field Research

Rush to Outcome

Often funders want to know that an intervention "works," and they want to know it soon, which can mean after the first cohort of participants completes the intervention. In other cases, the primary outcome is years away (e.g., school success, graduation, and leading a financially self-supporting life) when the intervention consists of an early care and education program, in which case intermediate goals and outcomes will need to suffice. The expectation of, or demand for, outcomes in the first cohort may be unrealistic, because new and complex programs often require the staff to experience two or three cohorts of participants before the program is implemented smoothly and effectively (Fixsen et al., 2005). Often it is helpful to have the funder in the planning and implementation group of stakeholders, and to have this collaborative establish not only a timeline for the implementation of the service or intervention but also a timeline of expected outcomes that represents a compromise between what can be reasonably accomplished and the patience and resources of the funder. Further, the first "outcome" is that the program is implemented faithfully and effectively; only then is it reasonable to expect beneficial outcomes for participants (Groark & McCall, 2008).

Independent Versus Participatory Evaluation

Historically, researchers often evaluated an intervention or service that they created and operated, but when field tests of potential public services became prevalent, policy makers and funders insisted that the evaluator be independent of the service provider. This often fueled attitudes of skepticism and mild antagonism between evaluators and service professionals, who perceived the evaluators to be testing and grading their performance. More recently, various forms of participatory evaluation have been emphasized (Fetterman, 1993; Fetterman, Kaftarian, & Wandersman, 1996) in which evaluators and program professionals collaborate to plan, implement, and execute a program evaluation.

Both independent and collaborative evaluations have some assets and liabilities. Funders often prefer "independent evaluations," because they provide the evaluation with a measure of credibility over service professionals who are assumed to be highly committed to the success of the intervention. But if the evaluation is conducted too independently, service professionals feel that the evaluation is being "done to them," and the evaluators, who have limited relationships with the service professionals or the participants, may not be able to collect the kind of data on program implementation and outcome that is desired.

Conversely, participatory evaluation can have the benefits of an involved professional staff members who can use their relationships with participants to obtain more personal and in-depth information on outcome and collect such information at less cost. However, motivating service providers to collect data can be challenging, they often lack the commitment to accuracy and comprehensiveness that researchers and their assistants have, and questions may linger about the validity and credibility of the results if the service providers have too much responsibility in collecting data. Also, sometimes a major stakeholder who is part of a collaborative team is actually responsible for a crucial component of the intervention or data collection (e.g., supervisory staff), and it may be their domain that is not functioning adequately. Such situations need to be handled as soon as possible, forthrightly, but discreetly, perhaps in private meetings between evaluators and this individual.

Of course, there are compromises between these two extremes. Researchers must be clever in training service personnel and designing data collection to make it useful to the service providers, monitoring of data collection needs to occur to ensure its accuracy and comprehensiveness, participants can mail to researchers questionnaires given to them by service personnel which they answer privately, and so forth.

Applied Research Designs and Strategies

In applied and practice studies, the researcher has much less control than in basic research, so comparison groups are often difficult to obtain, participants do not necessarily stay in their assigned groups, budgets and personnel change midproject, participants come and go at different ages, and so forth. Research designed for such projects may need to be quite different than for basic research and require considerable creativity to identify and obtain appropriate comparisons. A variety of old and recent textbooks and handbooks exist describing different research designs and strategies for these circumstances under the rubrics of "quasi-experimental design," "applied research methodology," and "program evaluation" (e.g., Cook & Campbell, 1979; Rossi, Lipsey, & Freeman, 2004). Newcomers to applied and practice research should become familiar with these strategies so they have an arsenal of tactics that can be creatively selected, combined, or modified to fit the circumstances of any particular applied or practiced study. A few of the more commonly used strategies are outlined very briefly in the following as an introduction, but advanced specialized references should be consulted before implementing these strategies (see "Further Reading").

No-Comparison Group

Practice researchers will often find themselves without an obvious comparison group. No-treatment controls are difficult and expensive to obtain, it is unethical to deny treatment that may be available to needy participants, there is limited benefit to participation for control individuals, and people who are denied treatment often seek it out on their own.

Posttest Only

Sometimes program evaluators are called in after a program has been in operation for several years and the only data available are essentially "posttest" or "outcome" data. In this case, nearly the only strategy is to compare treated participants with "norms" for the outcome assessment based on a standardization sample or a very large study available in the literature. For example, children reared from birth in orphanages are sometimes adopted into advantaged homes, and parents are asked to respond to questionnaires regarding their children's adjustment. The Child Behavior Problem Checklist (CBCL; Achenbach & Edelbrock, 1983) is often used, and mean scores and the percentage of children who fall into the borderline and clinical areas on the scales are often compared with the CBCL standardization sample of parent-reared American children.

Single Group, Pre- and Posttest

Sometimes researchers are able to obtain assessments before participants receive an intervention and again at some point during, immediately after the intervention is completed, or at a follow-up assessment some time later. If age-related norms exist for the assessment instrument, one can determine if participants moved up in percentile ranking or some other standardized score (T score).

However, if norms do not exist, the researcher is faced with the task of demonstrating the changes from pre- to posttest occurred because of the intervention, not because the children increased in age or some other factor that changes with the passage of time. A strategy to deal with this situation (Bryk & Weisberg, 1976; McCall, Ryan, & Green, 1999) can be implemented if children enter the intervention at different ages, even if they remain in the intervention for different lengths of time. A "residualized change score" can be calculated by regressing pretest scores on age, predicting for each individual subject their outcome score based on this regression using age at posttest as a parameter, and then using the difference between actual and predicted posttest score as the dependent variable reflecting treatment effect.

This approach can be very useful when participants are expected to change on the outcome measure simply as a function of time (e.g., low-income children are known to decline in mental test performance over the preschool years relative to the population). For example, one early childhood family support intervention for low-income children 3 to 6 years of age assessed general developmental status and found that mean performance actually declined between pre- and posttest. But when children's pretests were regressed against age, a negative relation was observed, indicating that such children would decline in performance even in their own homes with no intervention. When residualized change scores were calculated, however, children in the intervention actually declined less than would have been expected without the program, indicating that the program was "effective" in preventing decline (McCall et al., 1999).

Random Assignment With Waiting List Comparison Group

If an intervention has been demonstrated to be successful elsewhere, it may be unethical to deny treatment to individuals in a similar or replicated intervention. One strategy is to use a delayed intervention in which a group of worthy participants is selected, but randomly assigned to receive the intervention immediately or some time later. Both groups are assessed at the beginning, at the end of the first group's intervention, and after the second group's intervention. The delayed group constitutes the no-treatment comparison for the immediate group, and some assessment of longer-term benefits is possible.

Sometimes financial and personnel resources can only treat a limited number of participants, so participants are randomly assigned to treatment now versus a waiting list (i.e., treatment later) or perhaps no treatment if resources are very limited. Service professionals often want to treat the most needy, but if there are more needy than can be treated, they may welcome random assignment as a "neutral" strategy for deciding who is treated now and who is treated later or not at all.

Two-Intervention Comparison Design

One strategy that avoids not treating some potential participants is to simultaneously implement two contrasting interventions but to conduct pre- and posttreatment assessments of both treatment outcomes on both groups. The question is which intervention provides better results compared to the other, rather than compared to no intervention. The expectation is that Treatment A will affect Outcome A but not Outcome B, whereas the reverse will be the case for participants in Treatment B. For example, two different early care and education curricula, one emphasizing emergent literacy and the other emergent numeracy, might be implemented in different centers, but children are measured both pre- and postintervention on both literacy and numeracy. Children in the literacy intervention should be expected to improve on literacy to a greater extent than children in the numeracy intervention, but the reverse would be expected for the numeracy children. This strategy only works to the extent the treatments do not generalize to the other outcome.

No-Shows and Dropouts in Randomized Studies

Applied and practice projects, especially those using low-income and high-risk participants, often experience substantial no-show and dropout rates. Low-income families move often, participants do not attend all parts of the intervention, some tire of it, some perceive no benefit and drop out, and some regard it as more hassle than potential benefit. It is not unusual to have only a small percentage (less than 50% to 70%) of participants randomly assigned to treatment and comparison groups actually be exposed to the entire intervention or service program.

Promoting Participation

A major responsibility of intervention and service programs is to motivate people (which may be both teachers, caregivers, nurses who may implement the intervention on the one hand and client participants on the other) to participate in the intervention and in the control conditions. Not every potential participant wants to participate, especially in random assignment studies, even though researchers and service providers believe that they need it and should be motivated to participate. Incentives may need to be offered to participants in both groups, preliminary sessions may help build enthusiasm for participation, and these early sessions may be conducted before random assignment to weed out those who would quickly drop out.

How does one evaluate and choose appropriate research designs and methods for decision-making research that will provide measurable outcomes?

Intent to Treat (ITT) Analysis

Nevertheless, it is likely that all of those participants assigned to each group will not complete all of the intervention or comparison conditions but may nevertheless have both pre- and posttest assessments. It is often recommended, indeed insisted upon, that an intent to treat (ITT) statistical analysis is conducted in which all individuals who were assigned to a group (were intended to be treated) are included, regardless of whether they actually received all or any of the treatment. Such analyses produce estimates based on participants assigned to, not who received, the intervention or services.

Sometimes, ITT is indeed the appropriate analysis for the question at hand. For example, suppose a flu vaccine is offered free to a designated group (i.e., those over 60 years of age) in one community and not another, and the incidence of flu in that group, whether or not they actually received the immunization, is compared between the two communities. This comparison appropriately addresses the question of whether the free immunization reduced flu in the community. Notice the question is not whether the flu immunization is effective at preventing flu. ITT works best if the noncompliance rate is small relative to the total sample, outcome data are available on nearly all who were assigned to both groups, and the intervention benefits do not require much participant commitment.

However, the greater the dropout rate, the less sensitive to detecting treatment effects the ITT strategy becomes, because a progressively larger percentage of those assigned to the treatment actually did not receive all or any of it and cannot be expected to benefit from it. The most obvious response is to take only those participants who actually received all or most of the intervention and compare them to the control group, but critics argue that these are self-selected and more highly motivated people, and are not typical or representative of the target population or they might have improved with any program or even no program. Opponents argue that it makes no sense to include those who were not treated. One can calculate with estimates: The ITT result represents a lower estimate of intervention effectiveness, whereas the result for those who completed the program represents an upper estimate.

Alternatives to ITT

One strategy is to measure a variety of variables hypothesized to predict those individuals who stay in the treatment condition versus those who drop out, validate that these measures do indeed predict complete participation, select participants in the control group who match those who stayed in the intervention on the basis of these variables, and analyze the difference between completed intervention participants and their matched subset of control subjects (a type of "propensity score" analysis; Foster, 2003; Imbens, 2000; Rosenbaum & Rubin, 1983). Another simpler alternative is to use the treatment on the treated (TOT) approach (Bloom, 1984; Ludwig & Phillips, 2007) in which the TOT impact is equal to the difference in the average outcome of interest for children assigned to the treatment versus control group (the ITT impact) divided by the difference in program enrollments rates between the treatment and control group. This strategy is roughly equivalent to the complier average causal effect (CACE) analysis, which works best if one has both predictors of compliance versus dropout and outcome covariates (Frangakis & Rubin, 1999; Jo, 2002; Muthén & Muthén, 1998–2001; Yau & Little, 2001).

Statistical Strategies

Not surprisingly, the complexity in design and assessment strategies that often accompanies applied and practiced research must be analyzed with statistical techniques that match that complexity. Many modern statistical techniques have been designed to deal with these circumstances, including structural equation modeling, hierarchical linear modeling, latent growth-curve analysis, instrumental variables, propensity analysis, and so on. A list of references accompanies this chapter ("Further Reading") that includes articles that provide readable introductions to these and other statistical techniques plus some that describe how to implement and interpret such analyses.

Obtaining Tenure for Applied and Practice Research

Given the assumption that behavioral science, especially psychology, favors gold standard methodologies even when conducting applied and practice research, it is reasonable to ask if young scholars can obtain tenure, especially in a traditionally oriented psychology department, if they devote themselves to studying applied and practical problems. First, this depends on the tenured members of the department, the dean of the school, and the dean's school-wide tenure-review committee, all of which must approve the tenure decision. If these individuals are highly committed to basic research and have a low value for and negative attitude toward applied scholarly activities, the going is likely to be rough. Some candidates in this situation make tenure anyway if they generate enough basic research, literature reviews, grant support, grants from the "right" agencies, and publications in the "right" journals to merit tenure in spite of their applied activities. Instead of trying to conduct basic and applied research simultaneously, do it sequentially: Conduct basic research and do what is necessary to get tenure, and then conduct applied and practical research.

In any case, young scholars should try to pick a department that values the kind of scholarly activities they want to pursue. Not all psychology departments are very traditional; departments in professional schools (e.g., social work, education, public health), for example, may be much more receptive, understanding, and rewarding of applied and practice research than traditional psychology departments, although some professional schools believe the road to academic respect and increased prestige is through basic research. Some (McCall, 1996) have argued that the goal of all scholarship is to contribute to the benefit of humanity and other living things, and the distinction between basic, applied, and practice research is artificial in view of this common goal, but rarely do such arguments carry the day.

Some young scholars do not care. They are committed to contributing as directly as possible to the welfare of children, youth, and families, so they pursue their interests and career outside of traditional academics, for example, in a private research organization that specializes in applied research or in a public or private service organization large enough to conduct research and evaluation on services. Such organizations are often pleased to have people with such training, but at least some of these positions bring pressure on young scholars to obtain sufficient research funds to pay their own salary (but this pressure can also exist in universities).

Conclusion

Society needs researchers who study applied and practice programs and topics. Congress has called for such research for many decades, and the National Institutes of Health now dedicates substantial funding to "translational" research. Historically, however, applied research has been denigrated, partly because it is often less precise than basic research, conclusions of a single study are more ambiguous, and frankly some studies are methodologically sloppy and loose in drawing conclusions based on inadequate evidence. Applied and practice research deserves to be denigrated if it is done poorly, but there is a difference between "crude" and "sloppy" research. Society needs to base its policy and practice on the "best obtainable" evidence, even if not perfect, and sometimes even the "best available" evidence at the time the practitioner and policy maker must make their decisions. Because applied and practice research is more difficult, behavioral and social science disciplines need to "care enough to send their very best researchers to the task." Whereas the methodological challenges and profession frustrations may be great, so is the satisfaction and fulfillment of having one's professional activities more clearly contribute to the welfare of children, youth, and families.

References

Achenbach, T. M., & Edelbrock, C. (1983). *Manual for the child behavior checklist and revised child behavior profile.* Burlington, VT: Queen City Printers.

Armstrong, E. G., & Barsion, S. J. (2006). Using an outcomes-logic-model approach to evaluate a faculty development program for medical educators. *Journal of the Association of American Medical Colleges, 51,* 483–488.

Axford, N., Berry, V., & Little, M. (2006). Enhancing service evaluability: Lessons learned from a programme for disaffected young people. *Children and Society, 14*, 287–298.

Bloom, H. S. (1984). Accounting for no-shows in experimental evaluation designs. *Evaluation Review, 8*(2), 225–246.

Bryk, A., & Raudenbush, S. W. (1992). *Hierarchical linear models for social and behavioral research: Applications and data analysis methods.* Newbury Park, CA: Sage.

Bryk, A. S., & Weisberg, H. I. (1976). Value added analysis: A dynamic approach to the estimation of treatment effects. *Journal of Educational Statistics, 1*(2), 127–155.

Bush, V. (1945). *Science: The endless frontier.* Washington, DC: U.S. Government Printing Office.

Comer, J. P. (1988). Educating poor minority children. *Scientific American, 259*, 42–48.

Comer, J. P., Haynes, N. M., Joyner, E. T., & Ben-Avie, M. (1996). *Rallying the whole village: The Comer process for reforming education.* New York: Teachers College Press.

Cook, T., & Campbell, D. T. (1979). *Quasi-experimental design and analysis issues for field settings.* Chicago: Rand McNally.

Datta, L. E. (1994). Paradigm wars: A basis for peaceful coexistence and beyond. In C. S. Reichardt & S. F. Rallis (Eds.), *The qualitative-quantitative debate: New perspectives* (New Directions for Program Evaluation Monograph, No. 61, pp. 53–70). San Francisco, CA: Jossey-Bass.

Fetterman, D. M. (1993). Empowerment evaluation. *Evaluation Practice, 15*, 1–15.

Fetterman, D. M., Kaftarian, S. J., & Wandersman, A. (1996). *Empowerment evaluation: Knowledge and tools for self-assessment and accountability.* Thousand Oaks, CA: Sage.

Fisher, D., Imm, P., Chinman, M., & Wandersman, A. (2006). *Getting to outcomes with developmental assets: Ten steps to measuring success in youth programs and communities.* Minneapolis, MN: Search Institute.

Fixsen, D. L., Naoom, S. F., Blase, K. A., Friedman, R. M., & Wallace, F. (2005). *Implementation research: A synthesis of the literature.* Tampa, FL: University of South Florida, Louis de la Parte Florida Mental Health Institute, The National Implementation Research Network (FMHI Publication #231).

Foster, E. M. (2003). Is more treatment better than less? An application of propensity score analysis. *Medical Care, 41*(10), 1183–1192.

Frangakis, C. E., & Rubin, D. B. (1999). Addressing compilations of intention-to-treat analysis in the combined presence of all-or-none treatment-compliance and subsequent missing outcomes. *Biometrika, 86*, 365–379.

Groark, C. J., & McCall, R. B. (1993, Spring). Building mutually beneficial collaborations between researchers and community service professionals. *Newsletter of the Society for Research in Child Development,* 6–14.

Groark, C. J., & McCall, R. B. (1996). Building successful university-community human service agency collaborations. In C. D. Fisher, J. P. Murray, & E. E. Sigel (Eds.), *Applied developmental science: Graduate training for diverse disciplines and educational settings* (pp. 237–251). Norwood, NJ: Ablex.

Groark, C. J., & McCall, R. B. (2005). Integrating developmental scholarship into practice and policy. In M. H. Bornstein & M. E. Lamb (Eds.), *Developmental psychology: An advanced textbook* (5th ed., pp. 570–601). Mahwah, NJ: Lawrence Erlbaum Associates.

Groark, C. J., & McCall, R. B. (2008). Community-based interventions and services. In M. Rutter, D. Bishop, D. Pine, S. Scott, J. Stevenson, E. Taylor, & A. Thapar (Eds.), *Rutter's child and adolescent psychiatry* (5th ed., pp. 971–988). London: Blackwell.

Imbens, G. W. (2000). The role of the propensity score in estimating dose-response functions. *Biometrika, 87,* 706–710.

Jo, B. (2002). Statistical power in randomized intervention studies with noncompliance. *Psychological Methods, 7*(2), 178–193.

Joyner, E. T., Comer, J. P., & Ben-Avie, M. (Eds.). (2004). *Transforming school leadership and management to support student learning and development.* Thousand Oaks, CA: Corwin Press.

Ludwig, J., & Phillips, D. (2007). The benefits and costs of Head Start. *SRCD Social Policy Report, 21*(3).

McAllister, C. (1993). *The impact of the CCDP on communities in CCDP service areas: Family Foundation's Comprehensive Child Development Program, Ethnographer's Report #10.* Washington, DC: Administration for Children, Youth, and Families, Department of Health and Human Services.

McCall, R. B. (1996). The concept and practice of education, research, and public service in university psychology departments. *American Psychologist, 51*(4), 379–388.

McCall, R. B. (2009). Evidence-based programming in the context of practice and policy. *SRCD Social Policy Report, 23*(3).

McCall, R. B., & Green, B. L. (2004). Beyond the methodological gold standards of behavioral research: Considerations for practice and policy. *SRCD Social Policy Report, 18*(2), 3–19.

McCall, R. B., Groark, C. J., & Nelkin, R. (2004). Integrating developmental scholarship and society: From dissemination and accountability to evidence-based programming and policies. *Merrill-Palmer Quarterly, 50,* 326–340.

McCall, R. B., Larsen, L., & Ingram, A. (2003). The science and policy of early childhood education and family services. In A. J. Reynolds, M. C. Wang, & H. J. Walberg (Eds.), *Early childhood programs for a new century: Issues in children's and families lives* (pp. 255–298). Washington, DC: CWLA Press.

McCall, R. B., Ryan, C. S., & Green, B. L. (1999). Some non-randomized constructed comparison groups for evaluating early age-related outcomes of intervention programs. *American Journal of Evaluation, 2*(20), 213–226.

Millsap, M. A., Chase, A., Obeidallah, D., Perez-Smith, A., Brigham, N., & Johnston, K. (2000). *Evaluation of Detroit's Comer schools and families initiative.* Cambridge, MA: Abt Associates.

Muthén, L. K., & Muthén, B. O. (1998–2001). *Mplus user's guide.* Los Angeles: Author.

Olds, D. L., Henderson, C. R., Jr., Kitzman, H. J., Eckenrode, J. J., Cote, R. E., & Tatelbaum, R. C. (1999). Prenatal and infancy home visitation by nurses: Recent findings. *Future of Children, 61*, 44–65.

Olds, D. L., & Kitzman, H. (1993). Review of research on home visiting for pregnant women and parents of young children. *Future of Children, 3*, 53–92.

Reichardt, C. S., & Rallis, S. F. (Eds.). (1994, Spring). *The qualitative-quantitative debate: New perspectives* (New Directions for Program Evaluation Monograph, No. 61). San Francisco, CA: Jossey-Bass.

Rosenbaum, P. R., & Rubin, D. (1983). The central role of the propensity score in observational studies for causal effects. *Biometrika, 70*, 41–55.

Rossi, P. H., Lipsey, M. W., & Freeman, H. E. (2004). *Evaluation: A systematic approach* (7th ed.). Thousand Oaks, CA: Sage.

Schorr, L. B. (2003, February). *Determining "what works" in social programs and policies: Toward a more inclusive knowledge base.* Washington, DC: The Brookings Institution. Retrieved August 20, 2008, from http://www.brookings.edu/papers/2003/0226poverty_schorr.aspx.

Scott, K. G., Mason, C. A., & Chapman, D. A. (1999). The use of epidemiological methodology as a means of influencing public policy. *Child Development, 70*, 1263–1272.

St. Petersburg–USA Orphanage Research Team. (2008). The effects of early social-emotional and relationship experience on the development of young orphanage children. *Monographs of the Society for Research in Child Development, 73*(3, Serial No. 291).

Wandersman, A., Imm, P., Chinman, M., & Kaftarian, S. (1999). *Getting to outcomes: Methods and tools for planning, evaluation and accountability.* Rockville, MD: Center for Substance Abuse Prevention.

Wandersman, A., Imm, P., Chinman, M., & Kaftarian, S. (2000). Getting to outcomes: A results-based approach to accountability. *Evaluation and Program Planning, 23*, 389–395.

Weiss, C. H. (1995). Nothing as practical as good theory: Exploring theory-based evaluation for comprehensive community initiatives for children and families. In J. P. Connell, A. C. Kubish, L. B. Schorr, & C. H. Weiss (Eds.), *New approaches to evaluating community initiatives: Concepts, methods, and contexts* (pp. 65–92). Washington, DC: The Aspen Institute.

W. K. Kellogg Foundation. (1998). *W. K. Kellogg Foundation evaluation handbook.* Battle Creek, MI: Author.

W. K. Kellogg Foundation. (2000). *W. K. Kellogg Foundation logic model development guide.* Battle Creek, MI: Author.

Yau, L. H. Y., & Little, R. J. A. (2001). Inference for the complier-average causal effect from longitudinal data subject to noncompliance and missing data, with applications to a job training assessment for the unemployed. *Journal of the American Statistical Association, 96,* 1232–1244.

Further Reading

General Applied Issues in Practice and Policy

Groark, C. J., & McCall, R. B. (2005). Integrating developmental scholarship into practice and policy. In M. H. Bornstein & M. E. Lamb (Eds.), *Developmental psychology: An advanced textbook* (5th ed., pp. 570–601). Mahwah, NJ: Lawrence Erlbaum Associates.

Intervention Implementation

Groark, C. J., & McCall, R. B. (2008). Community-based interventions and services. In M. Rutter, D. Bishop, D. Pine, S. Scott, J. Stevenson, E. Taylor, & A. Thapar (Eds.), *Rutter's child and adolescent psychiatry* (5th ed., pp. 971–988). London: Blackwell.

Gold Standard Methodology

McCall, R. B., & Green, B. L. (2004). Beyond the methodological gold standards of behavioral research: Considerations for practice and policy. *SRCD Social Policy Report, 18*(2), 3–19.

Program Evaluation and Quasi-Experimental Designs

Cook, T., & Campbell, D. T. (1979). *Quasi-experimental design and analysis issues for field settings.* Chicago: Rand McNally.

McCall, R. B., Ryan, C. S., & Green, B. L. (1999). Some non-randomized constructed comparison groups for evaluating early age-related outcomes of intervention programs. *American Journal of Evaluation, 2*(20), 213–226.

Rossi, P. H., Lipsey, M. W., & Freeman, H. E. (2004). *Evaluation: A systematic approach* (7th ed.). Thousand Oaks, CA: Sage.

General Longitudinal Methods

Collins, L. M. (2006). Analysis of longitudinal data: The integration of theoretical model, temporal design, and statistical model. *Annual Review of Psychology, 57*, 505–528.

McCartney, K., Burchinal, M. R., & Rub, K. L. (2006). Best practices in quantitative methods for developmentalists. *Monograph of the Society for Research in Child Development, 71*(3, No. 385).

Growth Curve Analysis

Burchinal, M. R., & Appelbaum, M. I. (1991). Estimating individual developmental functions: Various methods and their assumptions. *Child Development, 62*, 23–43.

McCartney, K., Burchinal, M. R., & Rub, K. L. (2006). Best practices in quantitative methods for developmentalists (Chap. 5). *Monograph of the Society for Research in Child Development, 71*(3, No. 385).

Muthén, B. (2001). Second-generation structural equation modeling with a combination of categorical and continuous latent variables: New opportunities for latent class-latent profile growth modeling. In L. Collins & A. Sayer (Eds.), *New methods for the analysis of change* (pp. 289–322). Washington, DC: American Psychological Association.

Muthén, B. (2004). Latent variable analysis: Growth mixture modeling and related techniques for longitudinal data. In D. Kaplan (Ed.), *Handbook of quantitative methodology for the social sciences* (pp. 345–368). Newbury Park, CA: Sage.

Muthén, B. O., & Curran, P. J. (1997). General longitudinal modeling of individual differences in experimental designs: A latent variable framework for analysis and power estimation. *Psychological Methods, 2*, 371–402.

Muthén, B., & Muthén, L. (2000). Integrating person-centered and variable-centered analysis: Growth mixture modeling with latent trajectory classes. *Alcoholism: Clinical and Experimental Research, 24*, 882–891.

Raudenbush, S. W., & Bryk, A. S. (2002). *Hierarchical linear models: Applications and data analysis methods* (2nd ed.). Newburg Park, CA: Sage.

Propensity Score Analysis

Rosenbaum, P. R., & Rubin, D. (1983). The central role of the propensity score in observational studies for causal effects. *Biometrika, 70*, 41–55.

Complier Average Causal Effect (CACE) Versus Intent to Treat

Frangakis, C. E., & Rubin, D. B. (1999). Addressing compilations of intention-to-treat analysis in the combined presence of all-or-none treatment-compliance and subsequent missing outcomes. *Biometrika, 86*, 365–379.

Jo, B. (2002). Statistical power in randomized intervention studies with noncompliance. *Psychological Methods, 7*(2), 178–193.

Muthén, L. K., & Muthén, B. O. (1998–2001). *Mplus user's guide*. Los Angeles: Author.

Yau, L. H. Y., & Little, R. J. A. (2001). Inference for the complier-average causal effect from longitudinal data subject to noncompliance and missing data, with applications to a job training assessment for the unemployed. *Journal of the American Statistical Association, 96,* 1232–1244.

Instrumental Variable Analysis

Angrist, J. D., Imbens, G. W., & Rubin, D. B. (1996). Identification of causal effects using instrumental variables. *Journal of the American Statistical Association, 91,* 444–455.

Davidson, R., & MacKinnon, J. G. (1993). *Estimation and inference in econometrics*. New York: Oxford University Press.

Foster, E. M., & McLanahan, S. (1996). An illustration of the use of instrumental variables: Do neighborhood conditions affect a young person's chance of finishing high school? *Psychological Methods, 1,* 249–260.

Yoshikawa, H., Rosman, E. A., & Hsueh, J. (2001). Variation in teen mothers' experience of child care and other components of welfare reform: Selection processes and developmental consequences. *Child Development, 72,* 299–317.

Policy Relevant Statistics

Scott, K. G., Mason, C. A., & Chapman, D. A. (1999). The use of epidemiological methodology as a means of influencing public policy. *Child Development, 70,* 1263–1272.

CHAPTER 7

Ethical Issues and Challenges in Applied Research in Child and Adolescent Development

Celia Fisher, PhD, and Adam L. Fried, PhD
Fordham University

Introduction

During the last two decades, economic, social, political, and disciplinary factors have converged to foster increased attention to the social and applied relevance of the developmental empirical database. In response to societal demands, applied developmental science has broadened its techniques and populations studied to produce empirically grounded data that can inform policy and practices directed at improving conditions that pose risks to the development of adaptive and productive life skills (Fisher, 2002; Fisher & Lerner, 1994; Fisher & Masty, 2006; Fisher & Murray, 1996). Increased emphasis on conducting research that seeks to improve conditions for at-risk and vulnerable populations has resulted in novel questions and complex challenges for scientists, for which federal regulations for the protection of human participants and professional ethics codes may offer imperfect or incomplete answers (Fisher, 1999). As such, investigators often experience difficulty designing research procedures that adequately protect participants' welfare while maintaining the standards of good science (Fisher & Rosendahl, 1990; Fisher & Wallace, 2000). As we will discuss throughout this chapter, these goals need not and should not be competing, as good science exemplifies both.

How can investigators working with participants of at-risk and vulnerable populations design studies that protect participant welfare, respect autonomy, and maintain standards of good science?

Knowledge creation and acquisition derived from the scientific enterprise fuels the dynamic process of developing, refining, and implementing intervention strategies and social policy that promotes the development of individuals and families. The value of the knowledge derived through research is compromised, however, when study methods fail to adequately reflect the values and protect the rights and welfare of community participants. In this chapter, we describe how our personal and professional experiences led to us implementing a research ethic that builds upon shared understandings between investigators and participants. These experiences, illustrated throughout the chapter as case examples, have reinforced our conviction that employing strategies that seek to better understand the backgrounds of participants, including hopes, fears, expectations, goals, and comprehension of the specific study at hand, will contribute to an improved research design that protects participants' welfare, respects their autonomy, and by doing so increases study validity.

Authors' Background

Questions about research ethics have guided many of our scholarly interests, especially as they relate to better appreciation of participant perspectives on ethical challenges. Much of our research has been informed by direct work with study participants, particularly as they relate to issues surrounding research design, participant recruitment, informed consent, the research–participant relationship (including power differentials and coercion), participant risks, dissemination of study results, and responsibilities to participants after the completion of research.

Fisher's entry into examining the effects of research on participants was stimulated by her parallel experiences in studying infant perceptual development at the same time that she became a new mother. Motherhood transformed her worldview, leading to new ways of approaching research ethics. For example, instead of asking the question "Would I consent to participate in this study?" Fisher began to ask "Would I consent to having my child participate in this study?" (Fisher, 2000). Her ensuing research experiences with infant, child, adolescent, and impaired adult populations increased her awareness of the enormous struggles that parents and guardians experience in making the decision to give consent for their children to participate in research, and she appreciated more distinctly how participant, parent/guardian, family, and community diversity affected how individuals approached and felt about research. Fisher began to realize that researchers would not be able to adequately design and implement appropriate procedures that protect the welfare and respect the rights of participants without first learning about how the individuals themselves felt about research participation. To learn more about how participants approach and view research, she began to engage them in a dialogue to inquire about the ethical issues that were important to them (Fisher, 1999).

How can researchers balance their obligation to generate scientifically valid data with their responsibility to protect participant rights and welfare?

As first a research assistant and eventually a postdoctoral fellow working in Fisher's research lab, Fried has contributed to a number of studies that have examined the viewpoints, attitudes, and knowledge about research among a number of diverse participant populations. One of Fried's initial research experiences was assisting on a project that assessed the consent ability of developmentally disabled adults and the experience significantly altered the way he understood and valued informed consent procedures. Instead of viewing informed consent as a unidimensional, one-size-fits-all process, differences in how individuals understood and appreciated the components of informed consent demanded new approaches. As a result of his experiences, he has developed an interest in studying the factors that influence the degree to which decisionally impaired populations understand research concepts and their research rights.

Relational Ethics

Federal guidelines require that a research study maximize benefits, minimize harms, and provide a positive ratio between benefits and harms (Department of Human and Health Services [DHHS], 2001a). As outlined in the Nuremberg Code (1946), an "experiment should be such as to yield fruitful results for the good of society" (Principle 2). Investigators may find it difficult to achieve an appropriate balance between the rigorous standards associated with good science and their duty and responsibility to ensure the presence of research safeguards that adequately protect the rights and welfare of participants (Fisher, 1993, 1999; Fisher & Masty, 2006; Fisher & Rosendahl, 1990).

What methods do scientists engage in to design appropriate safeguards for participants, and what resources are available to researchers to assist in these decisions?

A common assumption, based on a traditional view of science, holds that professional ethicists and those in authoritative positions (such as senior scientists or members of an institutional review board) are solely responsible for science-in-ethics decision making (Fisher, 1999). Investigators' own worldviews, while often informed by scientific research, theory, and professional logic, may fail to consider important population and context-relevant considerations in the design of research. Too often scientists use their own moral compass (or that of their colleagues) in the design of protections, which may, unintentionally, neglect key factors and concerns relevant to the population of interest. Investigators also seek guidance from institutional review boards (IRBs) in designing procedures that safeguard participants from harm, but, similar to the investigators themselves, members of the IRB typically have their own moral views from which they make recommendations that may neglect considerations important to the community who is being asked to participate (Fisher, 1999). Further, given the diversity of populations with which applied developmental scientists may work, it may be extremely difficult for investigators, colleagues, or IRB members to adequately anticipate participant reactions, views, or attitudes toward research procedures (Fisher & Ragsdale, 2006).

Fisher's first empirical venture into understanding participants' perceptions of research ethics was humbling. She sought to grapple with the ethical problems associated with conducting deception research with undergraduates by conducting a paper-and-pencil study that asked students to judge the risks, benefits, and other ethical aspects of published deception studies (Fisher & Fyrberg, 1994). She naively thought that the opinions of her 18- to 20-year-old participants would provide the answers to the deception research dilemma. She discovered instead that some of the students' responses were ethically contradictory. For example, although they indicated on rating scales that most students would be harmed or suspicious of "dehoaxing" (explaining the true purpose of the study at the conclusion of the experiment), in their essays they saw dehoaxing as a way to make deception research ethically acceptable. Fisher realized that active dialogue with participants would be a more constructive approach to achieving participant-sensitive ethical procedures and at the same time recognized that participant opinions must inform research ethics procedures, but are not a substitute for the investigator's own ethical responsibilities.

Co-Learning: An Interactive Process of Learning and Teaching

Fisher's work has culminated in the development of a relational ethics framework, which promotes moral discourse between scientist and research participant. Influenced by a justice–care perspective that emphasizes beneficence, respect, and fairness, this approach capitalizes on the expertise of both researcher and participant, who, through a synergistic process of co-learning, can formulate ethical procedures that respects the rights and values of participants (Fisher, 1997, 1999, 2000, 2002; Fisher & Masty, 2006). This dialectical process of co-learning, by which both scientist and participant learn from each other, recognizes the role of research participants as moral agents and engages them as stakeholders in the research process (Fisher & Ragsdale, 2006; Fisher & Wallace, 2000). Such co-learning gives voice to participants that may inform important aspects of research design.

Scientific methods that result solely from professional logic or scientific inference, without the solicitation of participant perspectives or consideration of the research context, risk jeopardizing the welfare of participants. For example, research procedures that do not take into account community attitudes toward or beliefs about science may exacerbate participant misperceptions, misunderstandings, and skepticism about research goals or procedures (Fisher, 1997, 2002; Fisher & Wallace, 2000; Fisher & Goodman, 2009; Fisher et al., 2008). By engaging participants and their communities in a dialogue and partnership, investigators ensure that their study-related procedures and safeguards are not solely determined by the moral viewpoints and opinions of the investigators or other professionals with little to no connection with the population being studied, but rather are informed by the research-relevant values of prospective study participants and their communities. Co-learning methods recognize prospective participants, parents/guardians, and members of the community as important stakeholders in the design, implementation, and dissemination stages of research (Fisher, 2002; Fisher & Masty, 2006; Higgins-D'Alessandro, Hamilton, & Fisher, 1998; Tricket, 1998).

It is important to remember that engaging in a process of co-learning with prospective participants does not guarantee that investigators will not encounter complex ethical dilemmas, as moral principles, such as respect, beneficence, and autonomy, may, at times, appear to be at odds. The fiduciary nature of the relationship between scientist and participant requires the researcher to take responsibility for the research-related decisions that impact the rights and welfare of the research participants such that participant perspectives inform but do not override the ethical duties of a scientist (Fisher, 1999, 2000; Fisher & Fyrberg, 1994; Fisher & Wallace, 2000).

Participant Perspectives: Scientist and Participants as Moral Agents

Co-learning methods emphasize the interpersonal aspects of the relationship between participant and researcher and values the participant perspective as integral to good ethical decision making (Fisher, 1997, 1999). According to this framework, both the scientist and participant are moral agents engaged in a process of constructing scientific goals and procedures that share mutual values and are sensitive to the population and context. Failure to consider participant perspectives in the planning of research risks treating participants as "research material" and substitutes the investigator's judgment and worldview for those of the individuals who are being asked to participate (Fisher, 1997, 2000; Veatch, 1987). In the absence of participant consultation, investigators risk over- or underestimating study-related burdens, resulting in either precluding valuable research opportunities for at-risk populations or exposing vulnerable populations to risks and harms (Fisher, 1999; Fisher & Masty, 2006; Sugarman et al., 1998).

Consultation with community members can promote trust and enhance support for the overall study (Fisher et al., 2002; Melton, Levine, Koocher, Rosenthal, & Thompson, 1988). For example, investigators working with children and youth often find it difficult to determine what information to keep confidential and what to disclose, especially when working with ethnic minority populations (Brooks-Gunn & Rotheram-Borus, 1994; Fisher, 1994, 1999; Fisher et al., 2002; Scott-Jones, 1994). In Fisher's focus group and survey research (Fisher, Higgins-D'Allesandro, Rau, Kuther, & Belanger, 1996; Fisher 2003a; Fisher et al., 2002; O'Sullivan & Fisher, 1997), contrary to common assumptions regarding the confidentiality protections, both adolescents and their parents indicated preferences for disclosure to trusted adults or treatment referral if an investigator discovered during the course of research that an adolescent's health or welfare was in jeopardy. Fisher has expanded our understanding of participant perspectives through ethnic minority adolescents and their parents (Fisher & Wallace, 2000), college students (Fisher & Fyrberg, 1994), parents of children diagnosed with cancer (Fisher & Masty, 2006), and illicit drug users (Fisher et al., 2008). Examples of her work soliciting the perspectives of participants will be presented, illustrating the ways in which these viewpoints inform research design.

How do street drug users evaluate ethical issues in research involving treatment and placebo control groups?

A common criterion in evaluating the validity of consent is whether the individual adequately weighs the risks and benefits of participating and is able to communicate a decision based upon this analysis (Appelbaum & Grisso, 1995). But what if participants hold beliefs about research that might inhibit their ability to fully appreciate the risks and benefits associated with participation?

Many researchers mistakenly assume that participants share their judgments about the purpose of research, goals of a particular study, and risks and benefits of participation. Individuals, however, may differ with respect to their understanding of the purpose of research procedures, their classification of risks and benefits, their attitudes toward science, and motives of the sponsors of the research (e.g., government). For example, the aims of the study that are communicated by prospective participants may be met with skepticism as certain individuals may believe that the primary goal of any study is to promote the investigator's career. In addition, research that has the possibility of improving social programs and policy in a particular neighborhood may be viewed with caution by disenfranchised community members, who may fear that government officials may use the data to implement harmful government policies (Fisher & Wallace, 2000).

Fisher's National Institute on Drug Abuse (NIDA)-funded studies in collaboration with Merrill Singer, Meena Mahadevan, Matthew Oransky, Greg Mirhej, and Derek Hodge have shed light on the attitudes of street drug users toward participating in clinical research. In one study, 100 self-identified street drug users participated in 11 focus groups in urban cities to share their views about participating in randomized clinical trials (Fisher et al., 2008). To facilitate discussion, a 4-minute videotaped vignette depicting consultation between a medical researcher and prospective participant (who is addicted to cocaine and has expressed an interest in quitting) discussing a randomized clinical trial of an experimental drug designed to reduce cocaine cravings. In the vignette, the medical researcher describes some of the key elements of the study, including possible side effects of the medication, use of a placebo, random assignment to conditions, and the double-blind nature of the study. The participant asks the medical researcher questions about the methods and procedures of the trial; at the end of the consultation, it is unclear whether the drug user will consent to be in the study. Focus group participants discussed different aspects of the study, such as the motivations of both the participants and investigator, the purpose of research procedures, and the aspects of the research that are most important to the participant in deciding whether to participate. Several interesting themes emerged from these discussions.

Experimental Realism

The ability of participants to adequately understand the nature and purpose of ethically relevant components of the specific research protocol (e.g., random assignment) was termed *experimental realism*. Specifically, most participants were able to appreciate the concept of treatment uncertainty (expressing the hope that the treatment would work but uncertain of the actual outcome), methods of determining treatment efficacy, and purpose of placebo.

Therapeutic Mistrust

Many participants expressed a mistrust of investigators with regard to their motivations (e.g., using research solely for professional advancement), intentions with regard to participant care (e.g., treating participants solely as guinea pigs to further the interests of the study), and the integrity of researchers (e.g., not following stated treatment protocols in order to produce more desirable results). Focus group members with significant personal experience participating in clinical research were especially vocal about their beliefs that investigators are willing to "use" participants to further their own careers. For some focus group participants, therapeutic mistrust fueled their reluctance in believing that the medical researcher was uncertain about treatment outcome (with the regard to the effectiveness of the new medication), and some even indicated that the medical researcher was being intentionally deceptive and misleading in an effort to enroll the participant in the study.

Therapeutic Misconception, Misestimation, and Experimental Optimism

Participants evidenced beliefs consistent with what Appelbaum, Roth, Lidz, Benson, and Winslade (1987) have termed the *therapeutic misconception*, the idea that the intervention research is associated with a type of clinical care solely aimed at improving the participant's target condition, illness, or problem. They also demonstrated what Horng and Grady (2003) have labeled the *therapeutic misestimation* (over- or underestimating research risks and benefits) and experimental optimism (participants' hopes that participation in the study will lead to an improvement in their condition, problem, or situation for some participants and was expressed by some focus group members).

Broad Lessons

Content analysis of the statements of focus group members indicated that many poorly educated and impoverished street drug users are able to understand important concepts of randomized clinical trials research and make distinctions between research and clinical care. The data also demonstrated that participants may approach research situations with skepticism about the goals and motivations of the investigator as well as the integrity of the research enterprise in general. These findings highlight certain ethical vulnerabilities of these populations. For example, individuals who are at risk or present with drug use disorders may erroneously view participation in research as an opportunity to improve their condition or reject participation because of unsubstantiated mistrust of investigator motives.

For example, Horng and Grady (2003) distinguish the ethical permissibility of therapeutic misconception and therapeutic misestimation, arguing that although the therapeutic misconception is rarely acceptable because understanding the purpose and risks of the research is necessary for autonomous decision making, therapeutic misestimation is sometimes acceptable as an accurate comprehension of the exact nature of the risks and benefits of participation in research may not compromise the autonomous aspects of the informed consent decision. Experimental mistrust that leads to erroneous beliefs on the part of participants about the research (e.g., the purpose of the research is to further the investigator's career or that researchers will not accurately disclose the potential risks and benefits associated with participation) jeopardizes the integrity of informed consent, as it may deprive individuals (especially those who are economically disadvantaged and socially marginalized, and who may have few opportunities to receive treatment and services) from potentially helpful treatments and interventions (Fisher et al., 2008). As illustrated in these focus groups, some individuals may be more likely to believe that research is motivated by investigators' personal incentives (e.g., financial gain, career advancement) rather than scientific or altruistic purpose; these individuals may benefit from frank and honest conversations with research personnel about the nature and purpose of the proposed study, which may help to allay fears held by the participant of being used solely as research material (Fisher et al., 2008).

How do parents and youths view the risks and benefits of research on adolescent risk behaviors?

Adolescent risk has been widely studied by applied developmental scientists. Ethical dilemmas associated with this type of research have emerged, including the possibility of increased risk to participants that may result simply by agreeing to participate (e.g., stigmatization), unintended negative consequences associated with common research methods (such as negative affect and thoughts resulting from survey questions about emotionally charged issues), and concerns about confidentiality with regard to adolescent risk behaviors (such as drug use and unsafe sexual activities). The following example of co-learning through participant consultation with adolescents and parents illustrates how this type of dialogue can provide researchers with information that can be used to inform study design, including possible validity concerns associated with certain methods of data collection and the ways in which views about research might negatively affect recruitment and participation.

In 1998, Fisher and Scyatta Wallace led a series of 13 focus groups with 55 high school-age adolescents (ninth through eleventh grade) and 46 parents (Fisher & Wallace, 2000). Half of the sample of adolescents and parents were drawn from lower socioeconomic/ high-crime neighborhoods; most from this group were African American, Hispanic, or multiracial. The other half of the sample of adolescents and parents were drawn from an academically competitive public school with a diverse student body. The parents and adolescents in the group self-identified as African American, Hispanic, East or South Asian, and non-Hispanic White. Integrating video presentations with narrative examples of adolescent research, Fisher and Wallace asked participants about research risks and benefits across five types of research designs: survey, physical samples, school-based intervention, informant research, and the role of genetics in determining adolescent risk behaviors.

Both adolescents and parents communicated distrust of survey research findings, as they believed that adolescents often lie or exaggerate in attempt to provide socially desirable responses, to deceive the researcher, or because they are not answering questions seriously. Participants were equally skeptical of teacher or adult observations of students, arguing that peers and adults often base their observations on their experiences in one setting (e.g., school) and rarely have a good understanding of their behaviors in other settings (e.g., at home, at work). Focus group members were also concerned with confidentiality in school-based research. For example, there was concern that teachers who collect sensitive data about students may discuss confidential information with other teachers.

With respect to methods of data collection, students highlighted a number of validity concerns, including selection bias, honesty, and integrity in various methods of data collection. For example, with respect to research that collects bodily fluid, adolescents stressed that the only students who would participate in this type of research were those with "nothing to hide" (Fisher & Wallace, 2000, p. 106). Students also communicated that, in general, intervention research often attracts students who acknowledge that they are in need of help, and that participation in a study may result in increased stigmatization for these students. Finally, some adolescents expressed concern about research that probed emotionally distressing issues or traumatic experiences, noting that investigation of these topics may contribute to the poststudy negative affect.

Parents and adolescents from both schools distrusted researcher motivations when it came to risk prevention or intervention studies. Participants believed that researchers often use adolescents as guinea pigs or lab mice, and investigators were often motivated by financial considerations to produce research results that supported their theory. African American parents were especially likely to indicate distrust in research and its ability to benefit their community, with some citing infamous cases of research misconduct, such as the Tuskegee syphilis study (Jones, 1993) as a reason for widespread distrust of government-sponsored research and intervention.

Parents from lower socioeconomic/high-crime neighborhoods stressed that research that focuses on violence in these areas may give the false impression that violent crime is exclusively perpetrated by minorities living in the inner city and ignores the violence that occurs in suburban areas (e.g., antiminority, serial killers, antisocial behavior), by terrorists, or government agents. Many of these parents also expressed concern that scientists were extensions of the government whose goal was to conduct research that may be used to support racial stereotypes and as evidence to withhold support and services from economically disadvantaged communities.

Broad Lessons

There has been increased focus on the importance of mental health research with racial and ethnic minority groups (DHHS, 2001b). Broadly speaking, the contributions of representatives of prospective participant groups provided important insights regarding youth risk research. First, when designing research procedures with diverse populations, it is imperative for investigators to recognize and address vulnerabilities of members of particular groups in order to develop research procedures that adequately protect their rights and welfare (Fisher et al., 2002). To identify these vulnerabilities, investigators must view the research, and science in general, through the cultural lens of the population being studied (Fisher & Ragsdale, 2006; Fisher & Wallace, 2000).

Fisher has found that exploring the values and attitudes of research participants has forced her to acknowledge and confront her own ideas about race, culture, socioeconomic status, and risk-taking behaviors. Participant comments surfaced the fact that investigators' conceptualizations of race and ethnicity are incomplete without consideration of the political and social environments in which participants live, as many ethnic minorities have been victims of oppression, discrimination, and prejudice (Essed, 1991; Fisher et al., 2002; Fisher & Rosendahl, 1990; Fisher, Hatashita-Wong, & Isman, 1999; Fisher, Wallace, & Fenton, 2000; Helms, 1993; Parham, 1993; Sue, 1993). Failure to recognize this facet of a prospective participant's experience may result in researchers inadvertently asking participants to unjustly bear research risks (Fisher & Wallace, 2000). Research procedures and methods that ignore these factors may be unintentionally alienating, disrespectful, or fear producing.

Finally, adolescents provided helpful information about possible limitations to validity associated with certain methods of data collection, including selection bias and honesty of participants in answering questions. Focus group members also highlighted important participant protection issues associated with various types of research. For example, adolescents believed that participants who agree to enroll in intervention studies may be stigmatized as experiencing problems or disordered and that certain types of emotionally charged topics studied through survey methods had the potential to cause postexperimental harm by triggering associated thoughts, feelings, and memories.

How do you construct developmentally and contextually "fitted" informed consent procedures?

The relational ethic framework has applications to the informed consent process, seeking to preserve participant rights to self-governance and privacy, while ensuring that incompetent decisions do not jeopardize participant welfare (Fisher, 2002). Participants' voluntary informed consent to research has been viewed as the best means of preserving and protecting their rights and welfare (Freedman, 1975). Paternalistic approaches to informed consent have been tempered by an increasing recognition of the importance of participant autonomy, reflecting a respect for an individual's right to self-governance. For consent to be valid, it must be informed, voluntary, and rational. Certain participant conditions (such as mental disorders or developmental disabilities) may preclude individuals, however, from making autonomous decisions about participation research.

Drawing on applied developmental theory (Fisher & Lerner, 1994), Fisher has pioneered a "goodness-of-fit" approach to informed consent that conceptualizes consent capacity as a product of the individual and the context in which consent is being sought, rather than on an exclusive focus on the participants' consent-related abilities and limitations (Fisher, 2003b, 2003c). In effect, a goodness-of-fit approach to informed consent seeks to reframe the consent context itself through evaluation of the aspects of the research setting that may contribute to decision-making vulnerabilities and modification of the consent process or research environment to increase participant understanding of study-relevant topics and increase consent capacity (Fisher & Ragsdale, 2006; Fried & Fisher, 2007).

Research designs must be sensitive to possible participant vulnerabilities and the ways in which the study design (including the procedures to protect participants from harm) can be fitted to reduce such vulnerabilities (Fisher, 2003c; Fisher & Masty, 2006; Fisher & Ragsdale, 2006). To reduce or eliminate risks, scientists must be willing to alter or reconfigure experimental methods, recognizing that some procedures may represent higher risks, depending on the vulnerabilities of the population (Fisher, 1999). Goodness-of-fit approaches to informed consent are, by definition, context and population specific. Individuals may vary in the degree of consent vulnerability, depending on static and transient factors. For example, individuals with schizophrenia may present with fluctuating levels of consent capacity, depending on their symptoms or disease presentation at the time consent is sought.

Case Example: Goodness-of-Fit for Research With Developmentally Disabled Adults

Fried and Fisher have collaborated with Christine Cea and Philip Davidson on several studies focused on identifying the strengths and weaknesses of adults with intellectual and developmental disabilities (IDD) in consenting to participate in research (Fisher, Cea, Davidson, & Fried, 2006). Adults with IDD may present with more static deficits in their ability to understand and weigh the risks and benefits of participation and may require an enhanced or adapted informed consent presentation, such as forms written at a level appropriate for their cognitive ability. To investigate this we developed an instrument specifically for adults with IDD using the four standards of consent capacity proposed by Appelbaum and Grisso (1995):

1. Ability to communicate a choice about research participation
2. Understanding of the overall nature of the research
3. Appreciation of risks and benefits of participation
4. Demonstrating adequate reasoning about their participation choice

Before beginning data collection, we convened a community advisory board composed of a diverse group of community members (including researchers, physicians, parents, and caregivers) with expertise on individuals with IDD to provide recommendations and assistance at regular intervals throughout the course of the study. To assess consent capacity, we developed a hypothetical story (with questions assessing comprehension) about an individual who is asked to participate in a randomized clinical trial to test a new medication. The story was read to participants in one- to two-sentence segments, with a comprehension question after each disclosure.

The language and presentation of the informed consent material was simplified to a grade-school-level language, administered in small one- to two-sentence increments, and repeated to enhance comprehension. Participants included equal numbers of individuals diagnosed with mild or moderate IDD who were living in community group homes. As a comparison group, we administered the story and questions to college students to determine baseline scores.

To our surprise, a high percentage of mild IDD adults demonstrated good comprehension of the information presented, many within the range of college students, including questions tapping their understanding of the purpose of the hypothetical research study and appreciation of the consequences of participation. Nearly all participants, those with mild and moderate IDD, were able to communicate a choice about whether they believed the protagonist should consent to research. Some of the concepts that individuals had difficulty understanding included the right to withdraw from a study once it had started, confidentiality, the purpose of randomization (including the concept that assignment to the placebo group may not alleviate the protagonist's problems), and reasons not to participate.

Broad Lessons

Through this research, we learned a great deal about the consent strengths and vulnerabilities of developmentally disabled adults. First, the findings suggested that in many cases adults with at least mild IDD may be as able as nondisordered adults to make autonomous consent decisions regarding research participation. Findings also suggested possible consent vulnerability with respect to confusion over the distinction between ordinary treatment and research. However, as you recall, this "therapeutic misconception" is not unique to adults with decisional impairments. As the ethical implications of obtaining informed consent for the drug using populations described earlier in this chapter, investigators working with developmentally disabled populations must be aware of and take steps to remediate possible therapeutic misconceptions, or, more generally, the belief that the purpose of all doctors (with perhaps little to no distinction between researchers and physicians) is to provide clinical care and that doctors will always recommend the best course of action.

Several goodness-of-fit strategies may be considered to address potential consent vulnerabilities. For example, some methods to increase comprehension of poorly understood research-related concepts might be to educate prospective participants about the purpose and nature of the research study, the differences between a researcher and a personal physician, and to clearly outline how participation in research may or may not personally benefit the individual or result in improvement of a condition or problem. Another method (supported by the results of our research) is the use of simplified language to increase comprehension. For example, explaining confidentiality procedures by avoiding scientific jargon and using a few simple expressions (e.g., "keep things secret, won't tell anybody") to convey the idea that data will not be communicated to anyone outside the research team, or "flipping a coin" to indicate the random nature of assignment.

It is important to note that particularly vulnerable populations may require informed consent procedures to be repeated throughout the course of a study to ensure that participation is informed, voluntary, and rational. For example, to ensure that individuals understand their right to withdraw participation, investigators may find it useful to provide reminders throughout the participant's involvement in the research about their right to withdraw without penalty. For some individuals, the appointment of participant advocates or individuals (such as a representative from the participant's home or a trusted family member) could serve to ensure that consent is valid.

Conclusion

Applied developmental scientists work with diverse populations in a broad range of settings. Their work informs policies, programs, and laws that contribute to the betterment of society. Within a relational ethic framework, investigators and participants engage in a synergistic process of co-learning to ensure the implementation of scientifically valid and ethically responsible procedures within each unique research context that respects the rights, values, and welfare of participants. It must also be emphasized, however, that basing research design decisions solely on views and input solicited from participants and their communities does not absolve the researcher from his or her fiduciary responsibility to engage in sound, ethical decision making (Fisher, 1997; Fisher & Fyrberg, 1994).

In conducting research with at-risk and vulnerable populations, both novice and experienced investigators frequently encounter research challenges where cookie-cutter solutions may be insufficient to adequately resolve complex moral dilemmas (Fisher, Hoagwood, & Jenson, 1996). Research methods and techniques that may be appropriate for some populations may represent significant risk for others. The knowledge that can be gained through applications of relational ethics can provide significant and useful information that can serve to protect the ethical and scientific integrity of the research, while respecting autonomy and protecting the welfare of all participants.

Resources

Regulations, Guidelines, and Reports

American Psychological Association Ethics Code: www.apa .org/ethics

Belmont Report: http://www.hhs.gov/ohrp/humansubjects/ guidance/belmont.htm

Informed consent frequently asked questions (Office of Human Research Protections [OHRP]): http://www.hhs.gov/ohrp/ informconsfaq.html

Research involving children frequently asked questions (OHRP): http://www.hhs.gov/ohrp/researchfaq.html

Title 45 Part 46 (Department of Health and Human Services [DHHS]): http://www.hhs.gov/ohrp/humansubjects/guidance/45cfr46.htm

Mental Health: Culture, Race, and Ethnicity—A Supplement to Mental Health: A Report of the Surgeon General, by the Department of Health and Human Services, 2001.

Scholarly Articles

"Relational Ethics and Research with Vulnerable Populations" (Fisher, 1999)

"Participant Consultation: Insights into Parental Permission and Confidentiality Procedures for Policy-Relevant Research with Youth" (Fisher, 2002)

"Research Ethics for Mental Health Science Involving Ethnic Minority Children and Youth" (Fisher et al., 2002)

"Determining Risk in Pediatric Research with No Prospect of Direct Benefit: Time for a National Consensus on the Interpretation of Federal Regulations" (Fisher, Kornetsky, & Prentice, 2007)

"Ethical and Legal Issues in Conducting Research Involving Elderly Subjects" (High & Doole, 1995)

"Community Consultation in Socially Sensitive Research: Lessons from Clinical Trials of Treatments for AIDS" (Melton, Levine, Koocher, Rosenthal, & Thompson, 1988)

References

Appelbaum, P. S., Roth, L. H., Lidz, C. W., Benson, P., & Winslade, W. (1987). False hopes and best data: Consent to research and the therapeutic misconception. *Hastings Center Report, 17,* 20–24.

Appelbaum, P. S., & Grisso, T. (1995). The MacArthur Treatment Competence Study: Mental illness and competence to consent to treatment. *Law & Human Behavior, 19,* 105–126.

Brooks-Gunn, J., & Rotheram-Borus, M. (1994). Rights to privacy in research: Adolescents versus parents. *Ethics & Behavior, 4,* 109–121.

Department of Health and Human Services. (2001a). *Title 45 Public Welfare, Part 46, Code of Federal Regulations, Protection of Human Subjects.*

Department of Health and Human Services. (2001b). *Mental health: Culture, race, and ethnicity—A supplement to mental health: A report of the surgeon general.* Rockville, MD: Author.

Essed, P. (1991). *Understanding everyday racism: An interdisciplinary theory.* Thousand Oaks, CA: Sage.

Fisher, C. B. (1993). Joining science and application: Ethical challenges for researchers and practitioners. *Professional Psychology: Research and Practice, 24,* 378–381.

Fisher, C. B. (1994). Reporting and referring research participants: Ethical challenges for investigators studying children and youth. *Ethics & Behavior, 4,* 87–95.

Fisher, C. B. (1997). A relational perspective on ethics-in-science decision making for research with vulnerable populations. *IRB: Review of Human Subjects Research, 19,* 1–4.

Fisher, C. B. (1999). *Relational ethics and research with vulnerable populations. Reports on research involving persons with mental disorders that may affect decision-making capacity.* Rockville, MD: National Bioethics Advisory Commission.

Fisher, C. B. (2000). Relational ethics in psychological research: One feminist's journey. In M. Brabeck (Ed.), *Practicing feminist ethics in psychology* (pp. 125–142). Washington, DC: American Psychological Association.

Fisher, C. B. (2002). Participant consultation: Ethical insights into parental permission and confidentiality procedures for policy-relevant research with youth. In R. M. Lerner, F. Jacobs, & D. Wertlieb (Eds.), *Applied developmental science: An advanced textbook* (pp. 113–138). Thousand Oaks, CA: Sage.

Fisher, C. B. (2003a). Adolescent and parent perspectives on ethical issues in youth drug use and suicide survey research. *Ethics & Behavior, 13,* 302–331.

Fisher, C. B. (2003b). A goodness-of-fit ethic for child assent to nonbeneficial research. *American Journal of Bioethics, 3,* 27–28.

Fisher, C. B. (2003c). A goodness-of-fit ethic for informed consent to research involving persons with mental retardation and developmental disabilities. *Mental Retardation and Developmental Disabilities Research Reviews, 9,* 27–31.

Fisher, C. B., Cea, C., Davidson, P., & Fried, A. L. (2006). Capacity of persons with mental retardation to consent to participation in randomized clinical trials. *American Journal of Psychiatry, 163,* 1813–1820.

Fisher, C. B., & Fyrberg, D. (1994). Participant partners: College students weigh the costs and benefits of deceptive research. *American Psychologist, 49,* 417–427.

Fisher, C. B., & Goodman, S. J. (2009). Goodness-of-fit ethics for non-intervention research involving dangerous and illegal behaviors. In D. Buchanan, C. B. Fisher, & L. Gable (Eds.), *Ethical and legal issues in research with high risk populations.* Washington, DC: APA Books.

Fisher, C. B., Hatashita-Wong, M., & Isman, L. (1999). Ethical and legal issues in clinical child psychology. In W. K. Silverman & T. H. Ollendick (Eds.), *Developmental issues in the clinical treatment of children and adolescents* (pp. 470–486). Boston: Allyn Bacon.

Fisher, C. B., Higgins-D'Allesandro, A., Rau, J. M. B., Kuther, T., & Belanger, S. (1996). Reporting and referring research participants: The view from urban adolescents. *Child Development, 67,* 2086–2099.

Fisher, C. B., Hoagwood, K., Boyce, C., Duster, T., Frank, D. A., Grisso, T., … Zayas, L. H. (2002). Research ethics for mental health science involving ethnic minority children and youth. *American Psychologist, 57,* 1024–1040.

Fisher, C. B., Hoagwood, K., & Jensen, P. (1996). Casebook on ethical issues in research with children and adolescents with mental disorders. In K. Hoagwood, P. Jensen, & C. B. Fisher (Eds.), *Ethical issues in research with children and adolescents with mental disorders* (pp. 135–238). Hillsdale, NJ: Erlbaum.

Fisher, C. B., Kornetsky, S. Z., & Prentice, E. D. (2007). Determining risk in pediatric research with no prospect of direct benefit: Time for a national consensus on the interpretation of federal regulations. *American Journal of Bioethics, 7,* 5–10.

Fisher, C. B., & Lerner, R. M. (1994). Foundations of applied developmental psychology. In C. B. Fisher & R. M. Lerner (Eds.), *Applied developmental psychology* (pp. 3–20). New York: McGraw-Hill.

Fisher, C. B., & Masty, J. K. (2006). Community perspectives on the ethics of adolescent risk research. In B. Leadbeater, T. Reicken, C. Benoit, M. Jansson, & A. Marshall (Eds.), *Research ethics in community-based and participatory action research with youth* (pp. 22–41). Toronto: University of Toronto Press.

Fisher, C. B., & Murray, J. P. (1996). Applied developmental science comes of age. In C. B. Fisher, J. P. Murray, & I. E. Sigel (Eds.), *Graduate training in applied developmental science for diverse disciplines and educational settings* (pp. 1–22). Norwood, NJ: Ablex.

Fisher, C. B., Oransky, M., Mahadevan, M., Singer, M., Mirhej, G., & Hodge, G. (2008). Marginalized populations and drug addiction research: Realism, mistrust, and misconception. *IRB: Ethics & Human Research, 30,* 1–9.

Fisher, C. B., & Ragsdale, K. (2006). A goodness-of-fit ethics for multicultural research. In J. Trimble and C. B. Fisher (Eds.), *The handbook of ethical research with ethnocultural populations and communities* (pp. 3–26). Thousand Oaks, CA: Sage.

Fisher, C. B., & Rosendahl, S. A. (1990). Risks and remedies of research participation. In C. B. Fisher & W. W. Tryon (Eds.), *Ethics in applied developmental psychology: Emerging issues in an emerging field* (pp. 43–59). Norwood, NJ: Ablex Publishing.

Fisher, C. B., & Wallace, S. A. (2000). Through the community looking glass: Reevaluating the ethical and policy implications of research on adolescent risk and psychopathology. *Ethics & Behavior, 10,* 99–118.

Fisher, C. B., Wallace, S. A., & Fenton, R. E. (2000). Discrimination distress during adolescence. *Journal of Youth and Adolescence, 29,* 679–695.

Freedman, B. (1975). A moral theory of informed consent. *Hastings Center Report, 5,* 32–39.

Fried, A. L., & Fisher, C. B. (2007). The ethics of informed consent for research in clinical and abnormal psychology. In D. McKay (Ed.), *Handbook of research methods in abnormal and clinical psychology* (pp. 5–22). Thousand Oaks, CA: Sage.

Helms, J. E. (1993). I also said, "White racial identity influences White researchers." *The Counseling Psychologist, 21,* 240–241.

Higgins-D'Allesandro, A., Hamilton, M., & Fisher, C. B. (1998). Educating the applied developmental psychologist for community partnerships: The Fordham model. In R. M. Lerner & L. A. K. Simon (Eds.), *Outreach universities for America's youth and families: Building community collaborations for the 21st century*. New York: Garland Publishing, Inc.

High, D. M., & Doole, M. M. (1995). Ethical and legal issues in conducting research involving elderly subjects. *Behavioral Sciences and the Law, 13*, 319–335.

Horng, S., & Grady, C. (2003). Misunderstanding in clinical research: Distinguishing therapeutic misconception, therapeutic misestimation, and therapeutic optimism. *IRB: Ethics & Human Research, 25*, 11–16.

Jones, J. H. (1993). *Bad Blood: The Tuskegee Syphilis Experiment*. New York: Free Press

Melton, G. B., Levine, F. J., Koocher, G. P., Rosenthal, R., & Thompson, W. C. (1988). Community consultation in socially sensitive research: Lessons from clinical trials of treatments for AIDS. *American Psychologist, 43*, 573–581.

O'Sullivan, C., & Fisher, C. B. (1997). The effect of confidentiality and reporting procedures on parent-child agreement to participate in adolescent risk research. *Applied Developmental Science, 1*(4), 185–197.

Parham, T.A. (1993). White researchers conducting multicultural counseling research: Can their efforts be 'mo betta'? *The Counseling Psychologist, 21*, 250-256.

Scott-Jones, D. (1994). Ethical issues in reporting and referring in research with low-income minority children. *Ethics & Behavior, 4*, 97-108.

Sue, D. W. (1993). Confronting ourselves: The White and racial/ethnic-minority researcher. *The Counseling Psychologist, 21*, 244–249.

Sugarman, J., Kass, J. E, Goodman, S. J., Parentesis, P., Fernandes, P., & Faden, R. R. (1998). What patients say about medical research. *IRB: A Review of Human Subjects Research, 20*, 1-

Trickett, E. J. (1998). Toward a framework for defining and resolving ethical issues in the protection of communities involved in primary prevention projects. *Ethics & Behavior, 8*, 321-337.

Veatch, R. M. (1987). *The patient as partner*. Bloomington: Indiana University Press.

CONDUCTING RESEARCH IN APPLIED SETTINGS

CHAPTER **8**

Conducting Translational Research on Child Development in Community Settings
What You Need to Know and Why It Is Worth the Effort

Nancy G. Guerra, PhD, and Melinda S. Leidy, PhD
University of California at Riverside

Introduction

Conducting translational research on child and adolescent development in community settings can be both extremely rewarding and incredibly difficult. The rewards include the opportunity to make real differences in people's lives, to influence public policy, and to help bridge the gap between science and practice. The challenges include how to build connections in communities, maintain internal validity in less controlled settings, and fulfill the demands of an academic research career. The goal of this chapter is to discuss some of these challenges and opportunities in order to prepare young investigators for this type of work. Because I (Guerra) have spent my entire career trying to forge these linkages, I am happy to be able to share these experiences with the next generation of scholars. I am helped in this task by Melinda Leidy, a recent PhD and current postdoctoral researcher.

Like most psychology graduate students, her exposure to developmental research has been limited to work in controlled laboratory settings in a university. As she prepares for a career emphasizing research with children and families in community settings, she has numerous questions to ask—questions that are likely echoed by many new scholars of child development who want to work in real-world settings. I hope that by sharing my own experiences and lessons learned, I can help answer these questions.

The Big Picture: Connecting Research and Practice

I want to begin with a story that highlights both the importance and the challenges of blending academic and community perspectives. As a young faculty member I was pleased to be asked to participate in a conference sponsored by the National Institute of Mental Health on development and antisocial behavior. The purpose of the conference was to bring together researchers and practitioners to consider the role of development in understanding and preventing children's antisocial behavior. The first member of my panel, an esteemed scholar, discussed how development is linked to the etiology of antisocial behavior, displaying statistical models of developmental trajectories and highlighting how this behavior unfolds and escalates over time. For my presentation, I highlighted how preventive interventions could be developmentally sensitive by focusing on specific risk and protective factors linked to aggression and antisocial behavior for different age groups. The third and final presenter on my panel was from a national youth service agency. His comment on how his agency considered development in its work was, "We serve whoever walks in the door."

This story stuck with me as a powerful illustration of the need to build bridges between research and practice. In spite of a marked push toward applied, translational, and community-based participatory research over the last decade or so, we still frequently operate in separate worlds, speak different languages, and look at problems from distinct perspectives. Over the years I have learned to become more sensitive to these different orientations. I also have shifted from applied research to a more translational orientation.

You may ask, what is the difference? Albeit small, I believe that applied developmental research involves conducting studies in communities or practice settings that address real-world issues, whereas translational developmental research places more importance on the give-and-take process. It can be conducted in the laboratory or in the community—the important issue is the dialogue between research and practice. As a translational researcher, you must speak to scientists and community members simultaneously. This requires theory-driven research that considers real-world applications. In other words, theories must be relevant for practice, and practice must inform theory.

A clear strategy to maximize the relevance of theoretically driven research with children and adolescents is to conduct studies in community settings, allowing for active participation of those involved. Keep in mind that you can collect data on children and adolescents in community settings without such active involvement, for example, conducting surveys in schools. The school may agree to your request for data collection, but is not necessarily an active participant in shaping your research. This is an example of *community-placed research* (Minkler, 2005). In this case the school is your laboratory but you are treating it primarily as physical space. In contrast, *community-based research* requires active community engagement. A focus on the active involvement of participants is consistent with models of community-based participatory research (CBPR) that have gained popularity in public health and prevention (Faridi, Grunbaum, Gray, Franks, & Simoes, 2007; Katz, 2004; Weissberg & Greenberg, 1998). The challenge for community-based research is how to blend strong theory-driven science with community perspectives on the causes and solutions for preventing a particular behavior or outcome.

Getting Started: Is Translational Research in Community Settings Right for You?

From the outset, it is important to realize that this type of research can literally get "lost" in the translation. In some sense, this approach represents a middle ground that is unlikely to fulfill the internal validity demands of laboratory research or the external validity expectations of strictly applied research in clinical and community settings, for instance, evaluating an ongoing community-based intervention (Mankoff, Brander, Ferrone, & Marincola, 2004). Further, although translational research has gained considerable currency in the field of medicine over the last decade, it is still relatively new within psychology (Tashiro & Mortensen, 2006).

I believe that community-based translational research holds great promise, particularly for scholars interested in applied child and adolescent development research, because it provides a framework that validates the importance of contributing to both science and practice. If you are only interested in the science side of the equation, then working in community settings places unnecessary constraints on your academic research (although you can still maximize the translational relevance of your laboratory work by connecting with real-world issues). On the other hand, if you are only interested in working in communities, then you will be bootstrapped by the "publish or perish" demands of academia. Let me share with you my own experience and how it shaped my commitment to a translational research agenda.

I always wanted to make a difference in the real world. I had worked in community-based agencies for several years before graduate school. I spent most of this time listening to teenagers, their teachers, and their families as I tried to implement violence and delinquency prevention programs. I went to graduate school specifically to learn more about how to develop and evaluate programs. My goal was not to become an academic researcher but a better practitioner. Up to the day I defended my dissertation, I held fast to the idea of working in the community. Even though a distinguished member of my committee suggested a career in research, I clung to the idea of being part of the daily lives of youth in the real world instead of just writing about them.

However, I also realized that I wanted to participate in creating a knowledge base that would impact more than just the youth I worked with, to demonstrate beyond my own hunches or experience that we could help youth become productive citizens. This led me to think more seriously about an academic career and how I could blend my interest in real-world problems and community solutions with my interests in formalizing knowledge and shaping practices. I compromised by focusing my career on understanding and preventing childhood aggression and youth violence, an agenda with clear scientific and practical significance and great relevance to communities worldwide.

This has been extremely rewarding but not necessarily easy to navigate. Translational developmental research in community settings requires a theoretical grounding that can be mapped onto and can accommodate community concerns. To make matters more complicated, the "laboratory" where such research is conducted often is difficult to secure, requires building relationships with people and agencies, and offers preciously little control over the environment. If you actually are going to evaluate a prevention or intervention program that you develop, you will soon learn that the no-treatment control condition simply does not exist and that intervention fidelity is difficult to achieve. From a practical perspective, you must also design the intervention and oversee implementation, activities that typically do not build your record or advance your tenure case. I must admit that I sometimes daydream about what it would be like to sign up for a subject pool and conduct studies on campus with undergraduate students.

So why should you consider a career emphasizing translational research in community settings? First and foremost, the very best way to learn about the real world is to work in the real world. Academic researchers throughout their careers should get as much experience as possible in the worlds they want to understand—even if they confine their research to laboratory settings. Unfortunately, we sometimes get lost in a type of intellectual chain letter where we speak to one another through our journal articles but forget to include the very people we are talking about.

I remember being at a Society for Research in Child Development meeting early in my career where I spent the entire three days wondering if children had somehow been transformed into data points on graphs, mean differences in tables, and elaborate structural equation models; not once did I even see a picture of a child or hear a story about a child's life. Working in communities keeps you grounded in people's lives. It allows you to link theory and research to the actual experiences of the children and adolescents you want to study. If a theory says little about how people behave in their daily lives, it is of limited practical value. Conversely, developing laundry lists of daily experiences does little to help us make coherent predictions needed to advance developmental science.

Still, you may wonder how you can develop your own niche as an academic scholar and build a record for tenure with the added demands of working in community settings. How can you let the community define the problem and the solution? What if they do not agree with your theoretical orientation? How can you frame research questions in a manner that takes into account the theory and the community interests? Will this type of research be accepted for publication in top journals? An important first step is to follow a theoretical tradition that makes sense in the real world and is relatively easy to link with community concerns.

Theory Matters

Because I wanted do work in community settings, I was careful to align my work with a theoretical orientation that is relatively easy to translate into community-based intervention programs. In fact, although I had initially been interested in Kohlberg's moral development model, research suggested that level of moral reasoning was only weakly correlated with moral action. This rendered it quite difficult to build prevention programs from this perspective or promote inclusion of moral reasoning in behavior change programs. Fortunately, I shifted toward social-cognitive, social-information processing models of aggression and violence (for a review, see Guerra & Leidy, 2008). This approach, emphasizing discrete steps of processing social information and related cognitive schema that guide this processing, lends itself quite well to structured prevention and intervention programs. It also provides a clear theoretical grounding for an academic career. As a faculty member, not only is it important to publish in top-quality journals, but these publications must reflect a clear, coherent, and theoretically driven research agenda. Keep in mind that although your primary interest may be to help children, as a scientist and faculty member you are judged by your contribution to advancing research (which hopefully can also help children).

Building Community Support for Theory-Driven Research

How can you create linkages between theoretical models and community concerns? This includes using theory to guide your work in the community as well as learning from the community to build and refine your theory. First, let us consider how to transport a theory-driven intervention to a community setting. To begin with, if you have a very narrow focus or work in a specialized area, it can be more difficult to connect your perspective with community views. For instance, if you are designing a school-based violence preventive intervention to build self-control (based on studies linking low self-control and violence), it is important to engage in a dialogue with teachers and administrators to "explain" your theory and how it connects with their understanding of youth violence. If they believe that children are violent because of family problems (or other reasons), they may not buy in to your approach. To the extent that your theoretical orientation resonates with community understanding, the task of negotiating an agenda will be easier.

As an example, a social problem-solving focus emphasizes multiple and discrete social information-processing steps and their relation to aggression and violence. The model is comprehensive but at the same time offers something that everyone in community settings can relate to. Consider the robust finding that aggressive children are more likely to attribute hostile intent to others under ambiguous circumstances (Crick & Dodge, 1994). This is something that teachers and counselors observe daily—fights over a dirty look or a perceived sign of disrespect—so it is very easy for them to understand what hostile bias means.

Still, you do not want to approach communities by telling them about your theory. Keep in mind that people and agencies deal with needs and problems. Do they care about whether they provide evidence for a particular theory? Do they care if you are the first author of a *Science* article? No, they care about helping children do better in school, keeping kids off drugs, creating safe communities, enhancing well-being, and so on. Begin by engaging community members (or relevant agency participants) in a dialogue about their perceptions of the problem. Try to understand how they frame the issues and learn more about their lay theories of causality. Remember that academics often talk from the head, whereas community members often talk from the heart. Once you understand their perceptions of problems and how to solve them, you can find a common ground that allows you to address your scientific agenda in a meaningful fashion.

Second, think about how your theoretical framework (or some part of it) can help them clarify their understanding of the problem. For example, in my own work on youth violence I often hear community concerns that youth consider violence as an acceptable part of life; that they are bombarded with pro-violence messages in music, video games, and movies; and that they do not seem to care about the long-term consequences of their behavior. This fits together nicely in a social-cognitive framework where I can point out that all of the messages about violence are incorporated into how we see the world and solve problems, for instance, the more we observe violence around us, the more we come to see it as normative and acceptable (Guerra, Huesmann, & Spindler, 2003). I can also point out that one of the important components of problem solving is to help youth think more about the short-term and long-term consequences of behavior. If I am proposing an intervention, I also point out that we need to measure these thinking skills and see whether we can actually change them (a plug for the importance of research).

Engaging Community Partners: Building Relationships and Negotiating Responsibilities

At this point, you may be wondering how to get started. Unfortunately, there is not a simple solution or proven strategy for conducting community-based research in child and adolescent development. What you do depends on a number of factors including characteristics of the community you work in, how big it is, whether you have contacts or have just arrived, whether you are affiliated with a larger research group or center, and whether there is a likely source of available funding for your work. But first let me emphasize that the operative word is *relationships*. You must view yourself as a research partner. Here are some tips for building these partnerships.

Think of Yourself as an Equal

Keep in mind that academics and community participants each have their own unique knowledge and expertise to contribute. I often tell community members that they are the "experts," whereas I just help them organize their thinking and record it through writing. I emphasize that we can solve problems more effectively if we work together, combining our different perspectives. Build a team of equals. Be humble. This is particularly important for junior scholars who easily are seen as academic elites too young to have any relevant real-world experiences. For example, if you are working on a parent training program, parents may challenge you by asking whether you have children, suggesting that you cannot really know about parenting unless you have children. How would you respond, presuming you do not have children? You could point out that this is true, that there are some things you just cannot know until you have been there, but there are also things you can help with without having the experience, for instance, you do not have to have cancer to help people cope with cancer.

Speak in Plain Language

Even the most complex theories and empirical findings can be explained in language that community participants can understand. Sometimes I wonder if academics intentionally make things complicated so no one will understand or question their expertise. I recall one experience I had with a youth violence prevention coalition in a community in North Dakota. As part of a United Way project, the coalition had contracted with a local university professor to develop a logic model for their proposed violence prevention programs. I was there on a different project, and the coalition asked me to attend the presentation of the logic model. The professor spent about two hours explaining a model with at least 25 arrows going every which way. The coalition members nodded in agreement and looked pleased. After the presentation we went out for lunch and I asked them whether the logic model made sense to them. They looked at me and asked me whether it made sense to me. I replied, quite honestly, that I had not the slightest clue what all of that meant, to which they sighed a collective sigh of relief telling me that were afraid they were not smart enough to understand the presentation so they did not want to ask any questions. The moral of the story is if people do not understand what you are saying and are afraid to ask, it is unlikely that your work will have any meaning or benefits for them or the children they work with.

Listen and Observe

One of the most important skills you will need to work effectively in communities is the ability to listen and observe. There are many ways you can do this. For example, whenever I am asked to provide technical assistance or some other type of consultation in a new community, I begin by reading local newspapers carefully to find out about important youth issues. In small towns I may even browse through the yellow pages to get a sense of what type of youth services are available. Not only do you need to know what is going on in the community, but it helps to get a feel for the issues. Then I try to spend at least a day visiting different agencies, talking with children and adolescents, meeting with program administrators, and so on to get a true picture of how people in the community understand the problem and what solutions would make sense to them. This also helps me identify key individuals with whom I might discuss a proposed research or intervention project. This approach can be helpful if you are invited to a new community or just getting started in the community you would like to conduct your research in. Not only do you need to understand local perspectives, but you need to be able to speak the same language so your voice will be heard.

I will give you an example of what happened when I failed to do this. I was asked by a large national foundation to help frame positive youth development issues so that communities participating in a community-building initiative could organize services more strategically. My colleagues and I developed a very nice framework that highlighted key developmental tasks across age groups (from 0 to 18 years old) and suggested strategies for enhancing accomplishment of developmental tasks within communities. Each task was supported by several research studies, which we summarized clearly. We were asked to present this model at a conference of community participants whom we had not yet met or worked with. We arrived at the conference about an hour before our talk, violating the important mandate of getting to know the people you are working with before making any recommendations. The attendees were all grassroots community organizers and youth advocates with little interest in academic models (of course we had not yet realized this). We presented our model with diagrams and slides and then asked for questions. Staring out at a sea of blank faces, we soon realized that our presentation was disconnected from the perspective of conference participants. We did get one question. A brave community member asked us, "Where did you get that model? At Target [the store]?" In other words, we had not taken the time to listen to community participants and determine what would resonate most with them. I can assure you that I never repeated this disastrous performance again.

Give Yourself Some Time to Find the Right Match

If you want to conduct child and adolescent development research in partnership with communities, you will need to find a school, agency, or program to work with. This involves a type of courtship to determine whether you share similar views, get along with the staff, and can forge a working relationship. If you have a contact in an agency, begin there. If not, you can make a cold call to the program director, principal, or person in charge. Explain that you are a new faculty member and that you are anxious to partner with community agencies to help address important child or youth issues. If you work in a particular area, you should determine which agencies are the best potential partners. You may want to volunteer in some capacity in order to build these social connections.

A Word of Caution About Working With Schools

Over the course of my career I have found it quite difficult to work with schools particularly if you are reporting data that demonstrates the extent of a problem they have or the ineffectiveness of a program. Schools generally have a vested interest in maintaining a good public image and can present data selectively to make a good case. If you are simply asking to collect data that will be published in an academic journal without identifying the school, you may not have a problem. You can offer to present the findings to staff but assure school officials that you will not write feature stories in the local newspaper about your results (particularly if the results cast the school in a negative light). Again, this is a bit of a slippery slope. You want to advance science while they want to advance the image and performance of their school. This is not meant to scare you away from schools. Indeed, many academics have maintained positive relationships and built productive research careers working in schools. Chapter 9 in this book focuses on working in schools in detail.

Be Careful of Community Requests for Program Evaluation

What would you do if a community agency asked you to consult with it to evaluate a new program it has designed? At first blush this would seem like a fantastic opportunity to make connections with a local program. Do you see any pitfalls? I will say that early in my career I jumped at these opportunities. Sometimes this worked well and sometimes it did not. What I learned is that when agencies ask you to evaluate their program what they typically want is for a credible expert (translated: university professor) to show that their program works. They already know the program works and they want you to give it the official seal of approval. If you want to work with them, make sure at the outset that the agency understands the potential risks. If you find that the program is not effective they will have to live with the findings.

Further, if you want to publish this in a scientific journal (specifying the program but not the agency), the future of the program may be compromised. I would strongly recommend that you not only discuss this but develop a written memorandum of understanding (MOU) with the agency. This is a document signed by the agency and the researcher that includes what will happen in the event of no effect or negative findings, who "owns" the data, whether you can publish results, whether the agency must first approve the article prior to submitting it for publication, and what specific deliverables will be provided to the agency.

Collaborate With Senior Colleagues or Research Groups

Working in communities is time consuming and labor intensive. It is difficult to do this alone as a junior faculty member. In my own career I have benefited greatly from working with senior colleagues and mentors with shared interests. Senior mentors who have built a career on community-based research typically have extensive contacts and networks that provide entry into these settings, often have grant funding that facilitates this work, and can provide sage wisdom and guidance. If you have not yet accepted a junior faculty position, consider carefully who you will have as mentors and collaborators. When interviewing job candidates for assistant professor positions I am struck by the fact that they infrequently ask about potential collaborators. Instead, most candidates I have spoken with over the years ask about teaching load, buy out, office and lab space, quality of students, and so on. I would say one of the single most important considerations, particularly if you want to work in community settings, is who you will be able to work with.

However, you may have to compromise somewhat to blend your interests with that of your new collaborators. For example, I have always been interested in prevention of adolescent violence and wanted to conduct research exclusively with adolescents. However, as a new assistant professor I was fortunate to have several more senior colleagues who believed we needed to start with younger children. My colleagues were interested in testing prevention programs for elementary school children during the early grades (K–3) and invited me to join them. What would you have done? Would you have agreed to collaborate on early prevention in order to be part of a research group or held fast to your desire to work only with adolescents? Because they were interested in the same topic (aggression and violence), I decided to take the opportunity to learn about early predictors and interventions. I would say it was the single best decision of my career, leading to the Metropolitan Area Child Study, an 8-year development and prevention study funded by the National Institute of Mental Health. This research has resulted in over 100 publications on social cognition, violence exposure, early aggression, and prevention outcomes.

How to Get Funding for Your Work

One of the primary challenges to working in communities is that you need some type of funding. There are many possibilities. You will need to be creative. Think about what type of research you can conduct with very little money, perhaps start-up funds or a small university grant. If you want to collect data in a community setting such as a school, you can use graduate and undergraduate students to collect data, providing a small stipend to teachers or schools for participation. I find that it always helps to offer an in-service training for schools or to present your findings to participants. This is part of the give-and-take process that allows you to give something back (and does not cost you any additional money). If you want to work more collaboratively with schools or agencies but do not have funding, find out what programs they are already conducting and how you might be able to help (and collect data as well). One of the biggest challenges with prevention research is that running programs is costly and research trials typically must fund actual program operations.

What other strategies are effective? Fortunately, over the last decade or so federal funding agencies have become more focused on translational research. There are funding initiatives for translational centers, community-based participatory research, and related projects. Some federal funding agencies emphasize science–practice partnerships. For example, the Centers for Disease Control and Prevention (CDC) has built a large injury prevention research agenda emphasizing links between research and practice. Look for these opportunities. I have been fortunate to be part of an Academic Center of Excellence on Youth Violence Prevention funded by the CDC with an express mission of working with communities to develop effective programs that can impact youth violence. In general, if you are focused on a specific problem and want to propose an intervention, you will have a broader range of funding available.

Foundations are also sensitized to the need to conduct child development research in real-world settings. Indeed, several foundations have a specific directive to improve the lives of youth. For example, the William T. Grant Foundation and the Spencer Foundation fund research that impacts children's lives and the systems that serve them. Sometimes you can partner with agencies to garner local or state funds, particularly if you are developing and evaluating a new program targeted to identified priorities. We have received small funds from the city we work in as well as from the State of California to partner with them on community-based research projects.

How do applied researchers establish validity for methods that are designed in response to specific community contexts?

What About Internal Validity?

Recall that internal validity is the basic minimum needed to interpret an experiment. In intervention research this is the validity of inferences that observed covariation between the intervention (A) and the outcome (B) reflects a causal relation from A to B as the variables were manipulated or measured. The general consensus is that internal validity plagues community-based research, whereas external validity plagues laboratory research, with external validity concerned with the validity of inferences about whether the cause–effect relation holds over variation in persons, settings, implementation, and so forth (Shadish, Cook, & Campbell, 2002). However, intervention trials evaluated as demonstration projects (efficacy trials) still must address issues of external validity beyond the initial trial when they are tested on a wider scale in new contexts (effectiveness trials). This presents a larger issue in the pursuit of evidence-based programs and practices that has been a topic of considerable recent debate (Slavin, 2008).

Let us consider threats to internal validity in less controlled community settings. If you are simply using community sites in lieu of a laboratory setting, you can maximize control through careful planning. For instance, if you are conducting an experiment in a school, you can request a separate room, make sure that all participants come to this room, standardize experimental procedures, and so forth. However, when you are actually implementing a procedure or intervention that involves nonexperimenters (such as teachers), issues of standardization and control will arise. For example, a particularly difficult problem in prevention and intervention research in school and community settings is the issue of a "control" group, particularly when a no-treatment control condition is planned. When dealing with child and adolescent programs, it is virtually impossible to have a no-treatment control group for both ethical and practical reasons. In the Metropolitan Area Child Study, we assigned blocks of schools to a condition, with one block of schools being a no-treatment control group. However, over the course of the 8 years we worked with intervention schools on violence prevention, we could not tell the control schools not to prevent violence. Indeed, over the course of the research project, the control schools implemented a range of different programs, leaving us to document programs in the "control" condition and compare it to our intervention groups.

A related problem in evaluating preventive interventions is the feasibility of randomization. The often-cited "gold standard" in prevention research is the randomized controlled trial. Surely if you are a junior faculty wanting to make your mark in the scientific community you would prefer to conduct this type of study. If your intervention involves individuals, it may be possible to randomly assign them to treatment and control. However, more typically if you are involved in a community-based trial, you will need to provide your intervention at the school or agency level, that is, to all children in a given setting. A randomized controlled trial would thus require randomization at the school level, which requires about 40 schools (or classrooms if at the classroom level) for adequate statistical power using a nested design (Raudenbush, 1997). This is a daunting task for even the most seasoned (and well-funded) senior professor. Most likely, you will compromise with some type of quasi-experimental design. It is often more feasible to use some type of well-matched design with pretests as covariates (Slavin, 2008).

Another challenge that is particularly salient for intervention research concerns fidelity of procedures. Some interventions have lesson-by-lesson guidelines with programmed activities. A scientific test of the program requires strict adherence to these guidelines and activities. What would you do if you were implementing and evaluating a formal parent training program in a community agency and the parents decided they did not like one of the lessons and wanted to substitute something else? Or what if the agency started to implement your program but decided it would change the last three lessons? Would you tell the agency it could not do this or would you adapt your program to the agency's request?

I am sorry to say that I do not really have the answer. Obviously you want to stick as close as possible to the intervention as planned; however, if you could risk losing parent or agency cooperation you will need to find a compromise. I have found that you have to do this on a case-by-case basis. Let me give you a relevant example. One of the projects that our CDC-funded center is involved in is a community trial of the Families and Schools Together (FAST) with low-income immigrant Latino families. To implement this program, we partnered with a community agency that relied on trained community health workers to deliver the program. The intervention relied on parent–child interaction training to facilitate successful relationships, but did not include didactic parent training. However, during one of the implementation cycles, several of the parents requested specific lessons in behavior management and parent training. They felt this was necessary and did not want to continue without it. What did we do? We allowed for some flexibility and modified the program to add this content. Ironically, after we did this they subsequently realized that it did not fit with what they were learning and went back to the original program. The point is that there needs to be some level of flexibility in implementation. I have found that programs that emphasize system-level change and have room for customization are easier to implement during both the scientific evaluation and when disseminated more broadly. In the end, however, you will always need to make some compromises—the best you can do is to minimize the scientific damage.

Lessons Learned

What have I learned over the years that would be useful to junior scholars about to embark on a career in community-based research? What is the take-home message?

Take Advantage of Additional Training Opportunities

If your graduate career has been limited to laboratory research, try to get experience in communities before you develop your own research agenda. Community work is labor intensive. A postdoc with a large community-based research center would be ideal; if this is not possible, take advantage of summer institutes, brief training programs, and any similar opportunity. At a minimum, volunteer to work with a community agency for a few hours a week. If you are interested in child and adolescent development, spend some time with children and youth. I feel that I benefited greatly because I had worked in community and school settings for several years before going to graduate school.

I would like to use mixed methods to approach developmental hypotheses. How do you design qualitative methods for applied settings?

More recently, I have begun to conduct more qualitative research concerning children's bullying. In one study, I had expected to train a graduate student to conduct interviews and focus groups, doing the first few myself to get a feel for the issues and structure of the research. However, I found it so enlightening to talk with youth and hear their voices that I conducted all 14 focus groups myself, with assistance from students. For me, the dialogue with youth made me aware of issues I had not thought of before from reading previous studies. For example, I realized how much of bullying during middle school and high school focuses on sex, dating, and competition among girls. This is quite different from the typical picture of the big bully who targets the weak victim.

Compromise: Not Too Little, Not Too Much

Compromise is one of the most important skills you should learn. Of course, much of this will come with experience. You simply will not be able to work in a community setting without some amount of compromising research requirements with community needs. For instance, random assignment to treatment and control, even if it were possible based on logistics, is often difficult for community agencies to accept. Just as you want to account for nontreatment differences, they want to have a good name in the community and serve those most in need, not those in the control group. I have found in this case that you can use different quasi-experimental designs effectively, such as using propensity score matching to establish an equivalent control group (Slavin, 2008).

On the other hand, if you compromise too much you will be a community service provider and not a researcher. A key ingredient is to help communities realize that adhering to research standards does not increase their burden but has more potential long-term benefits beyond their own work. Sometimes this is quite easy. For example, agencies often want to learn something about youth or evaluate a program by coming up with a list of questions and giving youth a survey. Many times I have been shown a list of questions to measure a particular construct that was developed by a group of people sitting around a table. More often than not, the survey is 100 items long to measure a single construct such as self-regulation. I explain that researchers have been interested in this area as well and have developed some shorter scales that will be easier to administer and allow them to compare their findings with other projects (sans discussion of reliability and validity). This always works; they are more than happy to use my scale. But again, the idea came from the community; I helped shape it.

Be Strategic: Do Not Take on More Than You Can Manage

Keep in mind that as an academic in a university setting you will be judged first and foremost on your publication and grant record. Although some universities are more likely to recognize the importance and difficulty of conducting community-based research, at the end of the day, you still need to publish your work. I was able to take on a large-scale community-based intervention as an assistant professor only because I had a high-quality group of more senior colleagues. If I were starting over on my own, I am not even sure I would do much community-based research until I had tenure. More likely, I would try to work on some existing data sets either with faculty from my postdoc or national data sets that are publicly available. For my research on children's aggression, I would find out which schools in my community (or a community I would like to work in) are most concerned about this and contact one or two of them. I would suggest a small two-wave study, in the fall and spring of a school year, to get a longitudinal sample. I would probably also run focus groups to augment this research with qualitative data. I would offer to present my results to the faculty, setting the stage for more in-depth work the following year as well as building my reputation (principals and teachers talk to other principals and teachers).

Conclusion

My last piece of advice is know when to turn down opportunities. One of the most difficult things about being in academia is that it is hard to know what opportunities will pay off and which go nowhere. I am sorry to say that there is no easy formula to help you with these decisions; you will just get a feel for it as you mature. In my career, I have spent countless hours, days, and months working with schools and agencies on projects that never led to publications or any type of contribution, whereas other projects requiring less energy were quite productive. At some point, particularly if you are a junior faculty, you have to limit your involvement and focus on your own career development. If you feel overwhelmed by the demands of any project, you probably are. If you pace yourself for the long haul, your career will blossom and grow.

References

Crick, N. R., & Dodge, K. A. (1994). A review and reformulation of social information-processing mechanisms in children's social adjustment. *Psychological Bulletin, 115,* 74–101.

Faridi, Z., Grunbaum, J., Gray, B. S., Franks, A., & Simoes, E. (2007). Community-based participatory research: Necessary next steps. *Preventing Chronic Disease, 4*(3), 1–5.

Guerra, N. G., Huesmann, L. R., & Spindler, A. (2003). Community violence exposure, social cognition, and aggression among urban elementary-school children. *Child Development, 74,* 1507–1522.

Guerra, N. G., & Leidy, M. (2008). Lessons learned: Recent advances in the prevention and treatment of childhood aggression. In R. Kail (Ed.), Advances in child development and behavior (Vol. 36, pp. 287–330). Boston: Elsevier.

Katz, D. L. (2004). Representing your community in community-based participatory research: Differences made and measured. *Public Health Research, Practice, and Policy.*

Mankoff, S. P., Brander, C., Ferrone, S., & Marincola, F. M. (2004). Lost in translation: Obstacles to translational medicine. *Journal of Translational Medicine, 2,* 2–5.

Minkler, M. (2005). Community-based research partnerships: Challenges and opportunities. *Journal of Urban Health, 82,* 3–12.

Raudenbush, S. W. (1997). Statistical analysis and optimal design for cluster randomized trials. *Psychological Methods, 2,* 173–185.

Shadish, W., Cook, T., & Campbell, D. (2002). *Experimental and quasi-experimental designs for generalized causal inference.* Boston: Houghton Mifflin.

Slavin, R. E. (2008). What works: Issues in synthesizing educational program evaluations. *Educational Researcher, 37,* 5–14.

Tashiro, T., & Mortensen, L. (2006). Translational research: How social psychology can improve psychotherapy. *American Psychologist, 61,* 959–966.

Weissberg, R. P., & Greenberg, M. T. (1998). Prevention science and collaborative community action research: Combining the best from both perspectives. *Journal of Mental Health, 7,* 470–492.

CHAPTER 9

Applied Research in School Settings
Common Challenges and Practical Suggestions

David J. Schonfeld, MD
Cincinnati Children's Hospital Medical Center

Introduction

Children and adolescents spend a large percent of their waking hours in school (and for some a small amount of their nonwaking hours as well), and there is probably no other shared context for promoting child and adolescent development that exceeds the importance of school. Schools are therefore a logical site for conducting applied research in child and adolescent development—that is where we hope a lot of positive development will occur. But conducting research in schools is not without a host of challenges that require compromise, creativity, and flexibility on the part of the researcher.

This chapter will present common barriers and logistical challenges to conducting research in school settings and offer practical suggestions for how to overcome them. Although focused on school-based research, many of the points will be relevant to research conducted in other community settings. The chapter will outline some of the issues to consider in the selection of the research question, approaches to engaging the school community in the project, challenges and compromises required in the design of the study, other possible obstacles to conducting research in schools, and, finally, a reminder of the advantages of school-based research.

Selecting the Research Question

As in all research, questions should be both important and of interest to the researcher and funder. But in school-based research, the question also has to be of strong interest to the school community—the administration, school staff, students, and their parents. In child development research, the study often aims to make a small incremental step forward in our understanding of a basic phenomenon or process, which may not be of much interest to the school community. By designing a project that meets these needs of the researcher, while also providing practical information or services in a focused area of high relevance to the school community, the researcher is able to craft a project that is of interest to the school community as well. For example, an area of my research interest is to begin to develop a theory to explain how young children can most effectively be taught health education: to identify underlying and unifying health concepts; to have these concepts serve as the foundation for empirically derived and theoretically based health education curricula; and to test the efficacy of these curricula in randomized, controlled trials. As evidenced by the limited time devoted to health education, it is clear that students, parents, teachers, and school administrators do not share this basic interest. When I began this line of research in the late 1980s, though, there was a growing interest within the National Institutes of Health (NIH) to develop evidenced-based approaches to teaching children about HIV and AIDS and a strong interest in many school communities to teach children how to understand the illness and learn how to prevent its spread. By focusing on identifying young children's conceptual understanding of HIV and AIDS (a funding priority of NIMH at the time) and conducting a randomized, controlled trial of an empirically derived and conceptually based elementary school AIDS prevention intervention (an interest of the school community), I was able to advance my research goals within a funded project that received the support of the school community.

Researchers who have not conducted research in school settings often approach me with proposals for projects that they would like to conduct within local school systems. Their view is that children are a captive audience in schools and because there are large numbers of children in school during the hours that their research staff is most available, it stands to reason that it must be a convenient site for research. Both conclusions are naive. Yes, many students will agree that they are a captive audience; but the research team is not the captor. And I have heard experienced school-based researchers voice a number of descriptors for research in school settings, but "convenient" is not one of them. Given the challenges of conducting research in school (and other applied) settings, the ideal research question is one that is *best* answered in a school setting, rather than one that *could*, such as questions about educational interventions or processes, or social interactions that relate to group settings.

School-based interventions often aim to modify complex behaviors that have multiple determinants; as such, school-based interventions are often "weak" interventions. One area of my research aims to utilize classroom-based social development instruction to decrease the early onset of sexual behaviors in high-risk urban school settings. Since there are many other more compelling reasons to engage in sexual behaviors than we could ever hope to confront through relatively brief classroom-based programs, only a modest impact should be anticipated. This does not mean we should not conduct such research, since even a modest impact that could be delivered at scale could have a very significant public health effect at a favorable cost–benefit ratio. But it does mean that a number of the interventions will either "not work" (often because of unanticipated challenges that invariably arise during such a project) or will not yield statistically significant results. Therefore, whenever possible, information should be gathered that will be of interest even if the intervention effect of primary interest is not demonstrated. For example, one of my first research projects involved an attempt to demonstrate the impact of brief educational intervention in prekindergarten through second grade to advance young children's conceptual understanding about death. While the study (Schonfeld & Kappelman, 1990) ultimately did demonstrate a clinically and statistically significant increase in children's level of understanding of core concepts, data was also collected through that project to contribute to our understanding of new measures on how to assess children's conceptual understanding, utilizing a newly translated death concept semistructured interview previously developed for use in Israel.

The baseline data for this project also allowed for a cross-cultural comparison of American and Israeli children's understanding of death (Schonfeld & Smilansky, 1989). Therefore, even if the educational intervention had not "worked," the study would still have stood to advance our understanding in the field. Studies should aim to create the most theoretically based and robust intervention that has the highest likelihood of yielding a significant effect, but should also yield data and observations that will advance the field even if the intervention does not "work."

Engaging the School Community
Establishing the Relationship

For researchers who are not already a member of a school system, one of the initial steps is engaging the school community (and being a parent of a child in a school alone generally is not sufficient for engaging the school community—and from my children's perspective it may even be a contraindication for using the school as a site). Ideally, researchers approach their local school system to offer assistance and support prior to planning any research project. You are most likely to gain access into the system if you approach them with a *genuine* interest to help them meet *their* needs and address issues of highest concern to them. Researchers conducting school-based research should do more than research in schools, such as providing service and consultation. Each professional is likely to have a number of unique ways to contribute a service of high value to the school system: providing in-service training to teachers on an area of personal expertise, offering to provide technical assistance or consultation, helping to write a grant application for an area outside of your own research, assisting the school system in collecting or analyzing survey data of their choosing, and so forth. The goal is to identify something that will be of great benefit to the school or school system that you can provide at no or very limited cost to the school system and that you can do well. Make sure that you are able to deliver fully on your promises of assistance; young investigators may need to temper their enthusiasm so that they can fulfill all of these criteria. You are often remembered more for what you failed to deliver than by what you accomplished. My initial research in schools started after I began to volunteer to assist schools in responding to the deaths of teachers and staff and other school crisis events. The National Center for School Crisis and Bereavement (www.cincinnatichildrens.org/school-crisis) that I now direct is a continuation of this volunteer work that I began during my fellowship training over 20 years ago. Schools that I helped in the past, or were aware of the volunteer work that I had done elsewhere, were more receptive to seeing me as a partner in a project. Ideally, research questions and studies emerge from within a preexisting partnership, which increases the likelihood that the project will be of mutual interest.

Initial offers of assistance to the school or school system often can be made through preexisting contacts, such as a more senior faculty member or community leader that already has a positive and strong relationship. Be sensitive to any ambivalence or distrust that may already characterize these relationships before aligning yourself closely with another individual or group. Once the initial contact has been made, try to identify ways for you to establish your own personal identity and relationship with the system. Be patient. School systems can be complex and relatively closed organizations. Whereas you can earn the trust of individuals and form relationships with individual people relatively quickly, gaining the trust and support of an institution such as a school system can take a great deal more time and effort; it is the latter that may be needed for a moderate- or large-scale research study. In my experience, I offered to provide assistance in dealing with crisis events (as a free service) to one local public school system for over 5 years before I was more formally invited to provide training and consultation, even though individual members of the system long ago felt comfortable calling upon me for advice and assistance.

What is the best way to create a feeling of investment in research in schools, teachers, and families of participating children?

When you are ready to propose a particular research study, you will need to identify an appropriate and interested school to serve as the research site. Begin by exploring the level of interest among those in leadership roles in the school or school system in the issue you aim to study. If they feel that your project is worthy and important, but not something they wish to or feel they can undertake at this point, explore interest in other school systems. After conducting several projects in one school system, I approached them with a proposal to evaluate a cancer education initiative that focused on preventing the use of tobacco among middle school-age students. My contacts in the school system were comfortable enough with me to explain that although that was clearly an area of importance, it was not one of the few priority areas that they planned to focus on in their health education efforts for the next couple years. I therefore worked with them to find a project that aligned better with our mutual interests and identified other schools with a high level of interest in tobacco prevention efforts.

As you discuss your research idea and project with the school, make conscious efforts to shape the project to address the school's needs and minimize your own self-interest, but do not deny its presence. Although you may genuinely be conducting the research to help advance the field, and create or provide more effective services and programs to assist children, the reality is that the research will also advance your own personal career goals. Be honest about your professional needs (e.g., the need to publish your findings, the benefit of having a comparison condition rather than delivering the intervention to all students at the same time across the entire school system, etc.). Studies may be more readily accepted in some school settings if they are seen as "projects" rather than "research," but in no way should you attempt to deceive school administrators, teachers, staff, and students or their parents. If the project will involve a randomized, controlled design, for example, this must be clearly explained from the outset.

What methods should I utilize to gain access and cooperation for my research?

Obtaining Institutional Approval

When working with bureaucracies, it is often tempting to use your contacts to get around the system. Instead, make the effort and use your contacts to help you get through the appropriate approval and oversight processes. When working within school systems, you should anticipate that someone (whether staff, parent, or student) will at some point complain and when these complaints surface, the lack of appropriate institutional oversight and approval will become evident and can be fatal to the project.

Especially when dealing with potentially controversial subjects, it is critical to explore with school leaders and community leaders what concerns are likely to be raised and work to identify solutions before seeking permission from the system or consent from the parents. Actively seek parent input early in the process and be sure to include parents most likely to raise concerns or objections; it is better to become aware of their concerns early when you have the opportunity to address them, rather than once the consent forms have been circulated. Make yourself available to parents and other community members to answer questions; offer open houses at convenient times for parents at the school(s). Even if few or no parents attend or ask questions, the openness may respond to concerns they might have otherwise.

Leadership positions in public school systems are often elected or appointed by those who are elected, so political issues may heavily influence decisions. In one project I proposed to a school system within which I had a long-standing relationship, approval was initially not granted because of conflicts between a local agency whose administrator sat on the board of education and an administrator of a program at my university—none of which had to do with their support of the project or my research, but nonetheless had major impact on the ability to conduct the project. Concerns may occur even when the study does not involve controversial subjects, particularly when there have been negative experiences with prior research or there are preexisting conflicts between parents and teachers or school administrators. In one research study that involved interviewing children individually about concepts of health, one of the parents complained to a school administrator and other parents that her child had been audiotaped, despite having signed a written consent form that clearly stated the interview would be audiotaped and transcribed. When I spoke with the parent, she clarified that a teacher in school had audiotaped the class recently without parent knowledge to document student misbehavior and that her concerns were really not at all related to my project. Since I spoke with her immediately after the concerns first arose, I was able to minimize the disruption to the study. She volunteered to speak with other parents that she had already complained to so they would not similarly withdraw consent (because of this action, no other children were withdrawn from the study). In a similar manner, respond to every complaint and problem as an "adverse event";

take concerns seriously no matter who raises them and do not ignore rumors even if they are unfounded.

To the extent possible, partner with trusted school staff so that the project is seen as a joint initiative between the research team and the school staff. In my research projects, I have generally tried to provide a subcontract to the school system so that public school staff implements the project, rather than research staff from a university setting. This has increased the acceptance by teachers and administrators. Making funding available to hire school staff can increase the school system's investment in the project and maximize the likelihood (although not guarantee) that successful interventions will be institutionalized.

Gaining Teacher Support

In addition to obtaining institutional approval, it is critical to gain the support of teachers and other school staff. In your discussions, help the teachers understand how the project will help their students and themselves. Be prepared to sell the importance of the study and, if relevant, the proposed intervention. In one study aiming to decrease the early onset of high-risk sexual behavior through the delivery of social development instruction that included social problem-solving lessons, we were able to demonstrate that students in the intervention group, though equivalent at baseline, achieved significant gains in academic problem solving and greater increases in state mastery test scores. This data raised the level of interest of the school administrators and teachers and provided some increased support for implementation of the curriculum, despite pressure from national academic accountability efforts, which was crowding out available instructional time.

Even if you have earned the trust of the teaching staff, do not expect them to extend themselves on behalf of the study. Classroom schedules are increasingly overfilled and teachers will be hard pressed to give up too much classroom time, even for a very worthwhile intervention. The importance of maintaining fidelity to the intervention protocol is invariably of much more concern to the researcher than to the teachers—and teachers ultimately will decide what is being taught in their classrooms. Those conducting school-based research realize the need to modify intervention protocols to adjust to emerging realities, such as shortening the period of time required for classroom interventions or integrating them within other subject areas.

Expect teachers to spend little time outside of the classroom in preparation for the project. In my studies, I have done my best to anticipate their training needs and provide in-service training and create resources that will answer questions or address concerns. For example, in a project involving elementary school cancer education (Schonfeld et al., 2001), I prepared guidance documents on what to do if a child in the class has cancer or has a parent who is undergoing treatment, what to do if the teachers are uncomfortable teaching the content because of their own illness or that of someone they know, and how to provide support to a child who had a family member die of cancer or another serious condition. I reviewed this information during the in-service training and found that as a result, the resistance to teaching the lessons was far less than would have otherwise occurred. I provide contact information and invite teachers to contact me if any problems or concerns arise or if they wish to discuss any aspect of the curriculum or its implementation. Efforts should also be made to provide teachers with all of the supplies that will be needed for complete implementation. In one study, I provided a bag of dirt (i.e., potting soil) that was required for one of the demonstrations. Although it could be argued that it is not hard to find a handful of dirt, some teachers taught this lesson in the middle of the winter in a New England urban community, when the ground was frozen or covered in snow. When the experiment required an apple, I brought them apples (with enough extra for the students and staff to eat) or provided a coupon for a local grocery store where they could be purchased. In other projects, we photocopied all of the handouts or provided them with reams of paper, since photocopy paper may be limited in some schools. The goal is to anticipate and eliminate any possible barrier to full implementation. These efforts should also extend to office staff and school administration. If you are going to ask the secretary in the office to collect consent forms from classroom teachers, offer them a clearly labeled box for this purpose. Taking the effort to thank office staff and teachers for their assistance is an important part of the implementation strategy—a box of cookies in the teacher's lounge or at the secretary's desk with a thank-you note can go a long way toward maximizing the response rate.

Maintaining Support of the Full School Community

School professionals are doing extra work to assist you with implementation of the project. Be sure to acknowledge their assistance. Although incentives are often helpful to maintain interest in the project and maximize participation, become familiar with the school policies that may be relevant. For example, teacher union or contract rules may not allow teachers to be paid for work done during school hours. In one project, rather than giving the teachers a cash incentive for attending an in-service training, I instead provided them with a bookstore gift certificate (that could be used for books for their class) or gift cards to an office supply store (that could be used to purchase classroom supplies that were not covered by their budget). Honoraria may be allowed when reimbursement is not; continuing education credits for in-service training may be important to the teaching staff. Project budgets should incorporate these expenses and should include both incentives (to promote involvement) and small thank-you gifts as the project ends, which will facilitate reentry to the school system for further projects. Often these gifts can be very inexpensive; in one study teachers were given a small flower pot and flower seeds at the end of the school year with a note thanking them for helping to nurture the growth of social skills in their students. No matter how much money is available for such incentives, it is critical that they be paired with professional recognition. Throughout the intervention design and implementation, invite input from the teaching staff and school leadership; you will learn a great deal from their input that will improve the intervention. Invite them to review the intervention before it is finalized and seek their feedback throughout the study and at its completion. In several projects, I provided logbooks or incorporated logs for teacher feedback into the curricula.

Hire staff that is at least as sensitive to these issues as you are; your project will be known by your rudest staff member. One of my first research assistants was a former elementary school teacher. Her ability to anticipate and meet the needs of teachers did as much as anything I could do to increase the success of the project. She was invited to eat lunch with the teachers in their lounge, she knew how to use small incentives and activities to keep the students interested in the interviews, and she showed respect and gratitude for the office staff. As a result, the school staff all worked to ensure that she was successful in carrying out the tasks of the project.

For the project to be of success, it will also require the support of students. Involve them in the planning and implementation process to the extent possible and offer small incentives as appropriate. For example, distributing pop-a-point pencils for completion of surveys (which can then be kept by the students) costs little but may make elementary school-age students more eager to complete the survey. Recognize that incentives need not be limited to tangible items. In one project involving a cancer education project in a small elementary school, the students prepared a Web site (http://info.med.yale.edu/ycc/kidsinfo/) to teach other students about cancer and were able to share their results at a technology exhibit at the legislative office building at the state capital. Students were also interviewed about the project for public radio. In another project, students were interviewed for a television news story on the project. Their ability to see themselves as part of an important endeavor that might help others increased their interest in the study. Just as with teachers, seek students' input throughout the study and upon its completion. In one study that involved pilot testing a curriculum in a small elementary school, I completed focus groups with each of the classes that participated. Children were excited to be able to provide their feedback directly to me and often gave very important information that helped shape later phases of the study.

Familiarize yourself with the organizational culture within the school(s) and work within it. Learn the school schedule: find out the times when it is most convenient to contact teachers, when it is inconvenient to teach lessons (e.g., first month and last month of school year, during standardized testing, around holidays, etc.) or to remove children from classrooms for individual interviews, and so forth. Beyond such logistical issues, find out what are the important issues for the school community and be sure to address them. In a project that I conducted to explore young children's understanding of HIV and AIDS, we conducted individualized, semistructured interviews of children in kindergarten to sixth grade (Schonfeld, Johnson, Perrin, O'Hare, & Cicchetti, 1993) Two students who were hearing impaired attended kindergarten in the school and wanted to participate in not only the lessons, but also the interviews. Although their limited sign language made it virtually impossible for them to answer the questions in sufficient detail to allow inclusion in the study (and the research interview was not standardized for use in this manner), their ability to participate in the interview process was meaningful to them and important to the teaching staff.

Considering the Long-Term Implications

Although your project is of a time-limited duration, give careful consideration to the longer-term implications for the school. Very expensive interventions may be supported by research budgets, but schools may be unable to continue them in the absence of this funding. This has ethical implications and leaves schools reluctant to engage in projects in the future. If the intervention itself (exclusive of the research evaluation costs that are unique to the research project) is so expensive that it cannot be continued by the school system that has already invested so much in its implementation and seen firsthand its positive impact, then it is unlikely to be practical for use by other school systems. As such, it is not a feasible intervention to bring to scale. Make the plans for institutionalization part of your project implementation design. If you expect your intervention to be worthwhile, you should be working with the school from the beginning to plan on how to make sure the intervention continues after the study ends, if the school chooses to do so at that time. If you do not think it is likely to be worthwhile, you should not be doing the study. In projects where I expected to prepare or publish a curriculum, I have included an agreement that free copies would be provided for every teacher in the appropriate grade levels in both intervention and control groups (including requiring this as part of the contract with the publisher), have budgeted for instructional supplies for teachers in the control group, and have included in the plans in-service training for control-group teachers at the completion of data collection. If you do not leave something behind of value, you and your colleagues are less likely to be invited back by the school for future projects.

Think about your next study even before you implement the current project. A funded research study can be an effective means to collect pilot data for the next project. In my research on elementary school AIDS education, the semistructured interview regarding children's understanding of HIV and AIDS included questions about colds and cancer as comparison conditions. This data on children's understanding of cancer (or really lack of understanding) was important to obtaining external funding for a cancer education project and persuasive information for the school system regarding the importance of educating their students about this topic.

Challenges and Compromises in Study Design

Classroom-Level Interventions

Classroom interventions, by their very nature, are delivered to classes. From a research design perspective, it would be ideal if the researcher could construct the classroom units through random assignment, but obviously this is not feasible. As a result, the researcher is left with either randomizing by class, school, or district. Randomization by class (within the same school), as opposed to randomization by school or district, is more likely to result in control and intervention groups that do not differ systematically on key variables at baseline (to the extent that assignment to classes in a school is not done systematically because of intrinsic differences among students in variables related to the outcome measure of concern, which is often the case). But randomization at the classroom level introduces a major risk of contamination of treatment effect across group assignment, introducing a conservative bias that will limit the power of the study to demonstrate a true intervention effect. Furthermore, if a multiyear intervention is being studied, class assignment invariably changes from year-to-year, so that it becomes impossible to maintain group assignment in subsequent years. School-based research where assignment of intervention status is by class, school, or district often employs analytic techniques such as hierarchical linear modeling to control for such nesting, but this requires large sample sizes, which may exceed the entire cohort of students in even a moderate-sized school system. Those conducting applied research may need to address this issue in grant applications, at least acknowledging the limitations and their understanding of the implications.

Active Versus Passive Consent

As with research in any setting, recruitment of the greatest percent of eligible subjects possible is a critical challenge. One approach that is an option for some school-based research is to employ a passive consent process. Unlike active consent processes that require written informed parent consent (and often also child assent), passive consent involves notification of all parents and the option for parents to decline consent (the absence of a response from parents who have been adequately notified and provided ample opportunity to communicate their response is assumed to imply consent; student assent remains a required element as appropriate to the child's age and capacity). Passive consent is allowable in evaluations of educational interventions delivered by school staff that are not considered experimental, even if they are not implemented equally to all students at the same time (i.e., schools are able to implement a new curriculum in several classes on a pilot basis and can compare student achievement across classes before deciding to further implement the curriculum). In several research projects, I have partnered to assist the school system in evaluating the impact of a health education curriculum that the school system has approved for universal implementation but elected to implement in a phased manner; the curriculum has been taught by regular classroom teachers supervised by school system professional development staff; and the evaluation has utilized measures already employed by the school system to assess impact of their curricula. As such, these projects were able to employ passive consent procedures. With passive consent it is important that parents are adequately informed and given ample opportunity to deny consent (e.g., sending letters home through students without documenting parent receipt may not be sufficient in some settings, especially if the content of the intervention is potentially controversial). Passive consent can dramatically increase the participation rate and minimizes the likelihood seen in active consent that the highest risk students would not be provided permission to participate (e.g., in studies of high-risk behaviors, active consent processes also result in the exclusion of those students most in need of the intervention). Furthermore, it is not practical in most schools to devote significant classroom instructional time to lessons provided to only a portion of the class. A limitation of passive consent processes is that they restrict the data that can be collected by the research team to that data already being obtained by the school system for its own use. For example, in one project we intended to use school lunch status as a proxy measure of socioeconomic status, but just prior to the start of the study federal regulations changed that allowed the school system to provide a free lunch to all of its students, so the school system stopped collecting this data on an individual student level. Since we were employing a passive consent process we were unable to add this additional data collection. In several of my projects I have been able to employ passive consent for participation in the educational intervention and collection of data by the school system (which is then supplied to me in such a way to render it anonymous for my use), while active consent is sought for individual interviews or participation in particular components, such as serving as a peer educator. If active consent is required, then effort should be made to maximize recruitment, ensuring that such efforts do not place too much burden on the school and are not coercive (e.g., offering a pizza party to the class with the highest participation rate would be coercive, whereas offering the same incentive to the class with the highest response rate, irrespective of whether permission was provided or denied, may be acceptable).

Interventions Delivered by School Staff

After designing what you feel is the ideal intervention, it is often difficult to hand it over for delivery by others outside your control. Classroom interventions delivered by research staff may be delivered with higher fidelity but lack generalizability to natural settings where by necessity the interventions must be delivered by school staff. Lessons taught by research teams may also increase suspiciousness of parents and community members and in reality, often the individuals most qualified to teach students are their teachers. Furthermore, many curricular interventions, especially those aimed at advancing child development or altering student behavior, require reinforcement of lessons and principles outside of any structured curriculum; teachers are best able to do this if they also teach the curriculum itself. One limitation, especially for investigators early in their career, is that this insulates the investigator from the intervention and the students receiving the intervention. During one of my earlier studies, I taught a series of six lessons that comprised an AIDS prevention education curriculum to all students in the school (Schonfeld et al., 1995). I began with the lessons in kindergarten and then modified the curriculum for a grade level higher based on the feedback I received from the students. In this way, I could review and revise the curriculum as it was being implemented and I developed a much better sense of what was being learned (and knew what was actually being taught), than I would have if classroom teachers had taught the lessons themselves. In the following phase of the project, I provided a brief in-service to classroom teachers and was able to demonstrate that they could achieve the same results that I had achieved in the earlier phase (Schonfeld et al., 1996). The skills that I developed during the year that I taught the lessons myself proved invaluable to inform my future research designs and curriculum writing and gave me clear insights into how to provide effective in-service training to teachers, to help me anticipate the needs for guidance documents, and to develop an even deeper respect for the work that teachers (and students) do everyday.

When someone else (e.g., classroom teachers) is delivering the intervention, efforts are required to maximize the fidelity of the intervention. To the extent possible, interventions should be manualized. I have often found it particularly helpful to utilize in-service time to ensure that teachers understand the underlying theory and principles of the curriculum, so that they know not only what they are teaching, but why and what is most important to convey. Process evaluation methods can be used to monitor the degree of implementation and the fidelity of implementation. Measures such as attendance lists at training, logs of teacher coaching sessions, and structured observations of instructional technique are important to implement, but care should be made that observations of teacher training is seen as a way for the evaluation/research team to "understand" how the intervention is being taught and received, rather than an evaluation of the teacher's teaching ability. Such observations may be expensive (in terms of project staff time) and difficult to arrange (since you have to prearrange the time the lesson will be taught). An advantage of classroom observation, though, is that it increases the likelihood that teachers will teach the lessons on schedule and can help program staff identify teachers in need of additional support or encouragement (i.e., if you observe the class, you can often tell if the students have not received the prior lessons or at the very least did not learn the intended concepts or content). Teachers should be provided logs to document when lessons are taught and to provide a place for them to record comments about the individual lessons or student responses or behaviors that were observed. In addition to assessing the degree of teaching of the lessons, some measure of student attendance or even participation may be important. Teacher satisfaction surveys (such as at the end of the class year) not only provide important feedback from experienced users of the curriculum, but may also provide insight into the likely degree of implementation. Teachers who are more enthusiastic about the curriculum are more likely (on average) to have implemented the curriculum and completed the lessons with a higher degree of integrity.

One of the limitations of utilizing teachers to deliver a new curricular intervention is that the efficacy of the intervention is often being judged at the same time that the teacher is first learning the curriculum. Attempts to provide in-service training months prior to the date of implementation with a general request to "become familiar" with the curriculum prior to the first lesson may not be effective. Teachers often simply forget the material covered in the in-service session by the time they initiate the curriculum. One option that I have implemented in research projects is to provide teacher training on the curriculum one year prior to when the cohort is at that grade level (e.g., training sixth-grade teachers when the cohort is in fifth grade) so that when the cohort is promoted to that grade, it will be the second year that the teachers are teaching the lessons. The problems I have encountered with this strategy result from the additional burden this places on program implementation staff (i.e., they have twice as many teachers to train and coach each year, which is often complicated by the personnel reductions required by budget cuts) and the high staff mobility in many urban school systems, such that often the majority of teachers in a grade level in a particular school change by the following year (resulting in novice teachers teaching the cohort irrespective). This is, though, a reasonable approach in systems where stability of teaching staff is greater and training personnel resources are adequate.

Nonintervention Control Groups

An additional challenge to research design involves the difficulty of creating and maintaining a nonintervention control group. Schools (and parents) that are enthusiastic about the potential benefit of an educational intervention may be particularly resistant to a randomized, controlled design. In most situations, parents and staff are able to understand the importance of a nonintervention control group from a theoretical research design perspective and appreciate that in the absence of the research project, none of the children will receive the program. Whenever possible, I have created research designs that allow the control group to receive the intervention at the completion of the data collection, but this may not be possible if the intervention phase and follow-up period extends for a number of years. For example, one project looking at the impact of social development instruction in grades 3 through 6 aims to follow students until the end of seventh grade in order to look at self-reports of early onset of high-risk sexual behavior. In this case, the intervention could not be offered to the students in the control group until eighth grade, when a curricular intervention for third graders would no longer be appropriate. Instead, the school can implement the curriculum intervention in the first year in third grade in the intervention schools and at an earlier grade level in the control group (assuming that contamination across grade levels could be minimized) and train the third-grade teachers in the control schools the following year, so that the study cohort maintains group assignment, but all schools have teachers trained in the intervention. This is often what would be done in the absence of a research project, because schools rarely have the resources to train every teacher all at once in a curriculum, and phased implementation is generally the norm. When a staged implementation is utilized, it is necessary to continue to monitor for unintended contamination and to work with school staff to understand the importance of a nonintervention control group. In one project, a community-based agency that was working in one intervention school offered the service to a control school (not understanding the overall research design). In another situation the school professional development staff compensated for the lack of teacher support and training in a control school by offering added services to promote implementation of a comparable intervention. In both cases, these threats to the study design were identified through discussions at weekly team meetings and their impact minimized after open discussion. Explanations that the important contribution of this study would be lost if the control group was compromised helped to enlist staff support—if the study findings failed to demonstrate a positive impact of the intervention, then it was highly likely that the intervention would not be adapted by other school systems and would be abandoned by their school system. As with every research effort, communication among study personnel is critical.

A related challenge involves efforts to blind students and program staff to group assignment especially when determining outcome measures of interest. Teachers who know they are implementing a bullying prevention intervention may be biased to rate students as demonstrating less bullying behavior at the completion of the intervention, especially when they are the ones tasked with implementing the intervention. Blinded evaluations are therefore critical but are often difficult to maintain in school settings when teachers and students know what they were (and were not) taught—or least we hope they would. Utilizing independent measures obtained by independent (and blinded) staff is an important strategy in school settings.

Some Additional Obstacles

Expense and Other Logistical Challenges of Intervention Research

Intervention research in school settings, when done well, is very expensive and requires a large sample size and significant staffing. If there is insufficient staff to monitor and support implementation, major deviations from the protocol can occur unnoticed (or be noticed too late). In one research project involving a cancer prevention education initiative, teachers in one school delayed the curriculum implementation because of competing academic requirements, and when they went to teach the lessons, found it necessary to take shortcuts. One shortcut was to administer the food survey once, rather than as the intended pre- and posttest administration (to try to minimize bias, the teachers were not told explicitly during the in-service that changes in scores were a major outcome measure of the study). Staff will need to be on site frequently and will not be able to rely solely on phone calls, e-mails, or mail follow-up. The personal relationships developed through face-to-face interactions and the ability to monitor more broadly unintended obstacles to implementation are critical to ensure adequate fidelity of implementation.

One of the realities of all applied research is that interventions that are theoretically based and that sound ideal on paper are often incredibly difficult to implement in a real-life setting. In one project, we included a component of peer educators providing monthly sessions to classes at a younger grade level in order to model for students, through role plays, the application of social skills being taught by classroom teachers. For many reasons, this sounded like a great idea. But the reality of identifying and training peer educators and scheduling them for presentations in other schools was daunting—peer educators were drawn from middle schools throughout the city school system and needed to provide presentations once a month to 750 elementary school students in 14 different schools. According to school policies, peer educators could not be released from their classes unless parents and every academic teacher provided written permission *every time*, documented that the student would not be missing any tests on that date, and was maintaining academic progress in all core subject areas. This was further complicated by the fact that the school did not permit students to be transported in personal vehicles (such as those of the peer educator facilitators), which required the use of school buses (that could not otherwise be committed for field trips, athletic events, etc.). The logistical challenges of this process proved so great that the school system ultimately chose not to continue this at the end of the study, even though the peer educators, students, and school staff all thought it was one of the most effective components of the intervention.

Another common challenge in school-based research is the high mobility of students, especially those attending large urban school systems, which can result in very high attrition rates. Attrition is generally not random and underscores the need for a control group, but even when a control group is present, reviewers tend to be very critical of high attrition rates, even if they are due to student mobility and at rates comparable to what is seen independent of the research study. My research has involved attempts to decrease the onset of high-risk behaviors, and as such, my research has been conducted in communities where these risk behaviors are prevalent and high mobility is the norm. Unfortunately, this has limited my ability to publish the findings of this research. One option is to limit the duration of the intervention and follow-up to the minimum possible (which is almost always the case because of financial considerations alone), or at least collect yearly outcome measures so that some data will be available on the vast majority or at least a greater percentage of the students. One limit to this approach is the cost of repeated measures and the fact that students and school staff may resent the added measurement burden, especially if the measures are highly redundant.

Research in applied settings is more complicated than anticipated by traditional experimental research designs. You can never
measure all the determinants of human behavior in a social setting,
let alone control for them or attempt to intervene in all domains.
At some level, this is the case in all clinical research (e.g., even
clinical drug trials) and rarely do these studies attempt to measure
all the variables of interest either (e.g., social support, diet/nutri-
tion, exercise, etc.), which may have a significant impact on the
physical outcomes (especially when these outcomes are assessed
through self-reports of symptoms), yet I find they are not faulted to
the same extent as applied research in child and adolescent development. Reviewers, whether related to funding or publication,
generally look for what you have not done, and in applied research,
they find a lot, especially if they do not understand applied research
or are so focused on pure research design or analytical principles
that they fail to consider the reality of the context. For example,
I have had reviewers fault my research proposal because I did not
plan to obtain baseline measures of behaviors used as the outcome
measure when randomization was done by school; but this was in
the context of a study aiming to prevent the early onset of sexual
intercourse through social development instruction beginning in
third grade. Would anyone who thought about the reality of this
context still feel it important to survey 6- and 7-year-olds about
how often they have had sexual intercourse as a baseline measure?
Condom use would seem even more absurd and behavioral intentions for either would seem meaningless for this age group (even
if it were possible to obtain parent permission and school approval
to ask such questions). In a similar manner, my research has been
criticized because of the failure to obtain biologic measures and
the reliance on self-reports of sexual behavior; when monitoring
the rates of sexual intercourse among children in sixth and seventh
grade, it is unclear what else could be employed in a school setting
(especially when using a passive consent process). Pregnancy and
diagnosed sexually transmitted infections are rare among sixth and
seventh graders, and direct observation of sexual intercourse fortunately remains an uncommon experience. Researchers who do aim
to conduct applied research will often do well to explain why they
are not proposing certain methodologies that may be the norm
in more controlled settings, even if it seems obvious for someone
conscious of the context of applied behavior research. Sometimes
it helps to state the obvious.

Remaining Flexible and Creative

One of the main challenges of applied research is that it is research conducted in the real world, and "stuff" happens within the real world all the time. This requires that the researcher remain agile, flexible, and creative. In a study of an elementary school AIDS education intervention, students were enrolled into intervention or control groups based on whether they attended a local feeder elementary school of a middle school that was assigned to intervention or control groups; students were then followed through the transition into middle school. Just after the funding was awarded, the school system decided to implement magnet middle schools and eliminate the feeder elementary school system. As a result, we needed to move the intervention from fourth grade, the last year of the elementary school, to fifth grade when middle school started. (Because of federal policies the title of the project remained the same; that is, the Comprehensive Elementary School AIDS Education Project began in middle school.) Researchers should try their best to anticipate potential obstacles, but it is impossible to prepare for all contingencies. In my research study exploring the impact of death education in prekindergarten to second grade, one of the teachers was unexpectedly hospitalized in the intensive care unit for a presumed heart attack just prior to one of the lessons. One of the parents in another school died of cancer in the midst of the cancer education study. In each case, adjustments needed to be made, if only for ethical reasons. In another project, the school closed for an extended period just prior to the initiation of the health education curriculum under study because of the discovery that the building was built many years prior on a former landfill and toxic contamination was now being reported by the media along with parent calls to permanently close the school. I had not prepared for that contingency, but needed to quickly readjust and accommodate the new schedule.

One of the advantages of a well-designed evaluation component that includes process measures is that it allows you to monitor for unintended and unanticipated needs, outcomes, and influences. For example, in my project studying the impact of social skills education at the elementary and middle school levels on the onset of high-risk behaviors, ethnographic observations of classrooms intended to monitor fidelity of teacher intervention provided insight into barriers to effective implementation not initially addressed well in the protocol. It became clear to observers that teachers were unable to deliver much of the intervention curriculum (or any curriculum for that matter) because of difficulty managing disruptive student behaviors and classroom interruptions. Coaching and in-service training then was focused on classroom management skills, which was well received by teachers and allowed them to be more effective in teaching all of their lessons.

Conclusion

Despite all these obstacles, applied child and adolescent development research in school settings can be extremely exciting and rewarding. It may be the best site for studying processes or interventions of very high relevance and importance. After all, the most important things happen in real life. If the intervention is effective, it can have a very wide impact when it is able to be delivered in a school setting. Schools do provide access to a large number of children and adolescents that are often representative of the general population. And you can learn a great deal from doing this type of research through your collaborations with educators and school administrators and your direct interactions with parents and students. As much as it is challenging, applied research in school settings can be exciting and rewarding. It requires you to remain agile, flexible, and creative. Research in controlled settings is just boring by comparison.

References

Schonfeld, D., Bases, H., Quackenbush, M., Mayne, S., Morra, M., & Cicchetti, D. (2001). Pilot-testing a cancer education curriculum for grades K-6. *Journal of School Health, 71*, 61–65.

Schonfeld, D., Johnson, S., Perrin, E., O'Hare, L., & Cicchetti, D. (1993). Understanding of acquired immunodeficiency syndrome by elementary school children—A developmental survey. *Pediatrics, 92*, 389–395.

Schonfeld, D., & Kappelman, M. (1990). The impact of school-based education on the young child's understanding of death. *Journal of Developmental and Behavioral Pediatrics, 11*, 247–252.

Schonfeld, D., O'Hare, L., Perrin, E., Quackenbush, M., Showalter, D., & Cicchetti, D. (1995). A randomized, controlled trial of a school-based, multi-faceted AIDS education program in the elementary grades: The impact on comprehension, knowledge and fears. *Pediatrics, 95*, 480–486.

Schonfeld, D., Perrin, E., Quackenbush, M., O'Hare, L., Showalter, D., & Cicchetti, D. (1996). Success by regular classroom teachers in implementing a model elementary school AIDS education curriculum. In I. Schenker, G. Sabar-Friedman, & F. Sy (Eds.), *AIDS education: Interventions in multi-cultural societies* (pp. 179–187). New York: Plenum Press.

Schonfeld, D., & Smilansky, S. (1989). A cross-cultural comparison of Israeli and American children's death concepts. *Death Studies, 13,* 593–604.

Additional Resources

Cohen, L., Manion, L., & Keith, M. (2007). *Research methods in education* (6th ed.). London: Routledge.

Ross, J. G., Sundberg, E. C., & Flint, K. H. (1999). Informed consent in school health research: Why, how, and making it easy. *Journal of School Health, 69,* 171–176.

Thomas, A., & Grimes, J. (Eds.). (2008). *Best practices in school psychology V.* Bethesda, MD: NASP.

Thomas, G., & Pring, R. (2004). *Evidence-based practice in education.* New York: McGraw-Hill Education.

CHAPTER 10

Conducting Applied Research in Child and Adolescent Settings
Why to Do It and How

Lyndee M. Knox, PhD
LA Net, A Project of Community Partners

Introduction

Conducting applied and translational research in child and adolescent development in the clinical setting is an exciting and very rewarding experience. In this chapter, I am defining the term *clinical setting* as the medical health care practice environment. Research in the clinical environment can advance science in the area and lead to real improvements in practice and, as a result, in the lives and well-being of families and their children. It can also be frustrating, slow, and oftentimes messy. It is definitely not for the faint of heart, nor for the individual who likes precise, predictable, and carefully controlled scientific work. My goal in this chapter is to discuss some of the challenges and rewards of conducting research in clinical settings and to share some of the lessons I have learned over the years.

Where Does Clinical Research Fit in the Larger Research Continuum?

There is a serious problem with the process of health and behavioral health research in the United States and around the world.

Important discoveries that could have a significant and positive impact on the health and well-being of children and families in the United States and around the world never make it into standards of care in the practice environment. Balas and Boren (2000) estimate that it takes an average of 17 years to move medical innovation and scientific discovery from its initial discovery to standard practice in communities, and even then only 14% of new scientific discoveries ever make it into routine use. A classic example of this is beta-blockers. Although the benefits have been established for more than 25 years, a recent study of its use in 234 hospitals across the United Stated found that a significant number of hospitals still do not routinely prescribe the medication following an acute myocardial infarction (AMI; Bradley et al., 2005; Howard & Ellerbeck, 2000; Westfall, Mold, & Fagnan, 2007).

The movement of a medical or scientific discovery into practice takes place in three phases. The first phase of the process is the initial discovery through basic or bench research. The second phase is the translation of this discovery from bench and animal trials to carefully controlled human trials (bench to bedside), and the third phase is translation of the discovery into regular use in practice (bedside to practice). Additionally, some are now referring to a fourth stage of translation that moves from routine use in practice to actual patient (or family or community) outcomes. This process of moving research from its origins out ultimately into the community where it directly impacts child and family well-being is called *translational research*.

For the past 50 to 100 years, the research community has focused most of its attention on the first two phases in the process. Much less attention has been given to translation of medical and behavioral innovations into broader use in the community. Research on child and adolescent development is no different. Although there are any number of thoughtful, theoretically sound, rigorous basic science studies, and a similar amount of well-controlled efficacy trials, there are far fewer studies that examine the effectiveness of interventions in real-world practice environments with the types of complex patients and lifestyle realities that are excluded from early lab and efficacy trials. The same can be said about bringing successful interventions to scale so they do the most good for the most people. In the public health community this interest in effectiveness and dissemination research is referred to as "shifting to the right-hand side of the public health model."

Why does this gap exist? There are a number of different factors that have contributed to this situation over the years. Of course, the first is funding. Historically, funding has favored early stage research over their translation into practice, and researchers by necessity have followed the money. The way we train scientists has also contributed. Most graduate training programs emphasize basic science. Far fewer train individuals who are able to take existing evidence and move it into practice. Finally, the tenure process in universities has also favored more basic science over applied and translational science, discouraging young researchers from pursing careers in these areas and cutting short the academic careers of others who have.

Responding to pressure from the American taxpayer and others anxious to see the actual benefits of all the research they have been supporting through taxes, the National Institutes of Health (NIH) and other funders have begun to rethink the research process in the United States. In 2004, the NIH initiated an ambitious project to reform the way medical, behavioral, and social science research is conducted. The NIH Roadmap set out an agenda to redesign the medical research process to include a new emphasis on translating research into community settings. Funding was established to set up Centers for Translational Research aimed at bringing more resources to the translation of research into practice. Funders also began to pay greater attention to participatory research approaches that engaged community members and end users of research as partners in the research process.

What Is a "Clinical" Setting and Why Conduct Research There?

For the purposes of this chapter, I am defining a clinical setting as a place where health care services are delivered. A clinical setting can be a hospital, a specialty care or primary care practice located in or adjacent to a hospital, or a specialty care or primary care practice located out in the community. Specialty care encompasses areas such as pediatric oncology, pulmonology, and psychiatry. These settings can be good locations for your work if you are interested in a topic directly connected to a specialty area. For example, if you were interested in studying how children and families cope with a catastrophic illness like cancer, then a pediatric oncologist would be a logical partner.

In contrast to specialty care, primary care is a patient's first point of contact with the health care system and is focused on the delivery of basic preventive and acute care services. Primary care disciplines include family medicine, internal medicine, and general pediatrics. Emergency physicians by default also function as primary health care providers much of the time, especially for the poor who often lack access to primary health care in the community and therefore seek this care from the emergency department of their local hospital. Also serving low-income, underserved communities are community health centers (CHCs), nonprofit organizations that have as their primary mission providing health care to individuals who cannot afford health insurance or who are publicly insured. CHCs, comprised of one or many different practices, and academic health center practices (primary care practices located in a medical school) are referred to as safety net settings and provide the majority of services to the poor and uninsured in the country.

Because my interests have always been focused on concepts of social justice and on the effects of poverty on child and adolescent development and well-being, my work has focused in those areas, institutions, and geographies that can have the greatest impact with these youth and families. This has included schools, social service nonprofit organizations, jails, and most recently primary health care clinics. Ninety-five percent of medical visits by children each year take place in the community in primary health care providers offices (Dovey et al., 2003), making it a critical site for early preventive interventions, especially for the poor. Without exception, I have found the clinicians working in these settings to be committed to the same issues I am, resulting in a very good fit between my interests and theirs, leading to very productive and happy partnerships.

The primary health care setting can provide a valuable connection to young persons and their families and provide opportunities to intervene with parents prior to a child's birth during prenatal care and on through the life span. Most individuals in the United States visit their health care provider four times a year. These visits provide opportunities for screening, referral, and counseling on a wide range of topics that can impact the quality of family life and the parent–child relationship. With children and adolescents, mandatory school and sports physicals as well as acute care visits provide excellent opportunities for risk screening and detection, referrals into supportive services, and delivery of educational and other types of interventions. The health care visit can provide opportunities for counseling on topics that may be more difficult to address in school and community settings such as risky sexual behavior and relationship violence; it can also provide an opportunity for counseling and education with the parent on a wide variety of topics that are critical to healthy development in a young child ranging from detecting developmental delays, to healthy nutrition, to risk reduction in areas ranging from accidental injury or death due to firearms, to preventing motor vehicle injuries.

In fact, the health care environment can provide ongoing opportunities for developmentally linked preventive and other interventions from before birth, through adolescence, and into adulthood. Rosenberg and Knox (2005) recommend clinician-delivered counseling on positive youth development beginning during the prenatal period with strategic planning and counseling with young parents, on through childhood, adolescence, and into adulthood. The clinical environment can also be the location for critical behavioral health interventions such as programs to prevent violent reinjury of adolescents presenting in the emergency department with violence-related injuries (Cunningham et al., 2009). A recent study of a simple intervention in the pediatric office to screen children for risk factors associated with aggression and involvement in violence, and then referring their parents to a parenting hotline produced statistically and clinically significant improvements in child behavior over a 12-month period (Borowsky et al., 2004).

The American Academy of Pediatrics has developed an excellent set of resources designed to assist clinicians in ongoing counseling on positive youth development and preventive topics, such as violence prevention, called Connected Kids: Safe, Strong, Secure (www.aap.org/ConnectedKids/). The Health Services and Resource Administration Maternal and Child Health Branch sponsored development of tools to support these types of parenting and preventive interventions in pediatrics as part of its Bright Futures initiative (www.brightfutures.org/). The American Medical Association published a toolkit on screening and educating on violence prevention that is an example of any number of resources on behavioral health issues and opportunities in the clinical environment (Knox, 2002; Knox, Lomonaco, & Elster, 2005). Any of these resources can be an excellent starting point for applied research in pediatric behavioral health.

There are many reasons for conducting research in clinical settings. The clinical setting can serve only as a site for recruiting children and their parents for studies and as a physical space in the community for collecting data. Although this is probably the most common use of these environments, this narrow use dramatically underutilizes the potential of the clinical site, and can also do some fairly significant damage along the way, especially in mission-driven organizations like the community health centers, as clinicians will eventually grow tired of being used only to find patients, without any real value accruing to them and their patients.

The clinical setting can also be used to explore questions about the clinical environment and processes of care, such as patient–provider interactions or patient compliance with treatment recommendations, and to examine how these can impact a child's overall health and well-being. Finally, the clinical environment can be used as a site to test interventions designed to reduce risk factors and improve the physical and emotional well-being of their patients.

How do I gain a firmer grounding in the developmental perspective, including how psychosocial and biosocial developmental processes interact with proximate environments, such as family, clinic, school, and peers?

There is a natural synergy between applied behavioral research in child development and the clinical environment and in particular the primary health care environment. Some key concepts and ideas that underpin primary care practice that are useful to know when you are starting to look for research opportunities in these environments include *community-oriented primary care* (COPC), an approach to health care and prevention that starts with the health of the population (rather than the specific needs of an individual) and asks what services, resources, and environment is needed to support the health of entire communities or populations (Mullan & Epstein, 2002). Although not well realized in real-world practice environments, a COPC approach to practice is a continuing goal in primary care, especially among CHCs. The *biopsychosocial model*, a related concept of care that encourages a broad definition of health, considers the health (or illness) of a child or adult, not only at the biological and individual level but also within the context of that individual's family, community, and broader society, adding to a natural synergy between applied behavioral research and clinical care (Borrell-Carrio, Suchman, & Epstein, 2004). Finally, evolving definitions of what it means to be healthy make clear the importance of behavioral and social factors as a component of health, not only as mediators or moderators. The most recognized of these definitions is that developed by the World Health Organization as early as 1943: "Health is a state of complete physical, mental and social well-being and not merely the absence of disease or infirmity" (www.who.int/about/definition/en/print.html). Add to this the fact that 8 of the top 10 health care problems in the United States have strong behavioral components and there is a seemingly unending list of potential research partnerships that might occur in these settings.

One example of the potential clinical practice environments hold for applied child and adolescent development research is a study one of my colleagues conducted with her primary care practice partners in Monterrey County, California. A pediatrician in practice in a part of the county where there was a large immigrant population approached her with a concern he had that an abnormally large number of children in the area coming into his practice with elevated levels of lead in their blood stream. Lead exposure in children can have serious and lifelong physical and mental sequelae. Working in partnership with the pediatrician, my colleague determined that there was a substantially higher percentage of children in this practice with elevated blood lead levels compared to other areas of the county.

With this observation, both my colleague and her new research collaborator set to identify the source of the exposure. Traditionally, lead exposure in these communities had been thought to occur through improperly cured ceramics that the families used in cooking. By a variety of research methods (e.g., interviews, observations), pottery was found to be a factor but another source of lead exposure was discovered. These researchers determined that the *chaupalines*, or dried grasshoppers (a delicacy in the Oaxacan regions where these families were from), were responsible for the high lead levels. Grandparents were sending these treats to the children from Mexico or the children were consuming them on their visits back to Mexico. Chaupalines eaten by the children in this pediatrician's practice were from a single region in Mexico, known mostly for silver mining. The trailings from the mines were somehow leaching into the bodies of the grasshoppers in the area. Thus, the silver trailings were transmitted to the children when they consumed the grasshoppers. The results of this exploratory study led to the implementation of a binational health education project (between the United States and Mexico) to educate care-givers on both sides of the border about sources of lead exposure and its effects on the neural development of children. The study also led to a number of publications in public health journals.

Approaches to Conducting Research in Clinical Settings

Just as there are different approaches to carrying out research with and in other settings like schools and community organizations, there are different approaches to conducting research in clinical settings. They run the gamut from very detached, where the clinical site is viewed as a source of subjects or a place to test theories and interventions, to the other extreme where a participatory approach to working in the setting is assumed and involves clinicians and patients as partners and even leaders of the research endeavor. This participatory approach can go even so far as to engage clinicians and patients in generating the actual area of focus and research questions that you will then help them pursue. This latter type of research can be very rewarding and lead you in directions you never thought you would go, but it can also be very time consuming and present some challenges for you if you want to pursue tenure. I will address these challenges a bit later in the chapter.

Until recently, the majority of research conducted in the clinical setting could best be described as "helicopter" research. This is a somewhat derogatory term used to describe situations where researchers who have received funding for studies helicopter into a clinic with their funding and resources, collect their data, and then helicopter out when the study is over—usually leaving no sustainable improvements to the practice or the patient once the study is over. Although these types of arrangements are common, they greatly shortchange the research potential of the clinical environment and often end up creating more problems than good.

I remember very well an experience I had with this type of research early in my career. A well-respected, senior researcher had received funding from a federal agency to study the use of health educators for improving self-management behaviors of Latino patients with diabetes. During the study, this researcher hired three health educators to do the work at the site, provided training to sites, and set up a screening process to identify patients with poorly regulated diabetes to participate in the intervention. The clinicians were delighted. They were relieved to finally have someone who could help them with these patients. The patients who participated in the intervention saw solid improvements in their self-management skills and overall health and shared their excitement with other patients at the clinic. Physicians started asking to refer other patients into the study. The researcher wanted to help, but the study design (e.g., using the standard randomization to intervention and control) and the budget made it impossible. Although the physicians understood, they were also becoming uncomfortable with the process, feeling it was in conflict with their mission to provide the best care possible to anyone who sought care from their clinic. At year three, when the intervention period ended, the health educators left the clinic, and the services they were providing ended without a plan to sustain these services postintervention. Over those three years, the physicians had come to rely on these resources for their diabetic patients. In addition, because these physicians were referring to this intervention, they had lost their connections with other programs that might support these same patients. Finally, patients who had been participating in the program had no one to go to for continued support. When the researcher left, the physicians were left with a demand for the health educator's service that they could no longer fill. Although they were able to recalibrate fairly quickly and return to processes they used before the study, the experience left a bad taste in their mouth. The researcher published his results and even came to present them at the practice, but in the end the physicians felt that the only lasting thing they received from the experience was a brief note of appreciation in the researcher's article that was published in a medical journal they did not even read. The next time a researcher approached them to participate in a study, they said no.

How can researchers, even if in a position of "authority" take measures to ensure that the "voice" of the participants is heard, even at the level of planning the data collection methods?

A second, and I believe much more effective, approach to conducting research in clinical settings is called practice-based research (PBR). PBR has many similarities to community-based participatory research (CBPR) and grew out of similar frustrations with the traditional research process, such as the ones evident in the earlier helicopter research scenario. Like CPBR, PBR seeks to conduct research "in partnership with" clinicians working in these settings. In PBR, the emphasis is on conducting studies that are of immediate relevance to the practice environment and its patients. While studies that seek to develop or test theories have a place, the main goal of PBR in on "patient-oriented evidence that matters." This means things that will directly impact patient care and patient outcomes.

Traditional approaches to research begin with theory or the researcher's own line of inquiry as the starting point for a study. In PBR, the clinicians' and their patients' needs and concerns are the starting point. For many years, I have used a participatory engagement process called the *reflective practitioner* as a way to initiate a research project in a practice or group of practices and be true to the PBR paradigm. This process was developed by Drs. Mary Croughan and Margaret Handley at the University of California–San Francisco.

I have used this process a number of times over the past 10 years, and I have also found it to be very helpful to me personally. More than once it has helped me transition back to a participatory mindset and approach after participating in more academy-centric research activities. It is a very simple process and easy to replicate and can be a good way to help build relationships with a new clinical site. The five steps of the reflective practitioner are

1. Collect information from clinicians about topics of interest by paging, calling, or e-mailing them and asking what they have experienced in the past week in patient care that they would like someone to do research on or help them with.
2. Collate topics and organize by theme. Eliminate topics not suitable for research and identify topics that are already well researched that could best be addressed through a literature review rather than a research project
3. Hold a virtual or in-person forum to discuss the various topics and have participants vote on the topic they would most like to see research on.
4. Organize teams of clinicians, a researcher, and a facilitator to review the literature on the topic and develop a research question.
5. Send topics out to the group by e-mail for a vote. Conduct study on the winner. Disseminate findings to the group of practices.

As part of this process, the teams use six questions to evaluate topic and research questions before moving ahead. These six qualifying questions are:

1. Will the answer to this question change my practice?
2. Will it change my colleague's practice?
3. Is there a clinician champion (someone in the organization who is willing to advocate for and shepherd the project at the clinical site) for this project among the participating practices/clinicians?
4. Is the study feasible?
5. Is it fundable?
6. Is it publishable?

If the answers to Questions 1 and 2 are no, the topic is dropped and the team moves on to another one. If these are yes, the project can move to the next step but the team must evaluate the implications of the answers to the remaining questions and their implications for the ultimate success of the study.

One of the most interesting projects I undertook was as a result of this process. A clinician from a CHC in my practice-based research network asked a question about the complementary and alternative medicines his immigrant patients were using. He told us a story about an older Asian patient he had been seeing in his practice. The patient was complaining of fatigue and other symptoms, and the doctor had ordered blood work. The report came back showing the patient had impaired liver functioning. After an in-depth assessment to determine the cause, the doctor came to the conclusion his patient was abusing alcohol and that this was the cause of the out-of-range lab data. He screened the patient for alcohol abuse and dependency but the patient denied overusing alcohol. At follow-up visits over the next year he would ask the patient about alcohol use and carefully provide counseling and education on substance abuse and its treatment. Finally, during one of these visits, the patient casually mentioned an herbal supplement he had been taking for the past year and how helpful he thought it was. The supplement turned out to be the cause of his liver problems and this experience formed the basis of a two-year partnership with this clinician to study the use of Complementary and Alternative Medicines by immigrant patients.

A practice-based research network (PBRN) is a group of clinicians and practices that are focused mainly on patient care but who have come together for the purposes of conducting research that matters to their patients and patient care. There are more than 100 PBRNs across the country, with most housed in medical schools but a growing number in larger community health centers, HMOs, and nonprofit organizations. Most PBRNs are directed by clinicians who have moved into research full or part time and are focused mainly on conducting research. Your initial conversation with PBRN directors can be easier than with the clinician who is working full time in practice because they are often more experienced in research than the community clinicians and so will have a better understanding of your goals and also the scientific and organizational constraints you are working under such as requirements for the conduct of good science, what it takes to be competitive for research funds, and the pressures to publish on the tenure track. Although this is not always true, in many instances it is, especially among PBRNs that are housed within medical schools and universities, as most are.

You can find a list of primary care PBRNs in the United States on the Web sites of the National Federation of Practice-Based Research Networks (www.aafp.org/online/en/home/clinical/research/fpbrn.html) and the National Practice-Based Research Network Resource Center (http://pbrn.ahrq.gov/portal/server.pt?open=512&objID=969&mode=2).

Important Considerations About Working In and With Clinical Settings

Relevance

The most important thing to remember when working in clinical settings, especially in PBR, is relevance. If your work does not lead to improved pediatric care, or another outcome that the providers see as important to their work, it is unlikely you will be able to establish a productive partnership. To give you an idea of what this means in a primary care environment, the issues of most concern to my clinical partners today are things like accessing specialty care services for their patients, preparing for changes in health care reimbursement such as pay for performance, how to incorporate health information technology into their practices effectively, recruiting and retaining qualified health care providers in their organization, maintaining a viable business model in the current economic and health care climate, and public health concerns such as chronic disease management and obesity. Whenever possible I try to make sure that the studies we undertake speak in some way to one of these issues. For example, we recently began a federally funded study of sleep apnea in uninsured patients. Although the study is interested only in rates of diagnosis and treatment recommendations, we have built in a small piece to attempt to increase access to specialty services in this area for the uninsured in their practices. In another example, we are involved in a study of adult obesity prevention that we will eventually extend to pediatrics because of requests from several clinicians involved in the project.

A particularly useful research framework I have come to rely on in most of my clinical research projects to ensure the data we collect is useful to providers, and in particular to medical directors and decision makers in clinical environments who may be interested in replicating the intervention in new practices, is the RE-AIM framework developed by Russell Glasgow (www.re-aim.org/2003/publications2.html). RE-AIM helps direct the researcher's attention to core information that a physician or program director would need to know before deciding what programs to implement in their practices. Following is a brief overview of the framework:

R—Program reach. A program's reach refers to the number of patients (out of the total eligible) that an intervention can possibly serve and the number of clinicians willing to implement the intervention with their patients. If an intervention is highly effective but only 2 patients out of 2,000 eligible get the intervention, is it useful in the practice environment? If an intervention is effective and has a reasonably good patient reach but only 10% of the providers in an organization are willing to implement it, is it useful in a practice environment?

E—Program effectiveness. In traditional clinical research, which is typically focused only on studying the efficacy of an intervention, be it a medical drug, or a behavioral or health services intervention under as tightly controlled conditions as possible, this is often the only component of the study. While this is an essential first step in the intervention research process, it is precisely that, the first step. In the RE-AIM approach to clinical research, the goal is to evaluate the intervention in real-world environments under real-world conditions with real-world patients. Any practicing clinician will tell you that he or she has never seen a patient who "just has diabetes," for example. The adult patients they see in the real-world practice environment usually come to them with multiple health problems: the diabetic patient who is obese and also has major depression; the patient with heart disease who is also diabetic; the pregnant mother who has two other young children who is also a victim of domestic violence in her home. While most children typically do not present with such a complex array of health conditions, their care or preventive health services usually occur and must take into consideration a much broader range of issues than just the immediate practice environment. Preventive counseling on health risk topics such as relationship violence or unprotected sex occur within the context of the young person's school or work context, peer environment, family environment, community, and developmental stage, all of which must be considered in the intervention process.

E2—Economics. How much does the intervention cost to start and to maintain over time? If the intervention is effective and has a large reach, but is unsustainable in terms of cost, this is something that must be considered when one considers taking a particular clinical intervention to scale. From a public health perspective, in a system with limited resources, decisions must eventually be made on where those resources are best spent. For effective interventions, medical directors and other decision makers at the organizational level need to be able to estimate how much a particular program will cost in relation to its potential impact and reach and to make informed decisions about implementing the intervention.

A—Adoption. Adoption refers to practice-level implementation and examines the number of practice sites in a system that are able to implement the intervention, and especially the degree of fidelity.

I—Implementation. Implementing an intervention in the practice setting requires an examination into the process of implementation and any modifications and adaptations that must be made to the intervention.

M—Maintenance of program effects. Decision makers and clinicians also need to know how long an intervention works for their patients. Are the effects long term or short term? Are they seen immediately or is there a "sleeper effect," and they only become evident after a number of months or even years have passed? Do the intervention effects wear off after a period of time and so booster sessions of some sort are indicated? In most mental health and behavior interventions, there is often short-term improvement that dissipates over the following months. Many behavioral health interventions such as Families and Schools Together (FAST) plan up front for this and include follow-up sessions that are less intensive than the original intervention but designed to reinforce earlier gains. In the clinical environment, for example, if an intervention improves a parent's ability to manage asthma in her child and reduces preventable admissions to the emergency department in the first 8 months, but the positive effects begin to wear off after this time, this is important for clinicians to know in planning for the intervention, and bears on the overall cost and potential value of the intervention.

Time

The most important commodity in the clinical environment is time. You must take this into consideration in any study you decide to undertake in a clinical setting. It can be a brutal calculus. In the CHCs I work in, even 3 minutes of clinician's time per patient to fill out a patient survey translates to four fewer patients that doctor could see that day. The conflict for clinicians in a CHC environment is that they may feel they are already unable to see the number of uninsured patients in their waiting rooms that need care.

There can be serious financial implications for the clinician and practice as well even if you give them a stipend for participation. Someone still must be available to provide care for the patients; if your study is taking time away from this care in these environments there is rarely an underutilized clinician that can be redirected to provide that care. Usually CHCs are short on staff as it is. It is important to be mindful of these issues and work with the clinicians to design the study so that is as minimally intrusive as possible. In my own work, I try to make sure that studies are designed so that my staff and I do as much of the work as possible and minimize its impact on patient visit or provider time.

Methodology

As in community-based research, it can be difficult to implement studies that require randomization at the patient level. Clinicians and their staff may resist a study design that includes randomization because it may conflict with the clinic's mission to provide the best care to all patients. Often this can be resolved by using a comparison group, nonequivalent comparison, or wait list design instead of using a no-intervention control group.

Getting nonresearch clinicians and staff to adhere to complex research protocols can also be a challenge. Clinicians and staff may not understand the importance of adhering to a particular protocol and so fail to implement it correctly. Equally likely, the protocol may appear nonsensical or even contradictory to their mission of providing patient care. These are common occurrences and will require you to do a considerable amount of ongoing training and oversight to ensure the protocols are implemented correctly. In one study we conducted with nine CHCs, the clinicians were asked to conduct a limited physical exam as part of a research protocol involving the "types" of subjects, which were pregnant mothers, and 1-year- and 3-year-old children and their mothers. Because the exam associated with the research protocol was abbreviated, the protocol instructed the doctors to invite the mother to schedule another health care visit with the physician where the physician would then conduct the full exam. The physicians and nurse practitioners at the CHCs rebelled over this issue and refused to comply even though there were important timing and monetary reasons behind the need for an abbreviated exam. They explained that this might be the only exam their uninsured patients came in for and that they were unlikely to return for another visit. The study was part of a large multisite effort that covered the United States and involved dozens of practices. The study director did not take these issues into account when developing the design and protocols. After a number of lengthy phone calls to the study director, the study design was changed to accommodate the concerns of the clinicians.

Leave the Practice a Better Place

In all clinical research, but especially PBR, your focus should always be to leave the practice a little better than you found it. There are many ways you can do this including

- Dissemination of the research findings to the practice in a manner that makes sense to them and that they can actually use.
- Resources or other benefits you leave behind when the study is complete. This can be
  - A computer.
  - Brokering an important relationship for the practice.
  - Providing continuing medical education (CME) as a part of the study training.
  - Giving clinicians an opportunity to publish and present papers on the project.
- Providing opportunities for clinicians to engage in intellectual debate with their colleagues on the topic.

Compensation

I have always found it troubling that researchers approach practices and their clinicians to participate in a research study, where they have either received or are submitting a grant to receive funds to complete the study with absolutely nothing or almost nothing budgeted for the practice involvement. Even when you hire your own staff to collect the data, there is a significant amount of disruption that occurs in a practice as part of any research study and there are costs associated with that disruption. Just like your university requires facilities and administrative (F&A) costs, you should also consider the investment that has been made in developing the practice and its ongoing maintenance and infrastructure costs. If your research is a true collaboration and an equal partnership, the budget must be considered in the same light and appropriate compensation provided to the practices for their participation in the project. In instances where there are simply not enough funds to provide support to the clinical environment and still carry out the research end of the work, this needs to be explained to them up front, and other types of compensation or support considered. For example, you might work to obtain continuing medical education credits for the clinicians who participate in the project, or as mentioned earlier, provide support to a non-research activity such as helping the clinic expand its specialty care access options, helping with some evidence-based summaries in the general area of your project that could be distributed to staff, or even collecting data that is of interest to the clinic at the same time you are conducting your surveys.

Important Academic Considerations for Working in and With Clinical Settings

Conducting research in clinical settings and especially using PBR is very time consuming. It takes time to build relationships, and you will often need to undertake studies and projects in service of the partnership that may not be directly related to your research. You will need to evaluate your academic setting to determine if it is a supportive environment for this type of work. The best way to do this is to talk to your faculty mentor if you are assigned one or a representative from the dean's office or the appointments and promotion committee. This type of participatory work often requires more time to develop and begin publishing on than bench research or even traditional clinical research that uses practice environments only for patient recruitment or as a lab. More progressive universities have realized the critical role participatory approaches to research play in the successful translation of research to communities. These institutions are actively looking for ways to modify the tenure process to support young faculty members engaged in this type of work such as extending the tenure clock for participatory research, recognizing project roles more than standard authorship order, recognizing dual Principal Investigators, giving equal value to nonfederal sources of research funds such as the Robert Wood Johnson Foundation that funds a considerable amount of participatory work, and valuing and recognizing a much broader range of publication types and venues.

Because I am early in my career, I am framing questions using academic processes more than community inputs. I feel that I should not stray too far from my academically defined questions, or I risk slowing progress toward tenure. However, I want my community relationships to be productive for the community, not just for my academic career. How do I negotiate this?

Traditional tenure standards, especially in medical schools, often require publications in so-called A-level journals, and recognize the peer-reviewed manuscript as the primary means for communicating research findings. For participatory research, these are not the appropriate or even most desirable outlets for your research findings. If the goal is to impact clinical practice, then the dissemination methods must include approaches most likely to reach these audiences. These may not be the A-level journals but rather more practice-oriented ones, and the best format may not be a journal at all. It may be a curriculum, or a white paper, or some other type of report. Universities that are more committed to the type of participatory work with clinics that I am describing will typically make allowances around these broad areas within their tenure process. Ask about this specifically. Forewarned is forearmed in this case. If you find your institution has not made adjustments in any or most of these areas, think long and hard about undertaking this type of work until you have gotten through the tenure process.

If you are lucky enough to be located in one of these universities, seek out the individuals behind these efforts and get their advice and guidance as you develop your own research career. Almost every university will profess having a deep interest and commitment to its surrounding community and in participatory engagement. This interest can sometimes be quite superficial and exists only for political expediency or image management.

Whenever possible, find a mentor in your institution or in the area to work with that is interested in practice-based research. They can provide you entry into practice environments and save you a considerable amount of time. If you have a PBRN at your university or in the area, it is a natural partner for you. Some of the newly established Centers for Translational Science Institutes (CTSIs) funded by the National Institutes of Health have a mandate to focus at least some of their resources on community translation and are another potential place to find a mentor or enter into community practices. Many CTSIs also have a postdoctoral training program focused on translational research. In these programs, you cannot only gain faculty mentors and translational sciences skills but also potential funding for your research project. Do not be afraid to go outside of your department. Faculty from the disciplines of social work, sociology, psychology, family medicine, nursing, pharmacy, pediatrics, and psychiatry may not only be interested in child and adolescent development but also may have interest in the clinical setting. Do not be surprised if your search brings you to faculty in the disciplines of business, law, computer sciences, and engineering.

Publishing is a critical component of any academic career. Because of the time it takes to get up and launched, especially in practice-based research, it is important to get articles out and flowing quickly. You should consider publishing not only on the final results of your study but also on the participatory processes or methods you used to conduct it. In fact, I can still remember the day about 7 years into my career that it suddenly dawned on me that I had become as much a methodologist (in participatory engagement processes) as I had become a content expert. So do not forget the "methods" part of the work you are doing and your ability to publish articles on your processes. Even if you do not have publishable results yet from the studies you are involved in, the approaches you have used to build relationships with clinics, clinicians, and patients are equal fodder for publication. Make it a goal to try to write an article on an aspect of your engagement methods for each study you carry out. These can make solid contributions to the field and also help support your bid for tenure.

Authorship is another area to be considered. It is important that you advocate for yourself and the expertise you bring the project and when appropriate, to maintain the first author position. I made a mistake early in my career in this area that I later came to regret. Because I was young and a non-MD on an MD-dominated clinical project, I did not advocate for first authorship on several manuscripts that I had clearly put the work into to qualify for the position based on standards described by the various journals we were publishing in and also the American Medical Association's set of standards on this topic. This failure on my part had consequences for my career later on.

It is important to remember that in many instances, especially with clinicians in community practices, their career advancement may not depend on first authorship, whereas yours does. Often clinicians do not even know about the academic realities with which you must contend. My recommendation here is that you be up front with them and explain what you need to get out of the project from an academic career/tenure perspective. Equal partnership goes both ways. In other words, do not be shy about advocating for your own career needs. If this is approached in a professional and transparent way, this can easily be done without threatening the participatory process.

You will also need to maintain a careful balance with your academic colleagues. If you decide to develop a career in PBR, you will spend a great deal of time cultivating relationships with physicians and other health care providers in the community. In PBR, and even traditional approaches to clinical research, this will become your most important research asset. As a seasoned PBR researcher once said to me, "At the end of the day, your most valuable asset is your mailing list and your connections. Guard them as if they were gold." Although interdisciplinary collaboration is absolutely essential to good clinical research, and good relationships with other faculty are an important part of academic development and success, be cautious with whom you share your hard-won contacts. Your relationship with a clinic can easily be damaged by a clumsy colleague, and although hopefully very unlikely, a colleague who is more adept in those settings can walk off with your contacts. One example of this is an experience I had with a close colleague of mine. He was interested in working on a project I was conducting on pediatric asthma and also wanted to work directly with the clinics. Most of his work had been in early stage clinical research on tightly controlled efficacy trials. Because he had such excellent people skills and was a well-respected scientist, I thought he would do very well in the practice environment. But after only one visit to our partner clinic, I was getting disgruntled phone calls from the clinic administrator and the lead clinician there complaining about his approach, and the demands he was making on the staff. It took several long discussions and quite a bit of training before he finally began to understand the type of communication style, flexibility, and project pace needed to support a participatory approach to research in the clinics, and the type of concessions that were necessary in the study design to increase the potential relevance and generalizability of the research.

Another balancing act you will have to maintain, especially in participatory approaches to clinical research, is that between responsiveness and focus. Where the initial orientation in developing participatory partnerships must be on being responsive and saying yes to your community partners' interests, remember the expertise you are bringing to the partnership is the ability to situate these interests in a larger scientific discussion while not losing their local relevance, and eventually to help your team determine which of a likely myriad of project possibilities are most likely be high yield when undertaken as research. If you do a study about detecting developmental disability in primary care, think also of how this could connect to a particular theory of intervention/practice that you have published on and see if you can get a second article on this. For example, in a recent study I was involved in on obesity prevention, I began to see a number of parallels to the intervention approach we were encouraging parents to take with their food management and exercise, and with their children, and theories of effective parenting. Just from this connection, we were able to draft an article on how obesity prevention strategies and education for families and children could be informed by theories and research on effective parenting.

Conclusion

One final note, there will come a time when you are well established with your clinical partners, and many more requests will come in than you can or should handle. Initially you say yes, but at some point you will need to begin to say no. A head of state was once quoted as saying, "Saying yes is easy. It's knowing what to say no to that is difficult and also where leadership really begins." One way to do this is to "know your because." There are a number of different "becauses" in PBR especially. You can undertake a study because you want to build a relationship and capacity with a practice, or because this is an important project that is likely to be high yield clinically or from a research perspective, or because you need to publish. If you are clear with yourself about the reasons you are taking on a particular project, and realistic about how feasible it is to accomplish these aims through PBR and other participatory approaches, you are well on your way to a successful and likely very rewarding career in research.

References

Balas, E. A., and Boren, S. A. (2000). *Yearbook of medical informatics: Managing clinical knowledge for health care improvement.* Stuttgart, Germany: Schattauer Verlagsgesellschaft mbh.

Borowsky, I.W., Mozayeny, S., Stuenkel, K., & Ireland, M. (2004). Effects of a Primary Care-Based Intervention on Violent Behavior and Injury in Children. *Pediatrics*, 114, e392–e399.

Borrell-Carrio, F., Suchman, A. L., & Epstein, R. M. (2004). The biopsychosocial model 25 years later: Principles, practice, and scientific inquiry. *Annals of Family Medicine*, 2, 576–582.

Bradley, E. H., Herrin, J., Mattera, J. A., Holmboe, E. S., Wang, Y., Frederick, P., ... Krumholz, H. M. (2005). Quality improvement efforts and hospital performance: Rates of beta-blocker prescription after acute myocardial infarction. *Medical Care, 43*(3), 282–292.

Cunningham, R., Knox, L., Fein, J., Harrison, S., Frisch, K., Walton, M., ... Hargaten, S. (2009). Before and after the trauma bay: The prevention of violent injury among youth. *Annals of Emergency Medicine, 53*(4), 490–500.

Dovey, S., Weitzman, M., Fryer, G., Green, L., Yawn, B., Lanier, D., & Phillips, R. (2003). The ecology of medical care for children in the United States. *Pediatrics, 111*, 1024–1029.

Howard, P. A., & Ellerbeck, E. F. (2000). Optimizing beta-blocker use after myocardial infarction. *American Family Physician, 62*(8), 1853–1860, 1865–1866.

Knox, L. (2002). *Connecting the dots to prevent youth violence: A training and outreach guide for health care professions.* Washington, DC: American Medical Association.

Knox, L., Lomonaco, C., & Elster, A. (2005) The American Medical Association's connecting the dots to prevent youth violence training and outreach guide. *American Journal of Preventive Medicine,* 29, 226–229.

Mullan, F., & Epstein, L. (2002). Community-oriented primary care: New relevance in a changing world. *American Journal of Public Health, 92*(11), 1748–1755.

Rosenberg, M., & Knox, L. (2005). The Matrix comes to youth violence prevention: A strengths-based model for preventing youth violence. *American Journal of Preventive Medicine,* 29, 185–190.

Westfall, J. M., Mold, J. W., & Fagnan, L. J. (2007). Practice-based research—"Blue Highways" on the NIH roadmap. *JAMA, 297*(4), 403–406.

SECTION IV

HOW TO MAKE THE MOST OF YOUR APPLIED RESEARCH

CHAPTER 11

Getting Funded in Applied Child and Adolescent Development Research

The Art and Science of Applying for Grants

Daniel B. Berch, PhD
University of Virginia

Introduction: Why Grants Are Important and How to Get Started in Seeking Research Support

The preceding chapters in this practical guide offer excellent suggestions for generating applied research ideas in various domains of child and adolescent development. In addition, the authors of these chapters have provided you with a wealth of valuable advice as well as strategies for crafting a sound study design, engaging the appropriate community for recruiting participants, dealing with ethical issues and challenges, and disseminating your findings. However, applied research is often quite costly and time consuming. Indeed, successful execution of even a moderately sized project is likely to require at least some level of external funding to support the costs of research personnel and staff, equipment, data collection and storage, statistical packages, supplies, travel, and so forth. So, where do you start?

Well, to begin with, you might ask why one should even contemplate applying for a research grant beyond the obvious motive just mentioned. Fortunately, Robert Sternberg (2003) has provided such a list of reasons, in which he maintains that a research grant

- helps support graduate students, thus providing them with the opportunity to receive training,
- permits you to assign some responsibilities to others,
- can supply you with summer salary if you are compensated by your institution for less than a 12-month period,
- will signify that you are a serious scholar, and
- can be very important for purposes of promotion and tenure.[1]

So now that you are convinced it is worth applying for a research grant, what do you do next? With such a bewildering array of federal funding agencies, not to mention private foundations, the complexities associated with the world of research funding are intimidating enough to strike fear into the heart of even the most ardent new investigator. However, it can be advantageous to devote the time and effort required to learn about not only specific funding opportunities, but also the missions, objectives, and possibly even some characteristics of the institutions and agencies that offer these opportunities. That being said, this learning process may well be slow, oftentimes tedious, and frequently discouraging—especially if you spend the better part of a semester putting together a grant proposal only to be informed several months down the line that in addition to not being awarded a grant, your proposal was not even deemed competitive for funding. Somewhat similar to the process of submitting manuscripts for publication in a scholarly journal, getting funded requires persistence in the face of "failure." Indeed, you should take a lesson from Sternberg (2003), who points out that some of his colleagues had concluded his group must have a great track record in obtaining grants because they had been comparatively successful in getting funded. His response: "False! I can honestly say to colleagues that we have probably had more grant proposals turned down than any other individual or group of which I know. We just write more grant proposals" (p. 177).

Furthermore, entrée into the world of funding is complicated by the vast array of grant mechanisms available to researchers. For example, the National Institutes of Health (NIH) alone offers upward of 100 different grant mechanisms, not counting contracts or cooperative agreements (see http://grants.nih.gov/ grants/funding/ac_search_results.htm), although any given institute within this federal agency may only accept applications for some subset of these mechanisms. Obviously then, the novice investigator would do well to seek out a variety of sources of information about granting agencies and their funding priorities (e.g., Web sites, books, periodicals), where to find specific grant solicitations, how to contact program officials, the application process, proposal preparation, grant review procedures, the decision-making process, post-award regulations (e.g., purchasing, progress reports), and so forth. As space limitations preclude me from providing you with the requisite details for how to understand all of the elements associated with seeking and managing grant funds, I will try to highlight what I consider to be some of the most crucial steps in this process, and then direct you to other sources for more information.[2]

How do you identify and successfully apply for sources of funding to support the development of new studies?

Beyond the kinds of information I am providing you in this chapter, those of you affiliated with a research university should be able to receive assistance from various institutional offices and personnel. These kinds of units are usually located within the office of a vice president for research or an office of sponsored programs. Additionally, your central administration may also house a faculty development or advancement division that provides tutorials on how to get your research program off the ground. Furthermore, detailed information about grant policies and guidelines is usually available on the Web sites of these offices, which also serve a number of other useful functions: (a) they provide training in grantsmanship; (b) they inform you of various funding opportunities or help you search for them; (c) sometimes they provide seed funds for conducting preliminary studies; and (d) they can assist you in developing your grant proposal.

Finally, it has become increasingly important for assistant professors to seek external funding for supporting their research. Unfortunately, however, formal training in how to go after external funding is still sorely lacking in many doctoral programs.

My Own Career Experiences in Research Policy and Grants Administration

My advice in this chapter stems from having spent 11 years in the federal service during which I served in several different capacities related to behavioral science policy and grants administration. I began my federal career as a Society for Research in Child Development (SRCD)/American Association for the Advancement of Science (AAAS) Executive Branch Science Policy Fellow at the NIH's National Institute of Child Health and Human Development (NICHD). This experience was followed by a stint serving as a Scientific Review Administrator (now called Scientific Review Officer) at the NIH's Center for Scientific Review (administering grant review panels [i.e., study sections]), service as a senior research associate for the Assistant Secretary for Educational Research and Improvement in the U.S. Department of Education, chief of the Section on Cognitive Aging in the Behavioral and Social Sciences Program at the NIH's National Institute on Aging, and then associate chief of the Child Development and Behavior Branch at NICHD. In all of these jobs, I helped junior, midcareer, and even senior investigators develop their research ideas, build or change their research career paths, and craft specific grant applications for submission. And now, as the first associate dean for Research and Faculty Development at the Curry School of Education, University of Virginia, I continue to work closely with faculty, especially junior faculty, on the same kinds of issues: providing advice and counsel on how to find funding opportunities and apply for grants. And I also serve faculty in other departments and colleges at the University of Virginia who seek external funding.

Brief Overview of Related Literature

Many books and papers have been published to guide new faculty about how to apply for grant funding (see several relevant references and numerous other resources at the end of this chapter). Even a cursory review of the Web sites of major booksellers reveals many such guidebooks, ranging from excellent to downright awful. Although I will not take up space here reviewing any of these sources, suffice it to say that most provide at least some useful hints, and although they sometimes offer conflicting advice, prospective grant applicants can benefit from information they may not otherwise have considered important. You should also be aware that articles about getting funded periodically appear in *The Chronicle of Higher Education* (e.g., see http://tomprofblog.mit.edu/2006/03/28/710-finding-grants-where-to-start for a relevant piece written by the director of a university's research development office).

Other particularly useful training and educational resources are provided directly by federal granting agencies themselves, under labels such as "grants workshop," "seminar," or "technical assistance workshop." An example of this is the webinar venue provided by the U.S. Department of Education's Institute of Education Sciences, which includes tutorials and opportunities for answering questions pertaining to various types of requests for proposals (RFPs; see http://ies.ed.gov/funding/webinars/index.asp). This kind of format also permits the viewing of slides presented by program officials (which are archived on the Web site), and a question-and-answer session carried out electronically.

The NIH sometimes conducts similar technical assistance workshops or seminars in different regions of the country, which not only offer excellent advice from experienced federal officials, but also provide opportunities to interact directly with them as well as with your peers, who obviously attend such functions for the same purpose as you. For example, the NIH Office or Extramural Research (OER) annually sponsors two regional seminars on program funding and grants administration (see http://grants.nih.gov/grants/seminars.htm). Similarly, the NIH's Office of Behavioral and Social Sciences Research presented a technical assistance workshop on the topic of community-based participatory research on February 29, 2008, pursuant to a program announcement soliciting "grant applications that propose intervention research on health promotion, disease prevention, and health disparities that communities and researchers jointly conduct" (see http://grants.nih.gov/grants/guide/notice-files/NOT-OD-08-052.html). For those who are interested in this particular topic, the archived webcast can be viewed at http://videocast.nih.gov/Summary.asp?File=14325.

Talking to Funders

How to Contact Funders

Prospective grant applicants frequently want to know who they should talk to at funding agencies and foundations; whether they should write, call, or visit; how much detail they should go into;

and so forth. The answers depend in part on whether it is an agency or a foundation. If the former, then how best to initially approach a federal official about your prospective project may depend on the agency, the unit within the agency, and the penchants or preferences of a given program official. In my own experience and that of many of my former federal colleagues, as a rule, meeting with prospective grantees individually is usually not the most preferred way of providing assistance. Although in most cases, a face-to-face meeting with a program official is not disadvantageous, it is certainly not critical for getting funded. On the positive side, direct contact with such an official can help in laying the groundwork for future communications, which can be important for effectively handling additional questions and issues that may arise before the application is submitted, as well as after the reviews have been completed. However, program officials have a responsibility to ensure a level playing field, such that all prospective grant applicants have equal access to information and assistance they need in preparing their applications, receiving feedback about their reviews, and so on. Moreover, in the case of agencies such as the NIH, the program officials have no say in the assignment of reviewers, and it is the scores of the reviewers reflecting the scientific merit of your application that carry the greatest weight in determining whether it will be competitive for funding. Certainly, as program relevance is often an important consideration as well, ensuring that this official is familiar with your proposal and that he or she both recognizes and supports its program relevance should not be underestimated. Nevertheless, it does not take a face-to-face meeting to establish a good working relationship with a program official.

Although a telephone discussion with the program official is often highly recommended, it is important to initially send a letter or e-mail message before arranging a time for such a call. Generally speaking, your message should state an interest in the program followed by a précis of your prospective application. More specifically, the description should consist of at most one to two pages in which you briefly state the nature of the problem, the specific aims or objectives of the proposed research, the types of participants, a concise description of the research design and methods, and the anticipated results. This approach will help you in a number of respects. First, the official will already have a basic idea of your project before the call, thus reducing the need to describe it from scratch on the phone, not to mention the time required for the call. Second, this tactic will make it much easier for the administrator to understand the nature of your project and to be prepared to ask good questions or provide useful suggestions if he or she has had some time to review your proposed project prior to the phone conversation. Third, if the project is not a good fit for the program, institute, or even the agency, the program official can at least forward your project description to other federal officials who can assess whether it aligns well with their own mission and objectives.

Preparing to Talk to Funders

Many grant applicants know comparatively little about funding agencies prior to contacting a program official. Although it is certainly not necessary to carry out a thorough review of an agency's mission, objectives, and programs, it would behoove you to at least familiarize yourself with the basic characteristics, functions, and procedures of a given agency in order to ask the kinds of questions that are likely to yield answers that would be most beneficial to developing your prospective application.

What kinds of questions might you pose to a program official? In my own experience, and that of many of my colleagues, grant applicants have asked just about any question one could imagine, including some which seem to have nothing to do with research or grants. Nevertheless, I would suggest that when in doubt about any particular issue or topic, it is better to ask a question than inadvertently assume you can infer the correct answer. However, I would also recommend that you do your homework before beginning to query a program official. Showing that you have explored the relevant Web sites prior to your call demonstrates that you are serious about getting involved in the grants process and that you are willing to take on some of the responsibilities associated with learning the rules, policies, and procedures governing the steps involved in applying for federal funds, the review process, and the postaward responsibilities of a grantee. To this end, I have listed a number of online resources at the end of this chapter, many of which deal with the National Institutes of Health.

During your initial conversation with a program official, your primary objective should be to determine whether your project is a good fit for that given program area. Then, depending on your level of experience, you will want to get advice about the most appropriate grant mechanism for your career stage. If it looks as though the potential fit is good enough to begin developing a proposal, it is still likely that you will need to follow up that call with more specific questions (preferably by e-mail initially) as you begin to flesh out the details of your proposed project. In this regard, you may wish to ask about such things as the viability and clarity of your specific aims, the breadth and depth of your literature review, and the amount of detail needed for your project description and data analytic procedures. Thinking back, I can recall numerous questions I have received about these matters. Here is a brief list of some of the questions I have been asked:

- Do I need to spell out both the theoretical and practical significance of my proposed project?
- If my study is designed to test an intervention that could help ameliorate a common behavioral problem, is it still necessary to show that this approach is derived from a theory?
- How many specific aims should I include?
- How thorough should my review of the literature be?
- Is it better to write the background and review of the literature before the research plan?
- Is it always necessary to include a control condition?
- How much pilot data do I need to collect before submitting an application?
- How many experiments should I include?
- How detailed does my research plan have to be?
- If my study is focused on the topic of X in adolescent males, would I still need to include a group of adolescent females?
- Is my *N* large enough?
- Do I need to include a power analysis?
- Do I need a statistical consultant?
- How innovative does my project have to be in order to be competitive for funding?
- Do I need to form a scientific advisory board?

My most frequent answer to the vast majority of these questions began with "it depends." Don't get me wrong, because in some sense, there is no such thing as a dumb question. It is just that with a little thinking, you should appreciate that successful grant applications, even within the same field, may vary considerably in the nature of the research methods, the number and types of participants, the number of experiments, and the like. What counts, to put it colloquially, is that the whole project hangs together. In other words, there should be strong and logical links among your theoretical model (that frames the research questions your project is designed to answer), the background and literature review (which sets the stage for the goals of the project), the specific aims and objectives of the project, your study design, research methods, measures, data analytic strategies, and expected outcomes.

Learning About How Funding Agencies Develop Research Agendas

Among other topics, I think it is potentially important for you to understand some things about the ways in which funding agencies decide what kinds of research to support. First, most of them have an explicit mission, which they publish on their Web site. For example, NICHD's stated mission is to "ensure that every person is born healthy and wanted, that women suffer no harmful effects from reproductive processes, and that all children have the chance to achieve their full potential for healthy and productive lives, free from disease or disability, and to ensure the health, productivity, independence, and well-being of all people through optimal rehabilitation."

As is obvious, this kind of mission is broad enough to include an extremely wide range of research topics that have a bearing on children and adolescents in particular and development in general. More specific objectives of the branches, divisions, and programs that comprise any given funding agency can be found on its Web site. So, specifically how do such agencies decide what their funding priorities should be? As it turns out, the research agendas they set are influenced by a variety of people along with information, ideas, and suggestions culled from numerous other sources (Berch, 2004).

Initially, many agencies engage in a kind of activity that some have termed a *gap analysis*. As I once described in a presentation I gave on the topic (Berch, 2003), this phrase is used in a number of fields including land management and information technology. It refers to the study of the differences between two discrete information systems or applications often for the purpose of determining how to get from one state to a new state. A gap is sometimes spoken of as the space between where we are and where we want to be. Indeed, this is a useful way of characterizing how funding agencies frame questions when they bring people in who have expertise in various areas and ask for their opinions first about what we know in a given area, what we do not know, and finally what we should do to fill in the gaps in our knowledge.

At the NIH, the National Science Foundation, and the Institute of Education Sciences, the vast majority of program officials are researchers in their own right, and thus can frequently bring their own expertise to bear on the question of how to develop a research agenda. Coupled with their almost daily interactions with some of the best investigators in a given field, program officials can play a distinctive role in helping to shape the directions in which a field of study might evolve. As Friedman and Baldwin (1990) have pointed out, "Scientist-administrators are in a unique position that allows them to identify areas in need of special support" (p. 56). Furthermore, Friedman and Baldwin acknowledge that "through their [scientist-administrators] contact with advisors who are well aware of leading scientific issues, they learn about potential areas for breakthrough and important problem areas" (p. 56).

Another way of characterizing the process of setting a research agenda is the development of a so-called *scientific roadmap*, which consists of a far-reaching gaze into the future of a given area of inquiry compiled from the combined knowledge and imagination of the leading drivers of change in that field (Galvin, 1998). According to Galvin (1998), "Roadmaps can comprise statements of theories and trends, the formulation of models, identification of linkages among and within sciences, identification of discontinuities and knowledge voids, and interpretation of investigations and experiments" (p. 803). So how does a funding agency in general or a program official in particular go about developing such a roadmap? First, one should recognize that it is not only funding agencies that try to develop these roadmaps. For example, the National Research Council, which is the operating arm of the National Academies, continuously issues reports about specific research domains in which the study committees (made up of the most accomplished researchers) provide numerous recommendations for not only future research, but also particular funding needs to ensure that work in a specified domain can be adequately supported.

Again, Galvin (1998) has done an excellent job of summarizing the process of setting a research agenda: "The optimal process for gathering and selecting the content of roadmaps is to include as many practicing professionals as possible in workshops periodically in order to allow all suggestions to be considered and to objectively evaluate the consensuses that will more often than not emerge" (p. 803). Although most federal agencies organize such workshops and make use of other formal mechanisms for developing research agendas, program officials also develop ideas that emerge from informal exchanges and interactions with their federal colleagues, grantees, and prospective applicants. And sometimes, these agendas grow out of directives from the U.S. Congress, as well as advice and counsel from scientific societies and professional associations (Berch & Wagster, 2004).

Of course a variety of nonfederal, alternative sources of funding may be sought for supporting applied research in child and adolescent development. These consist primarily of private foundations and, less frequently, corporate sponsors. Examples of these can be found among the list of resources provided at the end of this chapter.

Budgeting for Time, Space, and Other Resources

In developing your grant proposal, you may encounter important challenges with respect to garnering departmental and institutional backing for carrying out your prospective research project, should you become the recipient of an external award. This typically requires negotiating in advance for time (e.g., release from teaching), space (e.g., for housing graduate students), and other needed resources. Consequently, when developing your budget and research plan, you will need to explore in detail, matters such as direct and indirect costs, and procedures for "buying out" some of your teaching load. In the following section, I describe these two issues.

Understanding the Distinction Between Direct and Indirect Costs

Even if you are successful at securing external funding for your research, you will not be able to charge some of your expenses to your grant as *direct costs* (i.e., those that can be specifically identified with a given project, such as salaries and fringe benefits or equipment). Rather, the so-called *indirect costs*, overhead, or more formally facilities and administrative (F&A) costs are those incurred by the university for common objectives rather than ones that can be designated as being specifically associated with a particular sponsored project or institutional activity. Nevertheless, F&A costs are real costs incurred by your department, school, and university that are attributable to shared services such as utility costs, libraries, administrative expenses, depreciation on buildings and capital equipment, maintenance and repair, and so forth. The F&A monies are distributed to various units within universities according to a specific formula. Your school and most likely your department or academic unit will receive a share. And in some cases your college may have a "research incentive" policy whereby individual principal investigators can recover a limited percentage of their own unit's F&A (to which they have contributed) for purposes of supporting existing and future research-related activities (e.g., travel to speak with potential funders, pilot work, student support, bridging research activities between grants). The following constitute some of the items and services that could be covered by the F&A monies:[3]

- Furniture, including moving it (e.g., desks, chairs, filing cabinets)
- General office supplies (e.g., pens, Post-it notes, stapler and staples, etc.)
- General operating software (Microsoft Office, Adobe Acrobat, Windows upgrade, etc.)
- Journal/magazine subscriptions (must be related to grant; check first)
- Miscellaneous office items (e.g., network splitter)
- Miscellaneous photocopying (e.g., grant applications, correspondence, etc.)
- Paper for printers (if used for nongrant specific purposes, e.g., e-mail)
- Phones (relocation, voicemail and new installation)
- Postage (letters of recommendation and miscellaneous)
- Rental space, electricity, heat

Negotiating Release Time From Teaching

Most colleges and universities have explicit policies regarding course reductions or buying out from teaching for faculty members who become recipients of a grant award.[4] More specifically, as you presumably know already, faculty at most universities are expected to teach a certain number of credit hours per semester.[5] The teaching load required by your institution will vary depending on whether you are employed by a four-year college where involvement in research-related activities is not all that high of a priority, or at the other extreme, a research-intensive university (what was formerly known as a Carnegie Research 1 institution), where a comparatively large number of doctoral degrees are granted, research is given a very high priority, and millions of dollars in federal funding are awarded annually.

How do young researchers survive in an environment where career development money is being downsized?

Either way, you will need to buy out of a portion of your instructional time at a rate specified by your institution. And generally speaking, neither the funding source (assuming it is an external sponsor) nor the kind of grant mechanism through which you receive a research award will influence whether you can buy out of a course, assuming that your budget can even cover this cost. However, there can be some exceptions to this broadly stated principle. For example, as most NIH Career Development (K-Series) Awards require that recipients dedicate a specified minimum percentage (usually 75%) of their full-time professional effort to the objectives of the career award, one's university may prefer that a faculty member who receives a K-Award devote at least some of his or her remaining professional effort to teaching, and thus not permit that individual to buy out of a course. Typically, to be released from one or more courses, funds from your grant will need to be provided to cover the costs of hiring a qualified instructor (e.g., adjunct professor) to handle your teaching responsibilities. This will usually amount to a standard rate specified by your institution's workload buyout policy, typically something like 12.5% of your base salary (plus fringe benefits). Finally, most universities require their faculty to fill out a course buyout form that must be approved by the dean and department chair. However, be apprised that you may not necessarily get to drop the course of your choice (e.g., your largest or least favorite class).

Top 10 Steps for Preparing a Competitive Proposal

Some investigators interested in applied research with children and adolescents have posed important questions pertaining to the topics of this chapter. In this section, I present one such question along with my attempt to provide a comprehensive and constructive answer: *How can I shape my applied child and adolescent development research questions and studies to best prepare me for (writing) successful grant applications?*

To the best of my knowledge, there is no magic formula for developing a line of research that will guarantee you a steady stream of funding. And it is generally acknowledged that coming up with a really good idea is the *sine qua non* of a viable grant proposal. That said, there are many important steps between developing such an idea and writing a proposal that not only translates this idea into a well-designed, significant research project, but also transmits the strengths and uniqueness of your proposed project in a manner that excites reviewers and convinces the funding agency that an investment in this work has a reasonable chance of bearing fruit. As to shaping your line of research to make the proposal more competitive, you really need to ensure that you align your work with the mission and goals of the funding agency, the interests of the funding program in general, and the objectives of a specific grant solicitation in particular. Even then, you should either try to develop an entirely new set of questions or a novel approach to solving a problem for which no solution has as yet been achieved. Covering already well-traveled ground to answer small questions with limited opportunities for generalizability of your findings, methods, or theory beyond the domain of your study proper is not likely to stimulate the enthusiasm of either the reviewers or the agency.

However, as noted earlier, you still need to craft a strong research proposal. If I were to try to specify the top 10 steps for preparing a competitive proposal, I could not come up with a better list than that provided by Robert Sternberg (2003):

1. *Tell a story*—Your application should have a narrative quality that begins with an important question that has not as yet been answered, discusses how or why prior approaches have failed, and ends with an account of how you plan to solve the problem.
2. *Justify the scientific importance and interest of the research*— Claiming that your project or approach to solving a problem has not been carried out does not by itself attest to its significance. Rather, you need to explain why the proposed research is worthy of being conducted.

3. *Be clear, and then try to be clearer*—Write for a reviewer in mind who is generally knowledgeable about your field, but has no particular expertise in your specialized research domain.

4. *Organize your proposal carefully*—Emphasize the major points that you want the reviewers to remember.

5. *Sell your ideas*—No matter how good your idea is, you need to convince the reviewers that the project is worthy of support. Do not expect them to discern it on their own.

6. *Be comprehensive but selective in your literature review*—Focus primarily on prior research that is directly pertinent to your proposed project and, if possible, cite researchers who you anticipate are likely to be selected to be reviewers.

7. *Be respectful in your literature review*—If you judge it is important to be critical of prior relevant work, then comment on this in a professional and respectful manner.

8. *Have a strong theoretical basis for your proposal*—You should not only provide a sound theoretical foundation for your project, but also make explicit how your hypotheses were derived from the theory.

9. *Follow directions*—Most federal agencies, especially large ones such as the NIH, have an extensive list of detailed rules that must be followed in order for your application to even be considered for review. Whether it is page limits, font size or width of margins, be sure to follow instructions to the letter.

10. *Make sure your budget is reasonable and matches the proposed research*—Do not try to overbudget or underbudget. Experienced reviewers may judge the former as signifying a greater desire for money than carrying out important research, and the latter as a sign of lack of understanding of the resources required to conduct your project.

By following these guidelines, along with having a little luck, your chances of getting funded should improve considerably. And to ensure that you try not to repeat the mistakes made by numerous grant applicants, see Table 11.1 for a compilation of common problems that have appeared in proposals as judged by NIH grant reviewers.

TABLE 11.1   Common Problems and Mistakes in NIH Grant Applications as Reported by Reviewers

Lack of new or original ideas

Absence of an acceptable scientific rationale

Lack of experience in the essential methodology

Questionable reasoning in research approach

Diffuse, superficial, or unfocused research plan

Lack of sufficient procedural details

Lack of knowledge of published relevant work

Unrealistically large amount of work

Uncertainty concerning future directions

Too little detail in the research plan to convince reviewers the investigator knows what he/she is doing

Problem more complex than investigator appears to realize

Direction or sense of priority not clearly defined (i.e., experiments do not follow logically and lack a clear starting or finishing point)

Lack of focus in hypotheses, aims, and research plan

Assuming proposed experiments will work

Methods unsuited to the objective

Investigator too inexperienced with the proposed techniques

A fishing expedition for which no basic scientific question is being addressed

Proposal driven by a method in search of a problem

A theoretical rationale for the experiments is not provided

Dense, repetitive writing

Boring!

Insufficient preliminary data

Old idea

Approach is not state of the art

Experiments too dependent on success of an initial proposed experiment; lack of alternative methods in case the primary approach does not work out

Relevant controls are not included

Proposal lacks enough preliminary data or these data do not support the project's feasibility

Insufficient consideration of statistical needs

Proposing incorrect statistical analyses

Not clear which data were obtained by the investigator and which were reported by others

Note: These comments have been drawn from several lists compiled by various program officials at the NIH over many years. Some of these can be found in tutorials posted on the NIH Web site.

Conclusion

In this chapter, I have attempted to provide you with numerous tips and guidelines for contacting funders, preparing grant applications, and avoiding common mistakes in an effort to assist you in seeking and hopefully obtaining funding to support your applied research on child and adolescent development. Naturally, as one size does not fit all, you need to consider these suggestions in light of your own research area, your prior experience in seeking external funding, the degree to which funded research is valued if not required at your college or university, and the kinds of support for internal seed funding as well as for the development of grant applications at your institution. At the very least, I hope I have helped demystify the external funding world and have provided you with a useful starter kit that motivates you to continue gathering the information you need to develop and submit a strong grant proposal. To this end, I have listed in the following section the links to a number of useful resources that I trust will be of some benefit to you. Good luck in your future research endeavors, and if after all the planning and preparation of a grant proposal you find yourself hesitating about whether to submit it, remember what the renowned hockey player Wayne Gretzky once said: "You miss 100% of the shots you never take."

Relevant Grant-Related Web Sites, Funding Opportunities, and Other Resources

Directories of Funding Opportunities (Mostly Consisting of Federal Agencies)

- Grants.gov—http://www.grants.gov/
- SPIN—http://spin2000.infoed.org/new_spin/spinmain.asp (SPIN permits indexed searching of every field in a grants opportunity database.)
- CFDA (Catalog of Federal Domestic Assistance)—https://www.cfda.gov (Provides access to a database of all federal programs.)

National Institutes of Health (NIH) Funding Opportunities and Other Resources

- NIH Regional Seminars—http://grants.nih.gov/grants/seminars.htm
- NIH Grants Process Overview—http://grants.nih.gov/grants/grants_process.htm
- NIH Grant Cycle: Application to Renewal—http://www.niaid.nih.gov/ncn/grants/cycle/
- NIH R01 Tool Kit—http://sciencecareers.sciencemag.org/career_development/previous_issues/articles/2007_07_27/caredit_a0700106
- Common mistakes in NIH applications—http://www.ninds.nih.gov/funding/grantwriting_mistakes.htm
- NIH Office of Extramural Research: Electronic Submission, Avoiding Common Errors—http://era.nih.gov/ElectronicReceipt/avoiding_errors.htm
- NIH: The Center for Scientific Review's Resources for Applicants—http://cms.csr.nih.gov/ResourcesforApplicants/
- NIH Mock Review Panel—http://cms.csr.nih.gov/ResourcesforApplicants/InsidetheNIHGrantReviewProcessVideo.htm
- NIH Career Development Awards—http://grants.nih.gov/training/careerdevelopmentawards.htm
- NICHD: Child Development and Behavior Branch—http://www.nichd.nih.gov/about/org/crmc/cdb/index.cfm

U.S. Department of Education Relevant Funding Opportunities

- Institute of Education Sciences—http://ies.ed.gov/funding/

National Science Foundation Relevant Funding Opportunities

- Developmental and Learning Sciences—http://www.nsf.gov/funding/pgm_summ.jsp?pims_id=8671&org=BCS&from=home

Private Foundations Funding Opportunities

- Foundations Center—http://foundationcenter.org/findfunders/
- Foundation for Child Development—http://www.wtgrantfoundation.org/funding_opportunities
- William T. Grant Foundation—http://www.wtgrantfoundation.org/info-url_nocat3042/info-url_nocat.htm
- The Spencer Foundation—http://www.spencer.org/

Other Funding Opportunities and Resources

- Funding sources for social psychology and related fields—http://www.socialpsychology.org/funding.htm
- Berg, K. M., Gill, T. M., Brown, A. F., Zerzan, J., Elmore, J. G., & Wilson, I. B. (2007). Demystifying the NIH grant application process. *Journal of General Internal Medicine, 22,* 1587–1595.
- Horner, R. D. (2007). Demystifying the NIH grant application process: The rest of the story. *Journal of General Internal Medicine, 22,* 1628–1629.
- Porter, R. (2003). Facilitating proposal development: Helping faculty avoid common pitfalls. *The Journal of Research Administration, 35,* 28–33. Retrieved from http://www.wpi.edu/Images/CMS/ORA/Avoiding_Common_Pitfalls.pdf
- Porter, R. (2005). What do grant reviewers really want, anyway? *The Journal of Research Administration, 36,* 341–351. Retrieved from http://www.srainternational.org/sra03/uploadedFiles/Vol36Issue2.pdf
- Porter, R. (2007). Why academics have a hard time writing good research proposals. *The Journal of Research Administration, 38,* 37–43. Retrieved from http://www.wpi.edu/Images/CMS/ORA/Article_on_Proposal_Writing.pdf

Guidelines for Writing Grant Proposals

- CFDA, provides guidelines for developing and writing grant proposals—https://www.cfda.gov/index?static=grants&s=generalinfo&mode=list&tab=list&tabmode=list
- University of Michigan's Proposal Writer's Guide—http://www.drda.umich.edu/proposals/pwg/pwgcomplete.html
- Books and articles on grant proposal writing—http://www.lib.uwo.ca/programs/generalbusiness/proposalwriting.html

Notes

1. Although being the recipient of a competitive grant award is generally considered to be a very important indicator of one's research-related competencies, several factors may be evaluated by those reviewing a dossier submitted for promotion and tenure: the amount and duration of the award; your role

(e.g., whether you are the principal investigator, a coinvestigator, or a consultant), the type of award or grant mechanism (e.g., career development grant, small grant, R01, etc.), and the source or sponsor. In addition, some institutions will give credit for the number of grant applications submitted, even if some of them were not funded. However, in such cases, the ratio of funded to submitted applications may also be considered an important metric.

2. To simplify this chapter, the guidelines and examples I provide are directed primarily to federal funding agencies rather than to private foundations or corporate sponsors. More specifically, I make reference predominantly to the National Institutes of Health and some of its institutes and centers. Finally, although I do discuss some aspects of grant budgets, such as direct and indirect costs, I have chosen not to provide detailed suggestions about how to prepare a budget.

3. I am grateful to Marianne Lampert for compiling this list.

4. Although some faculty would probably prefer to reduce their service load as much as if not more than their teaching responsibilities, most departments and colleges have no explicit policies pertaining to such an option. This is presumably because time and effort are frequently not calculated for service on department, college, or university committees (among other types of service), despite the fact that such service is usually part of what is required by universities for compensation via one's so-called base salary or institutional base pay. That being said, cases may arise where a department chair or college dean could permit a faculty member to buy out his or her time, which would be spent on a major, identifiable and measurable service commitment, assuming that a suitable replacement can be found.

References

Berch, D. B. (2003, July). *Gap analysis: Bridging the space between what we know and what we want to know.* Presented at the National Research Council's Workshop on Understanding and Promoting Knowledge Accumulation in Education: Tools and Strategies for Educational Research, Washington, DC.

Berch, D. B. (2004, April). *Funding programs and priorities: A perspective from NICHD.* Presented as a Presidential Invited Session to Division E (Counseling and Human Development) at the meeting of the American Educational Research Association, San Diego, CA.

Berch, D. B., & Wagster, M. V. (2004). Future directions in cognitive aging research: Perspectives from the National Institute on Aging. In R. A. Dixon, L. Backman, & L. Nilsson (Eds.), *New frontiers in cognitive aging* (pp. 333–355). New York: Oxford University Press.

Friedman, S. J., & Baldwin, W. (1990). Scientist-administrators at the National Institute of Child Health and Human Development as contributors to the scientific enterprise. *American Psychologist, 45,* 54–57.

Galvin, R. (1998). Science roadmaps. *Science, 280,* 803.

Sternberg, R. J. (2003). Obtaining a research grant: The view from the applicant. In J. M. Darley, M. P. Zanna, & H. L. Roediger, III (Eds.), *The compleat academic: A career guide* (2nd ed., pp. 169–184). Washington, DC: American Psychological Association.

CHAPTER 12

Communicating and Disseminating Your Applied Research Findings to the Public

Mary Ann McCabe, PhD
George Washington University School of Medicine
George Mason University

Andrea Browning, MPA
American Youth Policy Forum

Introduction

It is extremely important for developmental scientists to learn to share their research beyond academic journals. In many cases developmental science can be applied to improving children and families' well-being. Sommer (2006) has encouraged behavioral science researchers generally to strive for "dual dissemination" to both the academic world and various practical users of research knowledge. As he noted, "There is no single best outlet for all types of studies" (Sommer, 2006, p. 957). Among the possible goals for sharing developmental science beyond the academic audience are to inform the lay public, often through the mass media; to inform educational, health, mental health, legal, or other practice; to inform policy, at the local, state, and federal levels; to increase science literacy and enhance public awareness of the benefits of developmental science for public well-being; and to reinforce the importance of funding for developmental science. These goals are often overlapping. For example, translating research for practice, policy, or other public benefit is increasingly important to justify federal funding.

There is also a range of intermediary groups, or "knowledge brokers," involved in dissemination of developmental research, including think tanks, advocacy organizations, professional and science associations, university press offices, and journalists. These intermediaries have the credibility to disseminate research to policy makers and practitioners and are also trusted sources of research for the media and, therefore, the public. Working with intermediaries can greatly enhance a researcher's ability to reach different audiences. Many of the same skills and considerations are helpful in translating research for use by any of these groups.

The Society for Research in Child Development (SRCD) is one such intermediary in sharing research to educate the public and to inform practice and policy (McCabe, in press). It was founded by the National Research Council in 1933 with three goals: to advance research in child development, to foster an interdisciplinary consideration of substantive and methodological problems in the field of child development, and to encourage applications of research findings to improve children's and families' lives. The current SRCD strategic plan emphasizes dissemination of developmental science for the public, practice and policy, and it has a range of activities and products devoted to these aims.

This chapter will introduce developmental scientists to the key considerations for sharing research for practice, policy, and the public through the media. After describing the broad challenges for dissemination to nonacademic audiences, special attention will be paid to each of these three target audiences. We conclude with a list of recommendations to follow when sharing research beyond academic outlets.

Challenges

In preparing to disseminate your research more widely, it is critical for you to first clearly decide your *purpose*, from which you can determine the appropriate *audience*. Then it is critical to know that audience, in terms of its information needs, where science fits among its sources of knowledge, how/where it tends to learn new information, and the best timing for sharing your work. When disseminating research, it may be helpful for researchers to think of themselves as educators and to frame information with the needs of the specific audience ("adult learners") in mind.

To achieve your aims for dissemination to nonacademic audiences, it is important to accept, and work to overcome, five significant challenges. First, and perhaps most important for career planning, the academic reward and incentive structure does not usually recognize this type of dissemination activity. Landry, Amara, and Lamari (2001), as well as McCall and Groark (2000), both highlight this point. Career milestones such as promotion and tenure require you to think long term about the best timing for your investment in this type of dissemination activity and to be prudent about effective strategies for doing so.

Second, scientists are faced with challenges that stem from differences between nonacademic outlets and peer-reviewed journals, in terms of content, language, format, and length. For dissemination to be effective, you need to become familiar with specific outlets that reach a preferred target audience and to enhance your skills in translating science for the lay audience. It is important to recognize that research is more subject to misinterpretation outside the safety of scientific outlets and to take steps to ensure scientific accuracy to the greatest extent possible. Third, there are an unprecedented number of access points for the lay public to obtain research now. In addition to traditional sources such as books, newspapers, magazines, and local news networks, people are increasingly accessing scientific information through cable news channels, satellite radio, and Internet sources such as blogs and Web sites. The Internet enables the public to "cut out the middleman" and bypass traditional news sources. This enhances the rapid diffusion of research, but also reduces the amount of control that the researcher maintains over who obtains the information and in what form.

Fourth, it is easy for the *credibility* of research, and the researcher, to be questioned by nonscientific users, not on scientific grounds but rather on the basis of concerns such as bias, self-promotion, or lack of match between research variables and real-world contexts. Finally, as Shonkoff (2000) has aptly described, there are inherent cultural differences in the framing of "knowledge" and "evidence" in the cultures of science, practice, and policy. It is precisely because of these important cultural differences that we will devote the following three sections to highlight the issues in dissemination for the different target audiences of practice, policy, and the media.

Sharing Research for Practice

What is the process of disseminating research to practice?

There is a large and growing body of literature regarding sharing research for practice. Terms like "evidence-based practice," "knowledge utilization," and "knowledge transfer" reflect that the emphasis has moved beyond *passive dissemination* of research to *uptake* by practitioners. Understanding the process by which research knowledge is actually applied to practice (rather than ignored) has become an area of scholarship in its own right— sometimes called "implementation science." This complex field is beyond the scope of this chapter, but the reader is encouraged to explore it more fully to develop special expertise in effectively bridging science and practice. Here we will merely introduce the young investigator to the area of sharing research for the target audience of practitioners.

How do the policy and practice audiences differ from academic peer-reviewed journals and what are the implications for writing and disseminating research findings? What is a good model for dissemination and integration of highly scientific findings within traditionally applied knowledge settings? Given the large number of interventions available today, what can researchers do to make their contributions stand out?

There is literature about translating research to practice in a variety of fields that draw upon developmental science, including education, early childhood education, community-based programs, health promotion/prevention, medicine/health care, mental health, behavioral medicine, child welfare, and substance abuse. Unfortunately, the knowledge gained in one field is not easily shared with another, due to "silos" in the scientific journals, funders, agencies/organizations, services, service delivery systems, social networks, and professional outlets across these fields (McCabe, 2008). Further, in many cases it is not possible to make generalizations from one field to the next, since effective dissemination is so highly specialized for a given target audience and *context*. Consider, for example, that a process that might be effective for sharing developmental science with early childhood teachers may not work well for sharing research with mental health practitioners. The appropriate tools, processes, and venues for sharing research differ according to the practitioners' resources for obtaining information, opportunities for professional development, practice guidelines, supervisory and administrative oversight, and organizational systems.

There are still generalizations that can be drawn for sharing research for practice, particularly in terms of the challenges for doing so. The fragmentation of research, on a continuum from basic to applied to translational, can make it difficult to apply to practice. Across that continuum there are questions about what quality of *evidence* is sufficient to share with users. As Winton (2006) has reminded, "Clearly, not every research finding should be widely disseminated" (p. 79). Referring to education research, Lyon and Esterline (2007) have commented, "The consequences of disseminating research information of questionable quality and relevance to schools, teachers, parents, and policymakers are devastating" (p. 332).

Even for the gold standard of evidence for practice, the randomized controlled trial (RCT), concerns are raised by practitioners that external validity is often compromised for internal validity; that is, there is insufficient attention paid in the research to real-world settings and constraints, which in turn makes translation for practice difficult (American Psychological Association, 2008; Glasgow et al., 2006; Kazdin, 2008). Further, as Chambers has emphasized, "potential users need support for understanding the conditions under which the practices have been evaluated before choosing to adopt them within a particular service setting" (2007, p. 367). Glasgow and his colleagues (2006) have recently called for enhanced reporting of external validity factors "from which to judge the feasibility and cost-efficiency of replication in diverse settings and populations" (p. 106).

Similarly, program evaluation research, or other research that is closely tied to aspects of practice in real settings, varies in its readiness for application. As McCall, Groark, and Nelkin (2004) have noted, "Programs are not simply proven or not proven but rather have evidence that supports their effectiveness to varying degrees of certitude ... not all evidence is equal" (p. 333). Ideally, the research is informed by practice from the outset, for "practice-based evidence" rather than just "evidence-based practice" (e.g., Glasgow et al., 2006; Winton, 2006). In short, the young investigator must be certain of how their work fits into the larger body of research knowledge in the area, how it fits in real-world settings, and delineate realistic implications for practice according to the strengths and limitations of their study question and design.

Chambers (2007) has discussed the importance of "packaging" and "framing" in sharing research for practice: "Scientists often present evidence in ways they find compelling without considering whether clinicians require more support for interpreting the evidence the same way" (p. 368). He has also described criteria that have been proposed to determine whether research information will impact practice, including "relevance, timeliness, clarity, credibility, replicability, and acceptability" (p. 370). It is always preferable to share not a single study but a body of knowledge. For this reason, systematic reviews (and meta-analyses) may be ideal for bridging science and practice. "Users of the research literature seem to appreciate that summarizing findings across research studies using different settings and populations can provide more reliable and nuanced information ... than can a single study" (Trudeau & Davidson, 2007, p. 300).

A final challenge to be discussed is that the best available research evidence is merely one source of "knowledge" for the practitioner. As Winton (2006) has emphasized, "Practitioner values, beliefs, and experiences are valued sources of evidence that weigh heavily in decision making" (p. 93). She warns that practitioners may judge the utility of research on the basis of whether the results are practical, easy to understand, and congruent with their experience. Therefore, she suggests that intermediaries in a particular field might be needed to enhance effective dissemination: "Knowledge mediators play an especially important role as 'gatekeepers' of knowledge in that they are often entrusted to impart or share best available research findings and facilitate the *integration* [emphasis added] of that knowledge with wisdom and values" (p. 96).

Sharing Research for Policy

What are the best strategies for meeting the challenges of translating research to policy?

Like the application area of practice, there is a growing body of literature regarding sharing research for policy. (Again we will focus on the dissemination and translation of research, rather than cover the complex processes of knowledge utilization.) Some important observations can be generalized for dissemination of research at both the federal and state/local levels. First, a number of authors have described the challenges involved in sharing research for policy. Weiss (1980) has described the different frames of reference that scientists and policy makers employ to judge information as "knowledge" and to judge the trustworthiness of different sources of knowledge. Shonkoff (2000) has discussed the different rules of evidence and different degrees of influence from ideology and values: "Scientists generate data to advance knowledge. Policymakers mobilize information to support an agenda … science competes with values and 'common sense'" (p. 181). Choi et al. (2005) have also discussed the different "goals, attitudes toward information, languages, perceptions of time, and career paths" (p. 632) for scientists and policy makers.

How do the agendas of researchers and policy makers differ? How do the policy and practice audiences differ from academic peer-reviewed journals and what are the implications for writing and disseminating research findings?

Cohn (2006) has emphasized the importance of "policy windows" or the changing context of political and socioeconomic forces for decision makers. He stresses "policy-making being a more pragmatic pursuit than academic research—policymakers tend to search for *an* answer rather than *the* answer" (p. 13). Both Chelimsky (1991) and Cohn (2006) have noted that the challenges for bringing science to policy are inherent in a democratic society. As Cohn points out, "Even if academics are unanimous in their views, they are only one group with one form of knowledge trying to influence the policy process … democratic political processes are in fact a mechanism for reconciling multiple truths, or at least for selecting among them" (p. 20).

The literature also describes the various roles and uses for research in the policy-making process. Research can be used *conceptually* to (a) define a problem and "create an appetite for scientific information about it" (Huston, 2008, p. 8); and (b) warn that something is not going well, or provide direction for improving programs and policies (Weiss, 1988). Research can be used

strategically to (a) mobilize support, either from allies or opponents (Weiss, 1988), and reinforce commitment to a decision and
reduce uncertainties; (b) influence what issues are placed on the
policy agenda, how they are prioritized, which policy options
are considered, and what criteria are considered (Weiss, 1980);
or (c) legitimate decisions that are being made on other grounds
(Landry et al., 2001; Lavis, Robertson, Woodside, McLeod, &
Abelson, 2003; Weiss, 1980). Finally, from a *legislative* stand-
point, research can be used to (a) create legislation, regulations, or
government-funded programs; and (b) determine how legislators
vote on legislation that creates programs, reauthorizes programs,
or appropriates money. Cohn (2006) has clarified that the impact
of science on policy is best seen as "informing" policy making,
and usually through "schools of thought" rather than the work
of individual scientists. Weiss (1988) has introduced the notion
of "enlightenment," whereby ideas stemming from research can
help to inform policy simply by coming into "currency" with both
policy makers and interest groups.

Chelimsky (1991) has outlined the four types of decisions for
which policy makers might actively seek research: policy development; program development; policy and program monitoring; and policy and program evaluation. She has also described
three types of "mismatches" that prevent research from informing policy decisions, due to constraints on either the research or
the decision: (a) when political forces are overwhelming; (b) when
scientific information is sought, but the resources for, or context of, the research prohibit the necessary type of information;
and (c) when the best available research allows only inconclusive
answers. Regarding the latter, Chelimsky highlights, "In many
cases the question that most needs a response is precisely the one
that researchers cannot answer" (p. 228).

Huston (2005) has pointed out that the ideal research for the
policy audience may be "policy research," which she defined as
"framing questions around issues that policy can address; using
rigorous and multiple methods that inform policy; designing studies that produce information in a form that policy makers can use
and understand; considering costs and relative benefits of different
policy options; and being cautious about offering interpretations
that go beyond the data" (p. 3). She further emphasizes that for
research to be usable for policy, it may need to include information
about causal variables, about thresholds for good or bad outcomes,

and about the significance of effect sizes. Lavis and his colleagues (2003) have argued that "actionable messages" should be shared from a body of research knowledge, with a single study placed in context. Further, they caution that "not all research can or should have an impact. Some bodies of research knowledge will not generate a 'take-home' message, because either the research has no apparent application for decision-makers or the findings are not conclusive" (p. 223).

At the same time, McCall and Groark (2000), like Huston (2005, 2008), have emphasized that scholars should ensure dissemination of science relevant to policy. "In terms of public policy, the consequence of scholars failing to disseminate their knowledge is sometimes not simply that policy is formulated without information but rather that it is made with bad, wrong, or improperly interpreted information" (McCall & Groark, 2000, p. 201). McCall and Green (2004) have outlined the necessary steps and special expertise for effective dissemination for policy. Similarly, Sharpe (2007) has emphasized the importance of understanding the target audience (agency, committee, or legislator), how they typically get information, how they make decisions, and what timing would be useful for sharing given research. Lavis et al. (2003) have recommended that the strategy for dissemination needs to be fine-tuned according to the decisions audience members face and the environments they operate in. They pose questions to consider for deciding who to target with research information: Who can act on the basis of particular research knowledge? Who can influence them? With whom can you expect to have the most success and with what message? They note that sometimes multiple audiences should be targeted, with specific messages for each. Albert and Brown (2007) have advised that the researcher should anticipate questions about the research in advance and develop more than one product for dissemination: "a one-page overview, a five-page summary providing more details, and the full report for those few who have the time and desire to read through detailed findings" (p. 271). However, they caution that it is often difficult for those closest to the research to create brief descriptions, being steeped as they are in the details; this is often easier for intermediaries to do.

A final area of this literature addresses the mechanisms by which research makes its way to policy makers, even when they are not seeking it. Weiss (1988) has outlined at least five routes by which research comes to light: (a) information from policy staff; (b) reports from expert panels; (c) media coverage; (d) information relayed by intermediaries, such as advocacy groups and science organizations; and (e) research knowledge shared by the network of people within and outside government who have expertise on a particular issue.

One mechanism in this list worth elaboration is the role of intermediaries or knowledge brokers (noted earlier in regard to sharing research for practice). Cohn (2006) has argued that when academics make the findings of their research accessible to intermediaries, they improve their chances of influencing public policy. Knowledge brokers can also protect individual researchers from the risks they would otherwise face by becoming involved in advocacy efforts. Specifically, researchers can be perceived as a less reliable source of information and lose credibility if they promote their individual research with the policy audience. "Legislators can be suspicious of academics who come bearing data" (Weiss, 1988, p. 14). Because they represent a body of research, scientific discipline, or field of inquiry, science organizations (as knowledge brokers) can be perceived as trustworthy sources, provided that they remain bipartisan and objective. As Huston (2005) pointed out, "Professional organizations can serve as filters to help the public and policymakers identify reliable, high quality research findings" (p. 12). Landry et al. (2001) have suggested that knowledge brokers are also cost-effective, since they possess the necessary skills, products, and venues to effectively share research with policy makers. The costs of these activities can otherwise be high, relative to the actual demand, for any single investigator. Lavis et al. (2003) have similarly noted that establishing credibility and learning about decision-making environments can require a significant investment of time and financial resources.

Recall that Weiss (1988) also listed media coverage as a mechanism for sharing research for policy: "Policymakers know that the same story reaches all the other players in the policy game. They will be asked about it. They had better know about it" (p. 13). Similarly, McCall and Groark (2000) have argued for the critical role of the media for sharing science for policy: "The media tend to establish society's agenda … research information must be communicated through the media if it is to be part of the public decision process" (p. 201).

Finally, it is worth noting some additional considerations for sharing research at the state/local level. Albert and Brown (2007) have described three reasons why researchers may want to pay particularly careful attention to state policies and to foster relationships with state policy makers: "First, it is easier to reach state-level decision makers than national ones. Second, states play a critical role in determining *what* various projects, issues and concerns get funded and what level of funding each receives. When it comes to spending money, the rubber usually meets the road at the state level. Third, states often serve as the 'laboratories' where new and innovative policies are hatched" (p. 267). Among their recommendations to investigators, Albert and Brown emphasize "nothing tends to resonate as strongly with state-level leaders as research that contains a local component" (p. 272). A particularly effective approach for sharing research with state policy makers is illustrated by the Family Impact Seminars, which are a series of seminars, briefing reports, and follow-up activities that are aimed to bring research concerning families to public policies (Bogenschneider, Olson, Linney, & Mills, 2000). The topics are determined, in part, by the needs of the policy makers. In turn, the scholars seek feedback from the policy-maker participants to learn about the relative usefulness of research as a source of knowledge for this audience.

Sharing Research With the Public Through the Media

Once researchers identify important associations that influence children's development, how can they effectively disseminate these findings to practitioners and policy makers?

Communicating research to the public is not dissimilar from communicating research to policy audiences. Put simply, both audiences want to know what the research means and why it is important. Though the Internet has made research directly accessible to the public, researchers are often required to work with members of the media to convey findings to the public, an activity that is often daunting to them. There is scant research on how the public is affected by, and makes use of, news reports of research (Entwistle, 1995); however, much consideration has been given to the interactions between researchers and the media.

Much of the literature highlights the perceived cultural rift between scientists and journalists and addresses the negative stereotypes held by scientists about the inaccuracies of media reporting. Within the science community, the media is thought to be attracted to controversy. Sharing findings with the media may feel like turning over control of one's work to a reporter, which McCall equates to the scientist then becoming a subject in the media's data collection (McCall, Gregory, & Murray, 1984). Close involvement with the media might also put researchers at risk of "becoming suspect as serious scientists" (Phillips, 2002, p. 219). It is no wonder that many behavioral scientists have worried that cooperation with the media is "fraught with peril" (McCall & Stocking, 1982, p. 985). Whereas behavioral scientists select research questions for what McCall and Stocking (1982) refer to as reasons of theoretical importance, journalists are beholden by the public to report what is interesting or may relate to current events in the news. Additionally, researchers often worry that media coverage oversimplifies the science, leading to inaccuracies; however these errors are often omissions rather than incorrect statements (McCall & Stocking, 1982). Journalists face strict word limits and airtime constraints that make it impossible to include the caveats and qualifying statements that are often found in research reports (Entwistle, 1995).

Findings show that there are more similarities between scientists and journalists than each group perceives. When a survey asked scientists and journalists from different disciplines to rank the importance of accuracy, interest to readers, usefulness to readers, prompt publication, and uniqueness, both groups ranked all five of these items identically (Tichenor, Olien, Harrison, & Donohue as cited in McCall & Stocking, 1982). Also, in a recent survey of international scientists, though the respondents were critical of journalists, "they assessed their personal interactions with journalism quite positively" (Peters et al., 2008, p. 205).

Many scientists are unsure about whether their research will be seen as newsworthy by journalists. Tom Siegfried writes: "The newsworthiness of behavioral science is judged by the same three primary criteria as everything else: Is it new? Is it important? Is it interesting?" (2007, p. 151). He adds: "In the minds of many reporters, 'new' means 'not reported in the general news media yet'" (p. 152). According to Rachel Jones of National Public Radio, "The nexus between an issue researchers spend decades studying and one news organizations consider worthy of coverage can be boiled down to a few simple questions ... How does it affect real people? ... Is there a solution? ... In other words, 'What's the point?'" (2007, p. 142). Answering these simple questions may be helpful when considering whether your research is suited for media dissemination.

Despite the challenges of working with the media, scientists have much to gain from helping to make research available to the public. In the previously mentioned international survey of scientists, respondents cited "increasing the public's appreciation of science" as the most important benefit to working with the media (Peters et al., 2008, p. 204). Other goals such as achieving "a more positive public attitude toward research" and the motivation of "a better-educated general public" were also identified as benefits by nearly all scientists surveyed (93% and 92% percent, respectively). Building public understanding of research can also ultimately build support for public financing of scientific research. There is an added responsibility for researchers when results are "politically sensitive, controversial, or potentially inflammatory" (Phillips, 2002, p. 220). Researchers can be an important voice to help the public understand what conclusions can and cannot be made from the research.

Though having the skills to work effectively with the media can enhance the reach of research, journalists do not look favorably on promotion of one's own research. The general practice for conveying research to the media is through press releases of peer-reviewed, published work. An analysis of newspaper stories found that 84% of stories referred to journal articles mentioned in press releases (de Semir, Ribas, & Revuelta, 1998). University press offices are equipped to work with researchers to issue a press release and can help reach local journalists who take a particular interest in work being conducted at a local institution. Journalists rely on peer review to show them what is high-quality research and will generally cite the scientific publication, if not the name and affiliation of the lead researcher, in their coverage. In particular, journalists with no specialized science training who are less able to judge the credibility or importance of research rely on the peer-review process to help them select and develop stories (Entwistle, 1995).

With all of this in mind, we offer some general considerations for researchers who choose to work with the media. First, when it comes to reporting science for the public, not all journalists are created equal. General interest reporters may take up a story related to behavioral science or child development, but may have no relevant background for understanding the science. It may be helpful to a researcher to understand the degree of science-related expertise held by the reporter and recognize that it might be minimal. Second, researchers should also consider what type of interaction with the media they are willing to participate in. Interviews for print publications allow for more lengthy discussion and clarification, as opposed to a live radio or television interview, which necessitates precision and brevity, and may allow for questions from the public. This question-and-answer format may invite controversial or difficult topics. We have also included a list of tips for preparing for a media interview at the end of this chapter.

I am very interested in serving as a bridge in this gap between research, policy, and people. How does one facilitate serving in such a role?

Many new investigators want to ensure that findings are not exaggerated or taken out of context. Unfortunately, it is impossible to completely prevent this from happening. According to Phillips, "There will always be irresponsible (and ill-informed) journalists ... who distort, exaggerate, or selectively report scientific evidence for personal ... gain" (2002, p. 221). There are some general guidelines to keep in mind to encourage accuracy in coverage for the public, however. When discussing a set of findings, it is helpful to frame for a journalist the significance within the larger body of research and explain the implications for different users of information. When SRCD issues press releases for papers in the journal *Child Development*, the findings are contextualized by providing background such as relevant findings of prior research, as well as implications of the findings for different information users such as parents, teachers, legislators, or program administrators. Keep in mind that journalists may not have the training to interpret what technical findings (e.g., effect sizes) mean. Be sure to help reporters understand what can and cannot be inferred from your results. For example, consider a study that finds statistically significant differences in children's behavior, but this variation is still within the normal range. The observed differences might be statistically significant, but how important are the differences? Explaining the importance of these results would provide an opportunity to educate journalists and the public. Finally, nonscientific audiences often do not distinguish between correlation and causality. Be very clear about this aspect of your findings when talking to journalists.

Overall, a researcher's success in communicating science for the public depends on the ability to write and talk about his or her research in a way that highlights why the findings matter to the public. The editors of *Child Development* journal require manuscript authors to submit a public summary of their paper in order to translate for the lay audience and contextualize the significance of their work. Public summaries introduce a study's findings in nontechnical language, briefly mention how the study was conducted, discuss how the findings advance our understanding of the research area, and contextualize what this all means for the public (e.g., Do the findings have implications for learning, public programs, or parenting?). The SRCD Office for Policy and Communications often uses these public summaries when creating press releases. Researchers can expand the reach and use of their work by learning how to translate, contextualize, and discuss the relevance of scientific findings for public audiences.

Are there institutions or organizations that can help foster translational research activities? What range of activities or sources exist for disseminating applied research findings on children and families, and how should a researcher evaluate those different opportunities?

Conclusion

This chapter has outlined the most important issues to consider for sharing developmental science for practice, policy, and the public. It is imperative to think in advance about the challenges involved. It is then critical to identify a clear sense of purpose and determine the audience that is best suited to meet those aims. Each target audience will have important cultural nuances regarding science as a source of knowledge and distinct processes and timing that dictate how to proceed with dissemination for an effective message.

What follows are our key recommendations for sharing developmental science with lay audiences:

- Begin with research questions that are sensitive to the needs of your target audience, whether it be the public, practitioners, or policy makers; ideally partner with them in collaborative research so as to maximize the applicability of your research.
- Develop relationships with users (e.g., media, practitioners, policy makers) to tailor your dissemination.
- Become increasingly familiar with creative outlets to reach your preferred target audience, such as newsletters, professional development events, and so forth.
- Depending on your audience, seek to establish your credibility as a source of research information by
  - Identifying yourself very clearly in all your dissemination, so that your credentials (name, university, research funder) can be established.
  - Demonstrating unbiased reporting of research and the absence of self-promotion.
  - Disseminating only peer-reviewed research, preferably accepted for publication in a respected academic journal, proceeding more cautiously with material that has been peer reviewed for conference presentations.
  - Demonstrating an appreciation of the needs of your audience.

- Develop skills in translation and derive brief summaries of complex research.
  - These skills are included in training opportunities such as policy fellowships and media training workshops.

- Seek mentoring for dissemination, particularly for research that is either particularly important for the public or controversial.
- For ethical reasons, ensure that a single study is put in context with the larger body of literature.
  - Consider doing systematic reviews of your subject area for wider dissemination.

- According to your research design and the larger body of knowledge, carefully consider the implications of your research for the public, practice, and policy.
  - Specify limitations as necessary so the user can determine how applicable research is to them (e.g., causality, conditions under which an intervention was studied, etc.).

- Where appropriate, include personal stories or anecdotes that "bring your research to life."
- Anticipate users' questions, and prepare for those questions you particularly wish to answer.
- Prepare for timely dissemination whenever the opportunity arises.
- Become familiar with the range of intermediaries, or knowledge brokers, including think tanks, advocacy groups, professional networks, and professional and scientific associations, and their outlets for dissemination of research.

And some additional guidelines for media interviews:

- Notify your university press office if you are asked to talk with the media.
- Prepare a short summary of the key findings for your own reference. What would you say if you had only one minute to say it?
- Know the timeframe of the journalist (i.e., Is their deadline today at 5:00 or next Thursday?).
- Obtain information from the journalist:
  - What do they already know about the research area?
  - Who is the audience for the piece, and what will this audience want to know?

- Be able to quickly summarize what is already known about the research area and how the featured findings contribute to or contradict past findings.
- If you are asked to comment on an area beyond your expertise, do not hesitate to refer a journalist to a colleague who may have more relevant expertise.

- Use lay language, rather than technical terminology, to discuss your research.
- Do not say anything that you do not want quoted.
- Overall, be succinct!

The process of sharing research beyond academia is a challenging and gratifying endeavor, and the necessary types of collaboration promise to enrich your research as well. It is worth devoting time to the development of special expertise and networks for this purpose over the course of your research career. As Shonkoff (2000) has championed, "A commitment to 'cross-cultural' translation offers a potent strategy for enhancing both the generation of new research on child development and the application of cutting-edge knowledge to make a difference in the lives of children and their families" (p. 187).

References

Albert, B., & Brown, S. S. (2007). State your case: working with state governments. In M. K. Welch-Ross & L. Fasig (Eds.), *Handbook on communicating and disseminating behavioral science* (pp. 267–280). Thousand Oaks, CA: Sage.

American Psychological Association. (2008). *Disseminating evidence-based practice for children and adolescents: A systems approach to enhancing care.* Washington, DC: Author.

Bogenschneider, K., Olson, J. R., Linney, K. D., & Mills, J. (2000). Connecting research and policymaking: Implications for theory and practice from the family impact seminars. *Family Relations, 49,* 327–339.

Chambers, D. (2007). Disseminating and implementing evidence-based practices for mental health. In M. K. Welch-Ross & L. Fasig (Eds.), *Handbook on communicating and disseminating behavioral science* (pp. 365–390). Thousand Oaks, CA: Sage.

Chelimsky, E. (1991). On the social science contribution to governmental decision-making. *Science, 254,* 226–231.

Choi, B. C. K., Pang, T., Lin, V., Puska, P., Sherman, G., Goddard, M., ... Clottey, C. (2005). Can scientists and policymakers work together? *Journal of Epidemiology and Community Health, 59,* 632–637.

Cohn, D. (2006). Jumping into the political fray: Academics and policymaking. *IRPP Policy Matters, 7*(3).

de Semir, V., Ribas, C., & Revuelta, G. (1998). Press releases of science journal articles and subsequent newspaper stories on the same topic. *Journal of the American Medical Association, 280*(3), 294–295.

Entwistle, V. (1995). Reporting research in medical journals and newspapers. *British Medical Journal, 310*(6984), 920–924.

Glasgow, R. E, Green, L. W., Klesges, L. M., Abrams, D. B., Fisher, E. B., Goldstein, M. G., ... Orleans, C.T. (2006). External validity: We need to do more. *Annals of Behavioral Medicine, 31*, 105–108.

Huston, A. C. (2005). Connecting the science of child development to public policy. *Social Policy Report, 19*(4), 3–18.

Huston, A. C. (2008). From research to policy and back. *Child Development, 79*, 1–12.

Jones, R. (2007). National public radio. In M. K. Welch-Ross, & L. Fasig (Eds.), *Handbook on communicating and disseminating behavioral science* (pp. 141–149). Thousand Oaks, CA: Sage.

Kazdin, A. E. (2008). Evidence-based treatment and practice. *American Psychologist, 63*, 146–159.

Landry, R., Amara, N., & Lamari, M. (2001). Climbing the ladder of research utilization. *Science Communication, 22*, 396–422.

Lavis, J., Robertson, D., Woodside, J. M., McLeod, C. B., & Abelson, J. (2003). How can research organizations more effectively transfer research knowledge to decision-makers? *The Millbank Quarterly, 81*, 221–248.

Lyon, G. L., & Esterline, E. (2007). Advancing education through research. In M. K. Welch-Ross & L. Fasig (Eds.), *Handbook on communicating and disseminating behavioral science* (pp. 317–339). Thousand Oaks, CA: Sage.

McCabe, M. A. (2008). *The silo problem and questions to consider—Response to more than workshops, websites, and syntheses: Busting assumptions and building research-practice connections.* Paper presented at the Head Start National Research Conference, Washington, DC.

McCabe, M. A. (in press). Sharing knowledge for policy: The role of science organizations as knowledge brokers. In E. Banister, B. Leadbeater & E. A. Marshall (Eds.), *Knowledge Translation in Context: University-Community, Policy and Indigenous Approaches.* Toronto, Canada: University of Toronto Press.

McCall, R. B., & Green, B. (2004). Beyond the methodological gold standards of behavioral research: Considerations for practice and policy. *Social Policy Report, 18*(2), 3–19.

McCall, R. B., Gregory, T. G., & Murray, J. P. (1984). Communicating developmental research results to the general public through television. *Developmental Psychology, 20*(1), 45–54.

McCall, R. B., & Groark, C. J. (2000). The future of applied child development research and public policy. *Child Development, 71*, 197–204.

McCall, R. B., Groark, C. J., & Nelkin, R. P. (2004). Integrating developmental scholarship and society: From dissemination and accountability to evidence-based programming and policies. *Merrill-Palmer Quarterly, 50*, 326–340.

McCall, R. B., & Stocking, S. H. (1982). Between scientists and public: Communicating psychological research through mass media. *American Psychologist, 37*(9), 985–995.

Peters, H. P., Brossard, D., de Cheveigne, S., Dunwoody, S., Kallfass, M., Miller, S., & Tsuchida, S. (2008). Interactions with the mass media. *Science, 321,* 204–205.

Phillips, D. (2002). Collisions, logrolls, and psychological science. *American Psychologist, 57*(3), 219–221.

Sharpe, A. (2007). Working with the federal government. In M. K. Welch-Ross & L. Fasig (Eds.), *Handbook on communicating and disseminating behavioral science* (pp. 251–266). Thousand Oaks, CA: Sage.

Shonkoff, J. P. (2000). Science, policy and practice: Three cultures in search of a shared mission. *Child Development, 71,* 181–187.

Siegfried, T. (2007). Newspapers. In M. K. Welch-Ross & L. Fasig (Eds.), *Handbook on communicating and disseminating behavioral science* (pp. 151–159). Thousand Oaks, CA: Sage.

Sommer, R. (2006). Dual dissemination: Writing for colleagues and the public. *American Psychologist, 61,* 955–958.

Trudeau, K. J., & Davidson, K. W. (2007). Disseminating behavioral medicine research to practitioners: Recommendations for researchers. In M. K. Welch-Ross & L. Fasig (Eds.), *Handbook on communicating and disseminating behavioral science* (pp. 295–316). Thousand Oaks, CA: Sage.

Weiss, C. (1980). *Social science research and decision-making.* New York: Columbia University Press.

Weiss, C. (1988). Evaluation for decisions: Is anybody there? Does anybody care? *Evaluation Practice, 9,* 5–19.

Winton, P. J. (2006). The evidence-based practice movement and its effect on knowledge utilization. In B. Buysse & P. W. Welsey (Eds.), *Evidence-based practice in the early childhood field* (pp. 71–115). Washington, DC: Zero to Three.

CHAPTER 13

"I Am Pleased to Accept Your Manuscript"
Publishing Your Research on Child and Adolescent Development

Lynn S. Liben, PhD
The Pennsylvania State University–University Park

Introduction

To the outside world, it is probably perfectly plausible that I was asked to author a piece on publishing for this volume. Although I was not privy to the discussion that led to the invitation, it is not hard to guess that it was my editorship of the journal *Child Development* that lay behind it. At the risk of writing an inappropriately self-aggrandizing introduction to my own chapter, I acknowledge that I have, indeed, had a plethora of editorial experience. Prior to my 6-year editorship of *Child Development,* I was the associate editor and then the editor of the *Journal of Experimental Child Psychology* (spanning an 18-year period), I was the series editor of the Jean Piaget Society book series for 11 years, and I have served on various editorial boards. In addition, I have given many talks on "how to publish" and have published a variety of articles, editorials, books, and essays over the years.

But to the inside world (me), it is startling that I am writing this essay. To balance the self-aggrandizing first paragraph, I will confess that I did not always find writing easy. As a high school student, I finally quit the school newspaper because I hated the endless and immutable writing deadlines. As a freshman at Cornell, I dreaded Thursday nights because by 8:00 a.m. the next day (every week!) I had to have a two- to four-page essay typed and ready to hand in to my English teacher. As a brand new faculty member at the University of Rochester, I struggled for almost two years to turn my dissertation into an article. And for the first half-dozen years of my career, crafting an abstract to submit for a conference was a stressful weeklong job.

Happily, the first paragraph in the context of the second paragraph is not a sign of some deep-seated masochism that has led me to devote myself to something I despise. Instead it is a sign of my having come to love writing. It is true that I love conceptualizing research, collecting (at least some of the) data, devising coding systems (although I am quite happy to leave the tedium of their implementation to others), and the excitement of sitting down to analyze data and seeing what emerges. But I now also thrill over the process of turning prior stages of work into the written word. And I can now write a conference submission in roughly an hour.

The first lesson that I hope you take from this chapter is that even if you do not currently find writing rewarding or fun or easy, it may become so if you give it a chance. And even if you are beginning with a more positive frame of mind than did I, you can develop your writing skills more fully and enjoyably.

I am presuming that you have already completed the scholarship itself, and thus I have focused this chapter on the process of disseminating your work to others via publication, not on the process of developing and implementing the research itself (topics that are covered in other chapters of this book). My focus is on publishing articles in professional journals rather than, say, publishing popular books, textbooks, articles for popular magazines, briefing reports for agencies, or disseminating your work via other media. I also draw heavily on the discipline of psychology rather than other disciplines that are also relevant to developmental science (e.g., economics, sociology, pediatrics). Despite these foci, many of the points should apply across other publication outlets and disciplines.

I have organized the chapter so that it follows the sequence of steps you will encounter as you write a manuscript and continue through the review and publication process. First, I discuss some basic issues in approaching the writing project ("Motivating and Framing Your Manuscript"); second, I offer suggestions for the writing process itself ("Writing, Revising, and Revising Again"); third, I describe the process of editorial review, including not only the parts that you see as an author, but also the parts that operate behind the closed doors of editorial offices ("Demystifying and Managing the Review Process"); fourth, I discuss what happens once you receive a letter from the editor ("Reading and Responding to Editorial Decisions"); and, finally, I close with some suggestions to consider well after you have mastered the basics of the publication process ("In the Years Ahead").

In all cases, my comments are necessarily incomplete. Each individual topic deserves more discussion than can be included in a single chapter, and many topics relevant to successful publishing remain unaddressed. For example, to name only a few important but omitted topics, I have not addressed how to decide who should be included as an author and in what order authors should be named, how to write collaboratively with others, how to negotiate authorship when working with existing data sets or as part of large research groups, and under what circumstances similar ideas or data may be published in more than one venue. My advice is also undoubtedly somewhat idiosyncratic, having arisen from a unique collection of interests and experiences. In short, although this chapter provides a range of suggestions, it should be only one of many sources you explore as you seek to increase your enjoyment and success in writing and publishing.

Motivating and Framing Your Manuscript
Target Audiences

In addition to replacing any negative emotions (like viewing the writing process with fear and anxiety) with positive ones (like viewing it with a sense of excitement and opportunity), it is helpful to conceptualize your writing project in a way that works for you. The approach that works for me is conceptualizing the task before me as a puzzle (something akin to a jigsaw or a crossword puzzle) and a work of art (something akin to writing a short story or perhaps a representational painting with symmetry and balance). This framing allows me to enjoy (and justify to myself) searching for the organization, terminology, and turn of phrase that lead the pieces to fit together concisely, neatly, and—as best I can—elegantly, and it allows me to feel a sense of internal satisfaction with the product, whatever the critics may say. In some sense, then, it is important to serve yourself as audience by writing manuscripts that are true to your own passions with respect to both content and style.

But of course you are writing for others as well, and thus, before you can actually begin writing, you must have your audience in mind. Potential audiences will vary depending on the kind of work you are disseminating. I use two recent projects from my work as illustrations. One is a laboratory study (Myers & Liben, 2008) that examined children's developing understanding that an intentional agent assigns meaning to symbols (as when a cartographer assigns white squares on a map to stand for interstate exits). In this project research on children's developing understanding of intentional agents was of interest primarily for its implications for representational development. Thus, the target audience for this project is comprised of people who study various aspect of child development, especially those who focus on cognitive development in particular. Concentrations of such people are found within professional organizations such as the Society for Research in Child Development, the Developmental Psychology Division of the American Psychological Association (APA), the International Society for the Study of Behavioural Development, the Cognitive Development Society, and the Jean Piaget Society. It is true that anyone who relies on children's understanding of symbols (e.g., teachers, game designers, toy manufacturers) might ultimately profit from this research, but a single study of this kind, focused on basic theoretical questions of symbolic development and conducted in a laboratory setting, is not likely to be of immediate interest to an applied audience (although an article describing the findings in general terms and discussing implications for design issues might be a secondary route for dissemination).

The second example is an ongoing project on parent–child interactions at a museum exhibit on maps (Liben, 2009). Dyadic interactions are being studied in relation to the age of the child, gender (of parent and child), spatial skills (of parent and child), and qualities of the museum exhibits. This research also addresses questions specific to maps, asking, for example, how parents and children understand cardinal directions from

a compass rose symbol, and what they do when map orientation is atypical so that south, not north, is at the top of the
map. Given that this museum project is a complex, multifaceted
one that encompasses a range of theoretical and applied issues,
appropriate audiences include not only the developmental audiences mentioned earlier, but also people who study parenting,
design museum exhibits, study informal education, are geogra-
phers or geography educators, focus on gender studies, or are in
the field of education more generally. There are various professional organizations for each of these groups parallel to those
listed for developmental science.

Identifying Potential Journals

Most professional organizations produce one or more journals
that are distributed as part of membership, and thus, once you
have identified the target groups for your work, you have automatically identified a set of potential publication outlets. For
example, the professional organizations mentioned earlier with
respect to development and cognitive development (themselves
only a sample of organizations that could have been named) produce *Child Development, Monographs of the Society for Research
in Child Development, Perspectives on Child Development, Social
Policy Reports, Developmental Psychology, Human Development,
International Journal of Behavioural Development, Cognitive
Development,* and the *Journal of Cognitive Development.* In addition, many excellent journals are published completely apart from
professional organizations, typically as part of the journal division
of for-profit publishing houses. To continue using the research
project on representational development as an illustration, other
excellent journals to which manuscripts on the work could be
submitted include the *Journal of Experimental Child Psychology,
Developmental Science,* and the *Journal of Applied Developmental
Psychology.* Clearly the list of potential journals for the second
illustrative project would be even longer given that manuscripts
on this research could be suitable for journals in fields as diverse as
psychology, gender studies, geography, education, museum studies, and parenting.

How can you identify the range of options relevant to your
own work? One obvious avenue for identifying relevant journals
is to ask others who work in similar areas for advice. Another is
to examine the journals you drew from in developing your project.

If you used several sources from a single journal, it is likely that your work addresses an area of relevance to that journal. Another approach is to conduct a Web search with key words in the area of your research (e.g., using Google Scholar or your library resources), perhaps including the word "journal." Relevant journals are likely to appear in the list, either explicitly as journal Web sites, or implicitly as the outlets in which relevant research appears. Yet another route is to search via one of the relevant publication databases such as the Thomson ISI Web of Knowledge, which provides information on journals in science and in social science. This index provides lists of journals under broad topic areas (e.g., areas such as developmental psychology, education, and clinical psychology) and offers information about each that may help you in selecting a target journal, discussed next.

Selecting a Journal

There are three major kinds of considerations in selecting a publication target from your list of potential journals: first, the appropriateness of the journal for the substance of your work; second, the degree to which the journal meets your professional goals; and third, practical matters.

Substantive Fit

There are a number of ways to judge the question of substantive fit, all of which involve familiarizing yourself with each potential journal more thoroughly. An obvious starting place is to read the mission statement of the journal, which should explain the kinds of articles it seeks to publish. It is also useful to read at least a few articles in recent issues to make sure that the topics, scope, methods, populations, and traditions of the journal are well matched to those of your work. Also helpful is looking at the list of editors and any other published lists of editors or reviewers. Journals differ with respect to the specific terminology they use to refer to editors and standing reviewers (e.g., they may be referred to as associate editors, editorial board members, or consulting editors), but the basic rule of thumb is to look at the names listed on the journal masthead or the editorial page on the Web site. If you are familiar with at least some of the people named and believe that their work is at least somewhat related to yours, it is a reasonable indication that the journal is probably in the right ballpark for your work.

Professional Goals

There are various professional goals that you may have in seeking a publication outlet beyond the universal goal of getting your work into print. For example, if you wish to disseminate your work to a very broad audience, you may want to attempt to publish in journals that cover science in general (e.g., *Science* or *Nature*), or slightly more narrowly, those that cover psychological science in general (e.g., *American Psychologist*, *Psychological Science*). Instead you may wish to speak to a general developmental audience (as in, for example, *Child Development* or *Developmental Psychology*), or to still more specialized groups (e.g., *Social Development*, *Cognitive Development*). You may also have goals that relate to novelty. For example, at one end of this continuum you might find it particularly attractive to publish in a new, innovative journal that is establishing a new scientific niche. At the other end, you may find it appealing to publish in a well-established journal that offers widespread institutional subscriptions and more certainty that your article will remain archived well into the future.

You may also have goals inspired by your work setting. For example, many university departments and colleges use objective indicators of a journal's quality as part of their evaluations of faculty members' progress (e.g., for decisions about promotion, salaries, and honors). Thus, you may want to aim for a journal with a high citation index, high circulation, or with other criteria viewed as important by your institution (e.g., a high rejection rate, often viewed as an index of selectivity). One source of information on quality indicators like these is the ISI Web of Knowledge Journal Citation Reports (JCR) published by the Thomson Corporation. Its JCR Web site allows you to request journals that fit a particular subject category (e.g., education & educational research; family studies; health policy & services; educational psychology; developmental psychology). For each journal on the list that is returned there is annual information about "total cites" (the total number of citations that have been made to articles in that journal during the identified year), an "impact factor" (a ratio of the number of citations to the number of articles that appeared in that journal), the "immediacy index" (how long it takes before articles in that journal are cited), and the "cited half-life" (the median age of cited articles, with higher numbers typically perceived as better because they indicate their long-lasting impact; although lower numbers could be viewed positively as indicating quick attention to publications in that journal).

Of course, getting one's work accepted for publication in highly prestigious journals with high circulation, high impact ratings, and high rejection rates is difficult, and thus it is useful to be realistic about the quality of the journal to which you submit. It is fine to aim a bit high, but it makes little sense to submit to a journal that appears to have criteria that your work cannot meet. Such submissions will simply waste time and effort (yours in preparing the manuscript and then waiting for reviews; the editor's and reviewers' in arranging for reviews and then communicating the rejection). Again, it is important to read sample articles and try to assess the match to your potential article as well as possible.

Practical Matters

Another component of selecting a target journal involves practical matters. For example, journals differ markedly in how long they take to process manuscripts. Sometimes this information is available on the journal's Web site or in "information for authors" material. If not, it may be possible to get some sense of processing times from seeing whether articles published in a journal of interest include the dates of submission, revision, and acceptance. Another route is to call or write a note to the journal editorial office to ask the staff if it would be willing to give you some indication of the modal time to reach an editorial decision. Of course, even if a particular journal aims for a decision within a particular time, and even if the journal usually meets that goal, inevitably it will sometimes fail to do so, perhaps because of overdue reviews or idiosyncratic complications such as the illness of an action editor.

Like most things in life, there are trade-offs among these factors. For example, *Science* and *Psychological Science* are both highly prestigious publication outlets that reach broad audiences (across sciences and across subdisciplines of psychology, respectively), and each provides a speedy first-level editorial decision (i.e., a decision about whether it will be sent out for full review is made quickly, usually within a week or two). On the downside, however, journals like these allow only a small percentage of manuscripts through the initial filter (e.g., if you submit to *Science* you are far more likely to receive a quick rejection than news that your manuscript will be entered into the next step of the review process), and they usually have special requirements (e.g., very restrictive word limits), which mean that a manuscript rejected by that journal needs to be rewritten virtually from scratch before it can be submitted elsewhere.

Writing, Revising, and Revising Again

Getting Started

Having identified a journal, before beginning to write it is useful to reread the information for authors so that you keep the established parameters in mind. But knowing what you are aiming to do can carry you only so far. It can still be daunting to sit down to blank paper or screen. To help with this stage of writing, my advice is to read a book written by Anne Lamott titled *Bird by Bird* (1995). As explained on the back cover of the book, the title refers to an incident involving Lamott's father and her older brother, age 10 at the time. He was seated at the kitchen table, panicking over a project on birds that had been assigned three months earlier, due in school the very next day, and still not even begun. "Then my father sat down beside him, put his arm around my brother's shoulder, and said, 'Bird by bird, buddy. Just take it bird by bird.'" The message, of course, is to try to avoid overwhelming yourself by thinking about the enormity of the task and instead focus on one small, manageable step at a time. Bird by bird, section by section.

Although Lamott's book is aimed primarily at aspiring writers of fiction, much of it is just as applicable to aspiring writers of scientific journal articles. Among other tidbits, and with the hope that the volume editors will permit such language in the pages of this book, Lamott urges authors to write "shitty first drafts. All good writers write them. This is how they end up with good second drafts and terrific third drafts" (1995, p. 21). Of course, if your first drafts are elegant and professional that is great too. But the aim is to take the critical censor off your shoulder and not worry about the quality of your first draft so that you get something— anything—on paper (or screen). From there you have something to work with.

It is also helpful to remember that there is no law about where you begin. It thus makes good sense to begin with whichever part of the manuscript seems easiest to you so that you can feel a sense of accomplishment quickly. I, for example, often begin by writing the method section. There is no question about what was actually done, so the challenge (and, using the puzzle metaphor, the fun) is deciding how best to communicate the methodology to the reader so that both the overall structure and the details are clear and engaging. This comment about the reader segues into the next critical topic—taking the reader's perspective.

Perspective Taking 101

As you write, remember, you are writing for readers, importantly, a group that includes the editor and the reviewers. I will comment more about the details of the review process in the next section of this chapter, but even as you begin to frame your manuscript, it is important to keep reviewers' perspectives in mind, imagining yourself in their shoes. First, given that they are devoting time to your work largely for altruistic reasons, you want to make their jobs as easy and engaging as possible. This means attempting to introduce them to your work in a way that is intriguing and comprehensible. To be successful, it is critical to remember that readers and reviewers are not as immersed in and familiar with your work as you are. Imagine yourself hearing about this research for the first time. What terminology, methodology, and analytic strategies would be unfamiliar? Terms like *emotion regulation* or *theory of mind* or *attachment* or *mental rotation* are basic vocabulary to investigators working on these or related topics, but they are not necessarily known to your diverse readers and reviewers and must be defined, even if very briefly. Methods and tests whose purposes and acronyms are well known to you may be entirely unfamiliar to your reader. It is particularly critical to orient readers to basics if your work cuts across research areas. For example, to return to the illustrative museum study mentioned earlier, an article addressed to geography educators would not need to define *compass rose* but would need to define the spatial skill of *mental rotation*. An article addressed to cognitive psychologists would need the inverse. An article meant to reach both audiences would need to define both.

It is also important to imagine yourself in the role of critic. Reviewers are asked to evaluate the submission. They are trying to evaluate the importance of the work and the scientific quality of the work. With respect to the former, reviewers are unlikely to need to be convinced of the importance of the work if they are scholars working in a highly similar area of research, but such highly matched reviewers are the exception, not the rule. That is, you may have one reviewer who is an expert in your precise area of specialization, but you will almost certainly have at least one reviewer who is not, and your action editor—the person who is ultimately responsible for deciding on the fate of your submission—is particularly likely to fall outside of your specialization. Thus it is always important to begin by establishing why the particular area of your work is valuable, whether it is for theoretical or practical reasons (or both). As discussed in more detail later, it is helpful if your introduction and conclusions suggest, at least briefly, how your work is connected to domains that reach beyond your specialty area.

With respect to judging scientific quality, reviewers will be focusing on all components of the research—the clarity and tractability of the research question, the sample, the methods, the coding systems, the analyses, and, especially, the logical justification of whatever conclusions are offered. Thus, as you write, think about what concerns you would have if you were encountering this research for the first time and with a critical eye. No doubt you recognized some concerns as you planned and implemented your research, but for various reasons, you decided that the concerns were tolerable. For example, you might have seen the value of a larger or more diverse sample, of additional control groups, of the collection of longitudinal data after greater periods of time, or a more reliable coding system. Despite recognizing some limitations, you conducted the research and analyses. Perhaps you needed to balance ideal designs against limited resources (time, money, personnel), had to consider ethical and practical constraints (e.g., restrictions on what you could do based on what was permitted in light of parents, teachers, institutional review boards [IRBs], and your own sense of ethics), or faced some other kinds of practical constraints. Presumably you believe that there is much of value in your work, even despite its limitations. Why? Help your reader come to the same conclusion.

Although it is unwise to undercut your own work with an endless list of "limitations" like those often included in doctoral dissertations, it is wise to acknowledge key limitations as you go, explaining briefly why the work remains valuable despite them. What you are demonstrating is that you recognized and understood the limitations, that there is value in the work despite them, and that you have been careful to identify whatever limitations in conclusions might be necessary because of them.

Again, I will use the museum study described earlier as an example. As you may recall, the research was designed to observe parent–child interactions at a museum exhibit. Because it took place in an established children's museum, the sample was necessarily limited to families who had the financial resources, transportation access, time, and motivation to attend. In describing this work, it would be important to acknowledge that the sample is therefore not representative of the entire population of the city in which the museum was located, and thus that its findings cannot be generalized to parent–child interactions in general. Despite this limitation, it *can* provide information about the population of families who *do* choose to visit, and can offer insights into the way that museum exhibits are actually being used by families who visit.

It is also important to be prepared to recognize a fatal flaw in your work if it is there. That is, if in the course of writing you come to realize that there was, in fact, a serious and unacceptable flaw in sampling, methodology, or experimental design that makes it impossible to draw sound conclusions from the data, it is better to view the process as a learning experience, and, if circumstances permit, collect new or additional data that will overcome the problem before trying to disseminate the work.

Mastering the Genre

You are trying to master a *genre*, defined by *Merriam-Webster* (2008) as "a category of artistic, musical, or literary composition characterized by a particular style, form, or content." Probably the best way to develop a sense of the kind of writing that is appropriate is to read stacks of articles of the kind you are trying to produce. If you need to be convinced about the role of genre in writing, find several articles focused on the same substantive topic from different kinds of outlets. For example, look for articles on children's language or on friendships or on children's emotions in *Newsweek, The New York Times, The New Yorker, USA Today, Science, Developmental Psychology, The Young Child, The Elementary School Teacher,* and *Parents Magazine,* to name only some of the many sources in which you would be likely to find them. Although scholars of rhetoric and communication can probably offer formal analyses of how these differ, as a writer aiming for a particular genre, all you need to recognize is how different these articles are, and develop a good sense of the one appropriate for your target outlets. Fortunately, this job is made easier for us by the formulaic structure of empirical papers, at least within the discipline of psychology.

Thus, in addition to reading illustrative articles, you may also develop your expertise in the genre by reading material explicitly designed to teach it. One of the best resources is the *Publication Manual of the American Psychological Association* (APA, 2009). Most people think of the *Manual* merely as a reference book to consult for pesky details (Does the period go inside the quotation mark? Are units of measurement abbreviated? Are statistics italicized? Where do chapter page numbers go in the reference list?), but it is also a valuable resource on how to organize your article and on what information should be covered in which sections. Advice on scientific writing more generally is also helpful. There are often articles on writing in the general publications of scientific societies, for example, in *The Monitor*, published by the American Psychological Association; *The Observer*, published by the Association for Psychological Science; and *The Scientist*, published by Sigma Xi, the international honor society of science and engineering. A classic from the latter, "The Science of Scientific Writing" (Gopen & Swan, 1990), is packed with superb advice about writing for a scientific audience. And the even more general classics on writing have survived the test of time for a reason. Anyone who has not read (or recently reread) *The Elements of Style* (Strunk & White, 1959) would be wise to do so. A key lesson from this short classic (written when the generic masculine form reigned) is from the introduction: "Vigorous writing is concise. A sentence should contain no unnecessary words, a paragraph no unnecessary sentences … This requires not that the writer make all his sentences short, or that he avoid all detail and treat his subjects only in outline, but that every word tell" (p. xvi). Simplicity aids communication, whether the communication is linguistic or graphic (see Tufte, 2001, for excellent advice on the latter).

The Actual Paper

Thus far, my comments have been directed primarily to broad issues in writing. These all provide the principles on which to build your specific article that will describe your specific research. How do you apply these broad principles to write a specific manuscript?

Shaping Your Manuscript

The guiding principle in planning the specifics of your manuscript is that you want to have your readers share your understanding and excitement about the questions you are asking and about the answers you have found. You might think of your goals as making sure that readers leave with the intended take-home message and that they do not lose the forest of the main findings for the trees of specific methods and probability levels. To achieve this outcome, it is critical that you convey the key purpose and findings as intriguingly and compellingly as possible from the start (not only in the introduction but even in the title and abstract), and that you guide your readers to see the conclusions and implications as they finish reading (i.e., in the discussion and conclusions).

An hourglass is the ideal shape for your article. You begin your introduction broadly by pointing out important problems or questions (e.g., theoretical claims or controversies, important applied or policy questions—all linked to earlier literature as appropriate), begin to narrow the scope as you approach the introduction's end by identifying what particular questions you will address and what you hypothesize you will find, and then continue to tighten focus (the narrow part of the hourglass) on the study itself, describing the specific methodology and the specific findings (i.e., in the method and results sections). In the discussion, you gradually expand back out to larger issues, first, discussing findings in relation to your initial hypotheses, and then discussing their meaning in relation to the broader issues you had raised initially (e.g., more general theories; larger policy implications).

Organizational Transparency

It will help the communication process immeasurably if you can make the organizational structure of your work clear to the reader. Often the most important first step in doing so is making sure that the organizational structure is clear to you! Research projects often evolve in messy ways, with twists and turns, and by the time you go to write up the findings, you may yourself be lost among the trees. Thus, before you begin writing, it is helpful to prepare an outline that will concretize the major questions, major methods, and major findings in a formal outline structure. One (among many) ways to accomplish this might be to think of preparing a talk about the work, and designing overview slides that explain to listeners what topics you will be covering and the subtopics within each.

Once the structure is clear to you, it is a relatively straightforward matter to make that structure clear to the reader. One way to do so is to translate your outline structure into the heading structure for your manuscript, using the heading levels identified in the *Publication Manual of the American Psychological Association*. A second way to communicate the structure is by including overviews at the beginning of major sections. For particularly long sections, ending with a summary paragraph may be helpful as well. Finally, although you will probably write it last, the abstract should provide a very concise overview of the goals, findings, and implications of the entire project. As such, it serves to orient readers to what is to come. If you are having trouble writing the abstract, it may mean that your guiding questions and your take-home message are not yet sufficiently clear to you, and thus that you may need to give some additional thought to what it is that is really at the heart of your work and your contribution.

Feedback

There is no hard and fast rule about when to seek input from others except, perhaps, for seeking it at some point! It is particularly helpful to identify an individual or a small group of people who are willing to provide honest feedback. If you are just getting your feet wet in writing, it is probably best to seek feedback from someone (a colleague, a former mentor, a former graduate student peer) early in the process, perhaps when you have only a single section drafted, or, if you are having a serious difficulty getting going, even when you have only a couple of pages written. It is helpful to seek advice from two kinds of people—first, those who are expert in the substantive area in which you are working and, second, those who work outside your specialty area. The former are in a good position to evaluate your substantive argument, judge the appropriateness and thoroughness of the literature you cite, and offer ideas about the justification for your conclusions and suggested new directions. The latter are in a good position to find the spots in which you have not yet provided enough background information for the nonspecialist. Both should be people whose writing skills you admire, ideally those who have a record of publishing in the journals to which you aspire.

When seeking feedback, it is important to begin by encouraging colleagues to give honest, tough feedback, and then to accept it gracefully and gratefully when they do. It is far more helpful to have them return your manuscript covered with red ink (real or virtual) than to get an insincere "It's great!" You can be sure that the reviewers and editor will do the former, not the latter, and your goal is to avoid as many of those devastating criticisms in the real review as possible. Because you may want feedback at multiple points along the way, you probably want to space and limit your requests to any single individual. Doing so is in part to avoid overtaxing any one person, but it is also to ensure that you have fresh eyes reading the manuscript. Someone who has read the manuscript and discussed it with you often may come to suffer from the same insider's knowledge of the work that makes it difficult for you to take the uninitiated reader's perspective.

Checking It Twice, But Letting It Go!

I have suggested that you read what others have said about writing (e.g., consulting some of the sources I mentioned earlier) and that you seek feedback from others. But it is also important to be prepared to let go and send the manuscript off. One can be paralyzed by endless consultation and endless revision. Of course you want the manuscript to be as strong as possible, but undoubtedly there will remain some imperfections. The good news/bad news of the publication process is that it is almost unheard of for something to be accepted for publication as initially submitted. Thus it is virtually certain that you will have the chance to make revisions later, not only based on the editor's and reviewers' comments, but also based on your own rereading after the passage of time.

You do want to obsess enough to get all the pieces right, including a final proofreading (manually, not relying on word processing spell checks that miss problems like *their* for *there* or *trail* for *trial*); a formatting check against the *Publication Manual of the American Psychological Association*; a final check that all citations in the text have been included in the list of references; and a review of your author notes to make certain that you have thanked institutions or projects (e.g., those that allowed you to collect or access data), people (e.g., those who helped to collect, code, or analyze data and those who provided advice on writing), and funding agencies. Although spelling errors, missing or incorrect citations, format inconsistencies and the like may seem trivial, a reviewer who encounters more than one or two of these is likely to wonder whether your data collection, coding, entry, and analyses are similarly careless. There is no reason to engender this kind of negative response in reviewers.

To make it easier to see any remaining flaws, it is helpful to put a hard copy of what you believe is the final version of the manuscript into your desk drawer for at least a couple of days and then take it out and read it carefully one more time before you actually submit it. One last caution is to check that you have removed all the tracked changes before sending in the manuscript (assuming it is being sent electronically). In my 6 years as editor of *Child Development* I encountered many a manuscript that still contained records of changes and "hidden" comments among collaborators, not all of which were in language suitable for print, and many of which would have been embarrassing (and perhaps even career threatening!) had they reached certain reviewers. (Our editorial process included checking for and removing these, but not all journals follow this procedure.)

Transmitting the Manuscript

Instructions about submission requirements (e.g., the number of paper copies and a mailing address if the journal requests hard copies, the list of acceptable word-processing programs and URLs if the journal requests electronic submissions) are typically found on the journal's Web site and in every issue of the journal (e.g., on the inside back cover). These sources should also provide contact information for someone in the editorial office (typically a managing editor or editorial assistant) to whom you can address inquiries about difficulties or exceptions. If you encounter a problem, you should not hesitate to send a note or call. Although you do not want to be a nuisance, you should not simply assume that some legitimate problem cannot be addressed. For example, one of the submission requirements at *Child Development* is to submit manuscripts in either Word or Word Perfect, rather than as a PDF. The reason for this rule is that the electronic files in these programs simplify certain editorial and production processes. In the context of unrelated correspondence, I recently discovered from a would-be author that he had decided to submit an article that was appropriate for *Child Development* elsewhere, because he worked with different software. I am confident that we could have found a solution to the software issue if we had received an inquiry.

This particular problem can be avoided in the future by modifying the information for contributors, but undoubtedly there are other problems lurking that can be identified (and perhaps solved) only if authors bring them to the journal's attention.

Note that journals differ not only with respect to the form and submission process for the manuscript itself, but also with respect to ancillary requirements. For example, some journals require signatures from all authors at the time of submission, others do not require them until the manuscript has been accepted and is ready to enter production, and still others may not require them at all. Some journals require formal statements about sources of financial support for the research or about other conflicts of interest; some may ask for information about informed consent. Some require that you submit two versions of the manuscript, one with all author-identifying information included and the other with all such information removed (e.g., removing descriptions in the method section about recruiting participants at your home institution or community), others handle this "blinding" or "masking" process internally. It eases the editorial process (both for you and for the journal) if you fulfill the requirements when you submit your manuscript initially rather than having to be contacted to provide the missing information or change the format later.

When you submit, you may provide a cover letter (or perhaps fill in a comment section on a Web site) with additional information, including information that may affect the review process, a topic covered in the following section.

Demystifying and Managing the Review Process
Behind Closed Doors

As the preceding pages attest, there are many steps enabling you to get your manuscript written and submitted. But as this section will make clear, the process is far from over. Indeed, from the editorial perspective, it is only just beginning. Figure 13.1 presents a flow chart of the way that the editorial process typically progresses.

Administrative Processing

First, the manuscript must be processed for handling. To the degree that you prepared it in accord with the journal's requirements (e.g., followed APA style rules, kept within the specified

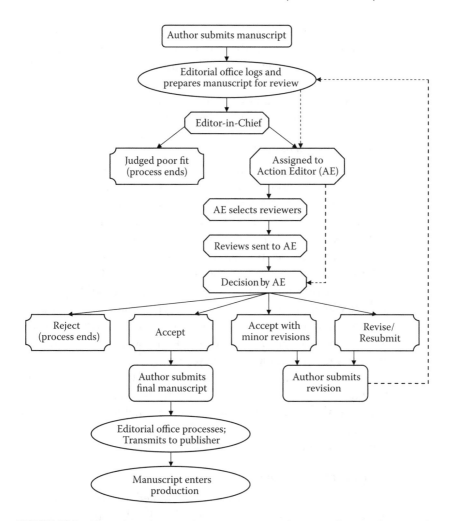

FIGURE 13.1   Flow chart showing the processing steps that typically occur between the submission of a manuscript and its rejection or acceptance. Dashed lines are used to show processing of revisions: Action editors may either recycle through the full review process (seeking external reviews) or may make a decision without external reviews. The latter becomes increasingly likely with later rounds of revisions.

page limits, and omitted information that reveals author identity), this step is likely to be quick, say, within a day or two, or perhaps a week or two. Delays might be longer if the journal is an unusually small operation, if the arrival of your manuscript coincides with a scheduled closing (something that commonly happens during universities' winter breaks), or if the journal were undergoing some unusual occurrence such as a changing editorial term or a new editorial staff. Initial processing is likely to be delayed by several weeks or more if the manuscript does not meet guidelines in some way, necessitating that the editorial staff contact you for additional materials (e.g., the signatures from all coauthors) or even for a revised manuscript (e.g., a shortened manuscript that does not exceed the journal's page limits).

Initial Editorial Screening

Next, the manuscript is transmitted to the editor-in-chief (EIC) who reads the submission (sometimes quickly, sometimes in detail) and decides how to handle it. For some journals, and as explained earlier, the EIC (with or without consultation with another editor, editorial board member, or other consultant) may make an initial screening or "triage" decision about whether the manuscript will undergo further review. Even EICs who do not routinely reject submissions at this point will typically reject submissions judged to be completely inappropriate for the journal (something that should not happen to you if you have heeded the advice given earlier on journal selection and genre). If the EIC decides not to continue the review process further, a letter is sent to the author explaining the decision, typically with little if any substantive explanation for the outcome. The negative side of this process is that you are not likely to receive helpful feedback. The positive side is that you receive the rejection quickly, and thus have lost little time.

Assignment of an Action Editor

Assuming that the manuscript is retained for further review, the EIC then determines who will handle the full review process. In some journals—those with relatively small numbers of submissions—the EIC always fills this role. In other journals—those with high submission rates or with specific editors assigned to handle specific topics—there are additional action editors (AEs), most often referred to as associate editors. There may be as few as one or two and as many as a dozen, and in rare cases even more (e.g., for the journal *Science*). Assignments to AEs are motivated primarily by the goal of achieving a good substantive match between the topic of the submission and the expertise of the editor, but they are also affected by AEs' current workloads and other less public circumstances such as AEs' vacation plans, medical emergencies, or potential conflicts of interest (e.g., an author who is or was the AE's student, collaborator, or institutional colleague). In most journals, once assigned to the manuscript, the AE has full control over the editorial decision. In some rare cases, the AE essentially serves in an advisory role to the EIC who retains all decision-making roles (including handling revisions).

Reviewer Selection

The assigned AE then reads the manuscript (again, with varying degrees of depth depending on the individual AE and the journal) and identifies a number of potential reviewers. AEs may do so based on their existing familiarity with the research area, by using a database or search engine such as PsycINFO or Google Scholar, by examining the list of references included in the submitted manuscript, perhaps reading one or more of those references or even references that are cited within those articles. Another resource for reviewers can be ones provided by the specific journal. For example, as part of my editorship of *Child Development*, I established a "reviewer database" that now includes thousands of potential reviewers. Scholars interested in reviewing are invited to register by providing information about relevant experience (e.g., academic degrees, publications, reviewing experience) and about areas of expertise (by checking all topics the individual feels comfortable reviewing). Editors of the journal can then enter topics individually (e.g., "perception") or conjointly (e.g., "perception + infancy + autism"), and a list of people with expertise in the named topic(s) is returned. In this database, the potential reviewer names are accompanied by information about each individual's past and current reviewer history (e.g., number of reviews completed in the last year, number of manuscripts currently assigned for review, average length of time to complete reviews, and number of manuscripts accepted versus declined for review), which may be factored into the AEs' decisions about whom to invite.

Reviewer Invitations

Various journals and even various AEs within a given journal differ with respect to the number of reviews they seek. Most aim for two or three reviews, but some aim for more, though rarely more than four. There is also variability in how AEs attempt to reach their target. Some AEs initially invite only the number desired, and turn to others only if and when an already-invited reviewer declines. Other AEs invite more reviewers than their target number from the start, assuming that not everyone will agree to review, and that not everyone who agrees to do so will actually produce a review, at least within the requested time frame. Journals and AEs also differ with respect to those time frames (reviewers may be asked to provide their comments anywhere between two weeks and several months) and with respect to how they handle late reviews (virtually all journals and AEs send out periodic reminders, but they vary with respect to if—and if so, how soon—they will go ahead with an editorial decision in the absence of a promised review). Indeed, extracting reviewers from consultants is the most difficult and time-consuming part of the editorial process that frustrates editors and authors alike.

Reviewer Tasks

Most journals and AEs ask reviewers for two kinds of feedback. First are comments addressed to the authors, and these are generally sent, as written, to the authors as part of the editorial decision. Second are comments or advice addressed confidentially to the AE. Such comments are often written less constructively than those written for the authors (although regrettably a small proportion of reviewers write less-than-constructive—sometimes even unconscionably destructive—comments to authors as well).

Many journals also ask reviewers to provide the editor with a confidential recommendation about the editorial decision. Reviewers are typically offered categories of reject (reject without the possibility of resubmission), reject/resubmit or revise/resubmit (reject this version but invite a revision), contingent accept (accept contingent on some relatively minor substantive changes), and accept (accept the manuscript as is, typically pending some very minor stylistic changes). Sometimes reviewers may be asked for more subtle distinctions such as asking reviewers who recommend revise/resubmit to add their opinion about the likelihood of success (e.g., selecting among optimistic, pessimistic, or neutral categories). These more subtle recommendations are likely to influence the tone of the AE's ultimate decision letter, which in turn should affect the author's decisions about next steps (discussed later in this chapter).

Editorial Decisions

Once all (or some minimum number of) reviews have been received, the AE thoroughly reads (or rereads) the manuscript, the reviews, and the confidential reviewer comments and recommendations to reach a decision. Journals and AEs differ in the way they handle reviewers' recommendations in their decision process. Some AEs see themselves as vote counters, viewing their decision as dictated by the majority opinion expressed in the reviews. Others see themselves as deciders, viewing their editorial decision as a judgment based on weighing their own opinion about the research and manuscript, a judgment about the importance of the work for the field, and a consideration of the various insights and recommendations made by the reviewers. A metaphor for the first approach might be editor as jury foreman; a metaphor for the second might be editor as judge. Although I have never seen public statements about whether a given journal or editor endorses one or the other of these models, a particular EIC might be explicit about this point when selecting and orienting AEs, but even then, particular AEs (assuming they have autonomy in reaching editorial decisions) may or may not implement that model. As an author, what is most important about this issue is recognizing that both of these models are common and both are considered legitimate. Thus, even if your manuscript receives what you would read as positive reviews (perhaps with what you view as easily addressed criticisms), that does not mean that an AE's decision to reject the manuscript is a travesty of justice that can and should be protested.

Once AEs reach a decision about the manuscript, they prepare a letter conveying the decision and attaching the reviews. Again, there is wide variability in the form of these letters. At one end of the continuum are AEs who merely convey the bottom-line decision (e.g., "I regret to have to tell you that I have decided to reject this manuscript") and refer readers to the reviews. At the other end are AEs who provide extensive substantive comments and suggestions. (As an illustration, as an author, I once received a revise/resubmit decision that included 11 single-spaced pages from the AE in addition to some 20 additional single-spaced pages from 4 reviewers!) Somewhere in the middle of this continuum are AEs who summarize and highlight what they see as the most important and critical points and suggestions in the attached reviews, perhaps adding a few additional comments of their own. As the decision is conveyed to the author, it is also recorded in the editorial office where all materials are typically archived for many years.

Revisions

As may be seen in the flowchart of Figure 13.1, if the decision was to reject, that is the end of the process (with potential exceptions, discussed later). If the decision was revise/resubmit, the next step begins when the author submits a revised manuscript.

In most journals, when revisions arrive back at the journal office, they are automatically sent back to the original AE (rather than to the EIC). The AE then decides whether to make a decision on the revision independently (very rare, unless the requested revisions were minor and the AE is an expert in the research domain) or to send the revised manuscript out for external review. In most cases, the AE will solicit reviews from one or more of the original reviewers. In a smaller number of cases, the AE will also request evaluations from one or more entirely new reviewers. Although some AEs request new reviewers for revisions routinely, most do so only under unusual circumstances, for example, when revised manuscripts draw on different theoretical, empirical, or methodological traditions (requiring different expertise); when manuscripts have been revised repeatedly (requiring fresh reviewers); or when original reviewers are unavailable. When a revision is sent to reviewers, it is typically accompanied by a copy of the author's cover letter (after identifying information has been removed), copies of the prior reviews and decision letter, and, if requested, a copy of the original manuscript.

As shown in Figure 13.1, the process described for the initial submission then recycles, each time with the same potential outcomes of reject, revise/resubmit, or accept. Minor substantive revisions are thereafter typically handled directly by the AE, and the managing editor or editorial assistant typically handles stylistic revisions. In most cases, the process repeats itself only two or three times, after which the manuscript has either been definitively rejected or accepted for publication.

Production and Beyond

Once the AE has accepted the manuscript for publication, it enters the production stage. Space constraints preclude discussion of the processes involved in moving your manuscript from an acceptance into the printed product (e.g., copyediting, handling permissions, copyright, figures, proofreading) as well as activities related to your article after publication (e.g., press releases, distributing the work to partner organizations, the public, and other researchers), but most of these processes are spelled out explicitly by the journal's editorial office and publisher.

Tracking and Influencing the Process

As suggested by the heading of the prior section, "Behind Closed Doors," authors have little chance to see most of the review process in operation, and even less chance to control it. But that is not quite the same as being completely without influence.

Monitoring

First, it is important to keep track of the process to make sure that it is functioning as it should. One critical issue is making certain that the manuscript you submitted was actually received. With Web-based submissions, there are typically automated acknowledgments. When manuscripts are sent as attachments to editors or editorial assistants, there are usually routine e-mail acknowledgments. When submissions are sent via hard copy, there may or may not be a routine acknowledgment (e.g., a postcard informing you of the manuscript's receipt, reference number, and perhaps the name of the action editor). Whatever the submission procedure may have been, if you have not received some kind of acknowledgment within a week or two at most, it is worth an e-mail, note, or phone call. Sometimes something goes awry, and you should not wait months to find out that the manuscript (or revision) was never received in the first place.

Relatedly, although you do not want to be a pest, you should also monitor the process along the way, and if some aspect of the process seems to be taking an inordinately long time, it is reasonable to communicate with the editorial office to inquire. Some submission Web sites may give you access to monitor the process yourself (e.g., seeing whether reviews have been received). Some journals make public their expected time frames. For example, during my editorship of the *Journal of Experimental Child Psychology*, the information for contributors published in each issue explicitly stated that authors would receive an immediate acknowledgment, and that "authors are welcome to send an inquiry to the Editor about the status of their manuscript if no decision has been returned within 3 months of the initial acknowledgement." Editorial office staff can often explain the cause for a delay, and an inquiry may lead the AE to work even harder to obtain an overdue review or perhaps decide to make an editorial decision without it. Again, though, it is important to avoid crossing the line into being a thorn in the staff or editor's sides.

Editors

Second, you may be able to have some influence on which of the potential action editors handles your manuscript. If you have taken the advice given earlier about examining the list of associate editors as part of selecting your target journal, you may have identified an editor or two whose substantive work, theoretical approach, or methodology seems especially compatible with your own. There is nothing wrong with mentioning in your cover letter that if it is possible, you would appreciate having that person serve as the editor for your submission, explaining why and noting anything that might be viewed as a potential conflict of interest (e.g., "Although we have never collaborated on research, we did work together on a conference program committee last year"). The EIC has confidence in all the AEs, and thus is not likely to have any objection to assigning your submission to that person (unless some other factor such as workload argues against it).

Reviewers

Third, you may also be able to have some influence on the selection of reviewers. One potential avenue is simply to offer the editor some suggestions, an approach that most editors would find useful rather than intrusive. For example, you might mention that persons X, Y, and Z are working in similar areas and you would expect that they would be in a particularly good position to evaluate the work. Of course, you should avoid suggesting anyone with whom you have a conflict of interest, or provide a short statement about current or past interactions that might be perceived in this way. In some cases, you may want to make suggestions about the inverse—reviewers to avoid. As editor, I have also had authors ask me to refrain from asking a particular person to review for some unnamed reason, and I honored those requests without asking for any additional justification assuming that there has been some personal conflict or relationship. Such requests become problematic only if the list is long (something that I have encountered only once in over a quarter century of editing). Sometimes you may want to point out a theoretical clash that you hope the editor will take into account when soliciting or weighing reviews. For example, if your manuscript is essentially a critique of an established program of work, it might be legitimate to point out your concern about obtaining balanced reviews. It would, however, be unreasonable to ask the editor to refrain from soliciting reviews from the established research group altogether given that it would be a source for the most expert consultants.

Reading and Responding to Editorial Decisions
Reading the Decision

The decision you receive (usually via e-mail) will typically include a letter from the AE, which, as described earlier, may range from a paragraph to a mini-manuscript, and one or many reviews. What happens now that you have the long-sought decision letter in hand? In answering that question, I am making the assumption that the decision letter did not say, simply, that the journal would be delighted to accept your manuscript for publication in its current form. This almost never happens (at least for highly selective journals, and at least not for mere mortals). Indeed, if your early experiences are immediate acceptances, probably you, rather than I, should be writing this chapter!

The first step, of course, is to read the letter and the reviews. As a mentor, I have come to appreciate how cryptic decision letters can be to novices largely as a result of two experiences. One was roughly 20 years ago when one of my graduate students had just received her first editorial decision letter (for a coauthored paper on which she was first author). She arrived teary-eyed in my office, holding the "devastating" reviews in hand, contemplating a change in careers. I took the letters from her, began reading, and started reassuring her that in actuality they were very positive reviews and there was an excellent chance that there could be a successful revision. By the time I finished them, I guiltily recognized that as a mentor, I had failed to provide enough transparency about the publication process from the author's perspective. I can still remember looking at her and saying: "You think *these* are negative reviews? Let me show you what negative reviews look like!" and I went to my file drawer and pulled out a set of reviews from an earlier paper of my own. They were effective in drying her tears both because they were far more critical than the new ones, and because we had the advantage of knowing that the earlier manuscript had indeed been revised successfully and published in that same highly selective journal. I now routinely share my own previously hidden publishing experiences with graduate students so that they are less shocked when they begin to encounter similar experiences.

The second experience was far more recent and illustrates the problem with assuming that the single word *reject* is necessarily ominous. The context was similar: a graduate student receiving her first decision letter from a highly selective journal. In his letter, the AE said that "I have decided that I must reject this manuscript for publication." But the AE went on to say that he thought it might be possible to revise the manuscript to address the reviewers' comments, adding that he was uncertain whether a resubmission would be successful and thus could not "guarantee an acceptance." I knew from experience—particularly on the editorial side of the process—that editors want to protect against the potential misunderstanding that an invitation to revise is tantamount to an acceptance upon receipt of a revision. Thus, whereas she interpreted the warning as ominous, I interpreted it as pro forma, and thus her anxiety in seeing a rejection contrasted with my elation in seeing an encouraging revise/resubmit decision.

Two major lessons derive from these anecdotes. First, it is important to develop a thick skin. An occupational hazard in the business of academic publishing is that when you submit a manuscript, your work becomes a ready target for reviewers. Although most reviewers remember that a human being—often a junior, inexperienced one—is at the other end of their reviews, a few regrettably do not, and they make no effort to offer positive comments before launching into negative ones, and no effort to convey their criticisms constructively. Although editors and others often admonish reviewers to be constructive, at least some are likely to ignore this advice, and thus it would be wise to toughen yourself in preparation.

Second, it is important to learn how to read the message of a decision. Sometimes a "reject" is really a reject. But sometimes a "reject" is really an invitation to revise and resubmit. With experience comes increased skill in interpreting letters, both with respect to the decision itself and also with respect to understanding what changes are essential versus optional.

To help in interpreting the decision, it is best to put it away for at least several days. When you pull it out again, your emotions (disappointment, anger, frustration) are likely to be under better control, and your cognitions are likely to be more productive. For example, you may begin to understand what was misunderstood and have some ideas about how the material might have been communicated differently; you might be able to recognize the legitimacy of the reviewers' competing interpretations of the data; you may be able to think of ways to recode, reanalyze, or amend the data to address some of the reviewers' concerns. With this frame of mind you are in a position to decide on your next actions. Obviously these will depend on whether the editorial decision was revise/resubmit or a rejection, discussed in turn next.

Responding to a Revise/Resubmit Decision

The revise/resubmit decision is the one you would have hoped for (again, because an immediate accept almost never occurs), but you still need to decide whether to attempt a revision. In reaching an answer, it is first important to identify the kinds of concerns that have been raised. Typically, some concerns are focused primarily on the framing and explanation of the research and other concerns are focused on the science of the research. As discussed in the following section, it should almost certainly be possible to respond to the first; there is more uncertainty about the second.

Communication Concerns

Some of the reviewers' concerns are likely to be the result of failed communication, and these can be handled by careful rewriting. In making revisions of this kind (and in explaining them to the editor and reviewers in your cover letter) it is far more helpful to presume that you had provided a misleading or incomplete description about your rationale, methods, findings, or conclusions than to presume that the reviewers were ignorant or inattentive to your text. Although as noted earlier, not every reviewer is careful and constructive, most will have made a concerted effort to understand your research and manuscript. Indeed, they are likely to be among the most careful, attentive, thoughtful readers you will ever have, and thus if they have misunderstood or overlooked something, it is probably wise to try to clarify or amplify your presentation.

Related are concerns about the way you have framed the rationale of your research or impact of your findings. Often reviewers will criticize a manuscript for overlooking connections to other theories or empirical literatures. These criticisms, too, are readily handled by expanding the links to other traditions in a revision. It is legitimate to resist suggestions to change the very theoretical foundations of your research, but it is reasonable and advantageous to agree to connect it to additional traditions. Such changes are likely to expand your audience and enhance the impact of your work.

A final criticism that falls within the communicative domain is one that asserts that the work is insufficiently novel, large enough in scope, or theoretically momentous. The evaluation of importance is truly a judgment call, and as such, is among the most difficult concerns to address. You may be able to do so by connecting to additional literatures and questions (see prior comment) and by giving more attention to implications, but your changes may or may not convince the editor and reviewers. On this issue, the best you can do is try to read the editor's letter as carefully as possible to try to evaluate the degree of optimism versus reluctance expressed in the decision, and to weigh your desire to publish in this particular journal versus trying to get the work into print soon. If you read the likelihood of success as low and view the importance of publishing quickly as important, you might be better off submitting to a slightly less selective journal that sees its role as publishing incremental findings rather than transformational work. If the balance is reversed, you might be better off revising and resubmitting to the same journal where at least you already know what other concerns must be addressed.

Scientific Concerns

A second category of concerns is focused on the science of the research. Among the kinds of issues that might be raised by the editor and reviewers are whether the measures were reliable and valid, whether coding was blind, whether the sample size was sufficiently large to allow the power to detect effects, whether the sample was sufficiently diverse to support the generalizations you have made, whether there were appropriate control groups to permit the elimination of alternative explanations for group differences, whether the sample was recruited in a way that was likely to introduce problematic confounds, whether critical assumptions were met for the statistics used, and whether effect sizes are large enough to suggest meaningful findings, to name only a sample of the potential arenas of criticism.

These are the kind of issues that you may well have recognized beforehand as limitations. Perhaps you had already noted them in your original submission (see "Perspective Taking 101"), and if so, it would be important to expand your arguments, hoping to be more persuasive. If you had omitted a discussion of these limitations earlier but have a response, you should include it now. Perhaps you believe that the concerns are unfounded, in which case your job is to explain why to the editor and reviewers, probably also amending the text to prevent future readers from mistakenly identifying the same problem.

It is also possible that the editor or reviewers have identified legitimate and significant concerns about which you had been unaware. This is a time for honest reevaluation of your research. Are there, indeed, serious flaws in the work? Are they so serious as to be "fatal" such that the best course of action is to reconceptualize your project as pilot research on which you will base your next study? Or might a possible response be to revise the paper so that it offers more conservative claims about the strength, definitiveness, or scope of the findings? Or might the criticisms lead you to realize that you must conduct additional or alternative statistical analyses or collect additional data? For example, perhaps you need to collect data from a greater number or diversity of participants, from participants in a comparison or control group, or from the same participants but on different measures (to assess additional constructs) or at different intervals (to assess longitudinal change).

There is no one right answer about which of these pathways to follow. You need to weigh the criticisms and potential solutions as well as practical matters such as your resources, time, and motivation to conduct additional work. If you are going to follow one of the more time-consuming paths (e.g., additional data collection) you should check with the editor to find out an acceptable time frame. Often if a revision is returned to the journal after too long an interval, it is treated as an entirely new submission, in which case it is likely to be handled by a new editor and new reviewers who will undoubtedly have a somewhat different set of concerns.

Formulating and Communicating Revisions

It is for the revision process that the cooling-off period suggested earlier is critical. If you have put the reviews aside for at least a few days, and if you can hold on to the idea that most reviewers seek not only to find flaws but also to suggest ways to make your manuscript better, you are likely maximize the benefits that accrue from their expertise. Taking a positive attitude also has the added advantage of allowing you to frame the revision process as an exciting opportunity rather than as a despised evil. With this attitude, you can go through the various criticisms and suggestions more productively, perhaps handling those that are relatively simple first (e.g., adding requested information about participants, task reliability, response variability) while you ponder those that will require greater reorganization and reconceptualization.

Your job is not only to revise the manuscript, but it is also to convince the editor and reviewers that you addressed their concerns adequately. Some authors find it useful to begin by preparing a letter to the editors and reviewers first, explaining how they "have" changed the manuscript to address concerns. They then actually make the changes they had already described. Others just dig into the task of making changes in the text, periodically go through the editorial comments to check off those they have addressed until the only items that remain are those that they judge to be unnecessary to change, and then compose a letter describing the changes.

Although there is no single format to follow, in general, it is helpful to provide a *brief summary* letter to the editor (likely to be under two pages) followed by a *point-by-point* response to the reviewers (with the addendum that if you have addressed a similar point in response to, say, Reviewer A, that you simply refer back to that response rather than repeat it for a similar point made by, say, Reviewer C). The key goal is to show that you have taken their suggestions seriously, thought about all of them, and responded to each, either by making changes in the text (giving page numbers when the responses are highly specific changes) or by explaining the reason that you believe that a suggested change is unnecessary. When you do the latter, the explanation should be substantive and rational, not accusatory and emotional. It does you no good to point out the stupidity, ignorance, or carelessness of a reviewer, all of which are less common attributes than authors might suspect.

It is also important to recognize that sometimes reviews are internally inconsistent, with one reviewer urging you to make a change in one direction, and another affirming the original or even suggesting a change in the opposite direction. Sometimes editors make clear in their decision letters which side they favor, and you should probably (but not necessarily) follow that path. Again, as in other responses, your job is to show that you have considered the issue, and provide a convincing argument about the path you decided to follow. For example, you might say something like, "As is evident from the comments of Reviewer A and C, it is clear that issue X was problematic, although each reviewer suggested a different solution to the problem. Given that [insert some rationale], my revision follows the suggestion of Reviewer C," perhaps adding some explanation of the change and where it may be found.

As a practical matter, assuming that you received the reviews as electronic attachments, you may want to simply insert your responses directly into the reviews, using different fonts, italics, or indentations to distinguish the reviewers' remarks from your own. As you go, it does no harm to thank reviewers or editors for particularly helpful suggestions or for the positive comments that may be intermingled with the criticisms. Throughout, try to keep your responses brief. Your goal is to reassure the reviewers that their concerns have been addressed, not to insert, piecemeal, the revised manuscript into the cover letter.

When the Decision Is a Rejection

Acting on a Rejection

The advice for a cooling-off period is even more critical when you receive a definitive rejection because your affective response is likely to challenge your rationality and self-control. Much of the advice given for revise/resubmit decisions applies even more strongly to rejections. Here, too, you are faced with the question of whether to revise the paper and submit it again, albeit to a different journal. Again, the most important critical first step is taking a hard, honest look at the criticisms.

If the reviewers point to communication oversights or to a mismatch between the journal and the submission (e.g., regarding substantive focus, scope, novelty, and so on), the next step is obvious: revise the manuscript based on those comments that you find to be useful, select a new journal (using criteria discussed earlier), make any journal-specific adjustments (e.g., concerning length limits), and send it off. Note that this advice is *not* to send off the identical manuscript to a new journal. Not only would you have wasted the opportunity to benefit from the close reading and suggestions from a number of experts, you run the risk that the editor of the new journal will seek a review from one or more of the identical reviewers. Few things irk reviewers more than getting an identical manuscript back from a new journal and seeing that the author has done nothing to address their comments. (Given the specialized nature of our field, this happens fairly often. Many years ago, for example, I received the identical paper, sequentially, from five different editors. How editors and reviewers handle this situation is another topic that cannot be covered here, but however they handle it is not likely to increase the author's chances of having the manuscript accepted.)

If the reviews point to scientific flaws, all the same issues raised with respect to revisions hold here. In essence, you should either reduce the range of your claims, conduct additional work (e.g., conduct additional statistical analyses or collect additional data), or put the manuscript away in your file drawer as a learning experience or as a foundation for your future research.

Should You Protest?

Faced with a rejection, the other possible response is to ask the editor to reconsider the decision. This is a path that should be taken extremely rarely, if ever, and probably not more than once or twice in your career. The circumstance under which it may be justified is when you truly believe that the rejection was based on a misunderstanding of a core component of the research. If this is the case, a letter explaining the issue and asking for reconsideration is not an outrageous action.

Some caveats are important. First, rejection letters and negative reviews often contain illustrative points rather than an exhaustive list of concerns. Thus, even if you believe you can respond to the particular issues, there may be additional reasons for the rejection, and thus the editor would be highly unlikely to reopen the case. Second, as noted earlier, manuscripts are sometimes rejected because the work is judged to be insufficiently important. This is an almost impossible issue about which to argue. Editors—who have seen hundreds and usually thousands of manuscripts and who have a particular vision for the journal they edit—are far better positioned to make judgments about importance than are individual authors who are, understandably, passionate about their research area. Third, your letter is highly likely to be sent on to one or all of the reviewers as part of the protest or reconsideration process. Thus, writing a hostile letter that complains about the stupidity or incompetence of the reviewers is not an effective strategy. Furthermore, if the journal does not use masked review, or if the manuscript eventually appears in another journal and the reviewer recognizes it, your professional reputation is likely to be tarnished. Again, remember the lessons learned from "Perspective Taking 101."

In the Years Ahead

Assuming that you will ultimately be successful in your submissions and will gradually acquire the experiences that allow you to look back on your early ventures with nostalgia and bemusement as I look back on my Thursday nights at Cornell, I close with a few final suggestions for what lies ahead.

First, enjoy yourself. Remember that you are excited and interested in your work. You are trying to share that excitement and your findings with others. Even as you negotiate the endless rules about format, learn the tricks of the trade, and revise again and again; try not to lose sight of the big picture. In this case, you do *not* want to keep your gaze on only the single bird or the single tree. Remember that even as you are writing for others, you are also writing for yourself. Keep a collection of papers that you like and try to figure out why you like them. Develop your voice not only with respect to your message, but also with respect to your style.

Second, even as your skills and knowledge progress, remember your past. Remember how you felt when you received your first set of devastating reviews. Remember what it was like to have to wait for months and months for editorial decisions. Use these memories to motivate your future actions. Share your own early uncertainties and setbacks with novices who are encountering these challenges for the first time. Agree to review others' work promptly and often. Prepare your reviews constructively and kindly, not arrogantly and hostilely.

And finally, remember that you are not alone, wherever in the process you may be. Seek others with whom you can share both the frustrations and joys of the process. Someday, you, too, may find yourself startled to be giving other people advice on how to write and even more startled to find yourself enjoying the chance to do so.

Acknowledgments

I thank faculty and student members of the Penn State Developmental Psychology Proseminar for providing helpful comments on this chapter, and Valerie Maholmes and the Fellows of the NICHD Summer Institute on Applied Research in Child and Adolescent Development for providing the impetus to write it.

References

American Psychological Association (2009). *Publication manual of the American Psychological Association*-6th edition. Washington, D.C.: Author.

Gopen, G., & Swan, J. (1990). The science of scientific writing. *American Scientist, 78,* 550–559.

Lamott, A. (1995). *Bird by bird: Some instructions on writing and life.* New York: Knopf.

Liben, L. S. (2009, March). *How parents guide their children's understanding of maps in a museum exhibit.* Symposium paper at the biennial meeting of the Society for Research in Child Development, Denver, CO.

Merriam-Webster (2008). Merriam-Webster online dictionary. Retrieved December 10, 2008 from http://www.merriam-webster.com/dictionary/genre.

Myers, L. J., & Liben, L. S. (2008). The role of intentionality and iconicity in children's developing comprehension and production of cartographic symbols. *Child Development, 79,* 668–684.

Strunk, W., Jr., & White, E. B. (1959). *Elements of style.* New York: Macmillan.

Tufte, E. R. (2001). *The visual display of quantitative information* (2nd ed.). Cheshire, CT: Graphics Press.

CHAPTER 14

Conclusion and Future Directions

Valerie Maholmes, PhD
*Eunice Kennedy Shriver National Institute of Child
Health and Human Development*

Carmela G. Lomonaco, PhD
Inspire USA Foundation

We started this volume with a focus on some of the essential and most frequently asked questions posed by early career investigators. These were the centerpieces of the chapters in this volume and each author addressed these questions based on their experiences conducting research and offered insights and important lessons learned. We conclude by asking additional questions that reflect areas where applied studies on children and adolescents may need to focus.

The literature on children and adolescents emphasizes the important and influential roles that context play on developmental outcomes. To fully explore and potentially disentangle the effects of these influences, researchers must be prepared to ask questions that take into account the physical and psychosocial ecologies within which development occurs. Child and adolescent researchers are becoming increasingly aware of the school as an important context not only for studying academic achievement and curriculum and instruction, but also as a vital part of a child's social ecology that influences development in critical domains, through significant milestones and across a significant span of life. Work by Comer (1995) and his colleagues have a long history of using child development research to inform the ways in which schools coordinate mental health and social support services for students. His work also examines how dimensions of school climate affect a child's sense of academic self-efficacy and ability to cope (Haynes, 1990). Evaluations of this work shed light on the challenges of using particular methodologies to determine the efficacy of such interventions as pointed out by McCall and Groark in Chapter 6. Schonfeld (Chapter 9) argued that school-based interventions often aim to modify complex behaviors that have multiple determinants and suggested that the ideal research question is one that is *best* answered in a school setting, rather than one that *could* be answered in this context.

Questions for future research may include

What are the most appropriate methodologies to study how targeted interventions might play a role in facilitating a child's sense of academic and social efficacy in school thereby improving academic and behavioral outcomes?

What evaluation strategies are most effective in studying the impact of programs that bring services into underresourced schools?

Fisher and Fried (Chapter 7) noted that increased emphasis on conducting research that seeks to improve conditions for at-risk and vulnerable populations presented complex challenges for applied researchers and resulted in such novel questions as

Are there critical or sensitive periods in childhood and adolescence at which cognitive, behavioral, or social interventions are most effective?

To what extent do certain vulnerabilities associated with family environment and neighborhood context, for example, place children at risk for long-term health consequences and for transmitting these risks across generations?

Pursuing answers to questions such as these require a fundamental integration between basic and applied research as Lerner pointed out in Chapter 3. Blachman and Esposito (Chapter 2) supported this assertion and suggested that to promote health and well-being, there is a need for integration across multiple levels, from the cellular and molecular through the psychological and behavioral and to the economic, cultural, and social.

Increasingly more attention has been placed on the disparities in health between minority and majority populations. The 1985 Report of the Secretary's Task Force on Black and Minority Health (U.S. Department of Health and Human Services, 1985) called for more research to understand the nature of these disparities, as well as the underlying mechanisms and indicated that minorities had not benefited fully or equitably from the fruit of science or from systems responsible for translation of science. Likewise, the broader education community seeks to understand why substantial gaps in educational achievement persist between Black and White children despite funding for programs to close these gaps (Rouse, Brooks-Gunn, & McLanahan, 2005).

Of necessity, applied research to address these issues must be sensitive to the particular cultural values as well as the more fundamental and basic processes. Participatory methods that engage the population to be studied are becoming more widely utilized to examine the complexities of these disparities alongside the nuances of culture and context.

Spicer (Chapter 5), Knox (Chapter 10), and Guerra and Leidy (Chapter 8) discussed how they use community-based participatory research to identify critical attitudes and behaviors that need further study. In his work with Native American populations, Spicer considers the tribal participatory research as an important strategy to remedy many of these problems. He asserted that participatory approaches such as this seek to rebalance power within the research enterprise by including community expertise in all phases of the study, recognizing that community expertise is as, if not more, valuable than that of the scientist. Fisher and Fried (Chapter 7) asserted that when designing research procedures with diverse populations, it is imperative for investigators to recognize and address vulnerabilities of members of particular groups in order to develop research procedures that adequately protect their rights and welfare, and investigators must view the research through the cultural perspectives of the population being studied. Questions to address the complex issues associated with disparities in education and health may include

What are the strengths and weaknesses of these approaches? In what ways are participatory strategies effective in understanding disparities among racial and ethnic groups? Are there more effective approaches?

How are these participatory approaches utilized to understand problems associated with childhood and adolescence? Are there more effective/appropriate approaches?

An insight we gained in putting this volume together is that there are gaps in funding and training for individuals interested in pursuing careers in applied research. In her chapter, Knox asserted that historically, funding has favored basic research over translation into practice, and researchers by necessity have followed the money. Berch (Chapter 11) further pointed out that applied research is often quite costly and time consuming, making it difficult for early stage investigators to both compete for external funding while at the same time preparing for the exigencies of achieving tenure. Blachman and Esposito (Chapter 2) discuss important funding mechanisms for early career investigators to consider as they seek support for their work. We encourage faculty mentors and senior colleagues to support young scholars in the use of these mechanisms to fund applied research.

Several authors in this volume not only describe their applied research, but also share how they came to pursue their particular line of inquiry. Most often, they expressed a desire and perhaps even a responsibility in some small, but hopefully consequential way to improve the lives of children and families. They emphasized the importance of sharing findings from their research beyond the academic community to the practice, policy, and lay communities as well. Whereas Liben (Chapter 13) focused on the mechanics of publishing research findings, McCabe and Browning (Chapter 12) outlined the particular strategies for disseminating research to specific audiences to enhance awareness of the benefits of developmental science for public well-being and to reinforce the importance of funding for developmental science. Educators as well as policy makers, parents, and other lay stakeholders need objective and informative overviews of current research in child and adolescent development and appropriate application in their respective contexts, with clear rationales for those applications.

Finally, there are many more questions to be asked about child and adolescent development research that are beyond the scope of this volume. Our aim was to use the questions submitted by early career investigators as a starting point for new investigators making their first foray into applied research in child and adolescent development. We expect this volume to be an important resource for understanding the complexities of conducting such research and, most important, as a tool to inspire more questions.

Acknowledgments

The opinions and asserations presented in this chapter are those of the authors and do not purport to represent those of the *Eunice Kennedy Shriver* National Institute of Child Health and Human Development, the National Institutes of Health, the US Department of Health and Human Services or the Inspire USA Foundation.

References

Comer, J. P. (1995). *School power: Implications of an intervention project.* New York: Free Press.

Haynes, N. M. (1990). The influence of self-concept on school adjustment among black middle school students. *Journal of Social Psychology*, *130*, 199–207.

Rouse, C., Brooks-Gunn, J., & McLanahan, S. (2005). Introducing the issue. *School Readiness: Closing Racial and Ethnic Gaps—The Future of Children*, *15*, 5–14.

U.S. Department of Health and Human Services. (1985). *The Federal Task Force on Black and Minority Health.* Washington, DC: Author.

Author Index

Subject Index